THE SENSATION OF SECURITY

A volume in the series
Police/Worlds: Studies in Security, Crime, and Governance
Edited by Kevin Karpiak, Sameena Mulla, William Garriott, and Ilana Feldman

A list of titles in this series is available at cornellpress.cornell.edu.

THE SENSATION OF SECURITY

Private Guards and Social Order in Brazil

Erika Robb Larkins

CORNELL UNIVERSITY PRESS   ITHACA AND LONDON

Copyright © 2023 by Cornell University

All rights reserved. Except for brief quotations in a review, this book, or parts thereof, must not be reproduced in any form without permission in writing from the publisher. For information, address Cornell University Press, Sage House, 512 East State Street, Ithaca, New York 14850. Visit our website at cornellpress.cornell.edu.

First published 2023 by Cornell University Press

Library of Congress Cataloging-in-Publication Data

Names: Robb Larkins, Erika, 1977– author.
Title: The sensation of security : private guards and social order in Brazil / Erika Robb Larkins.
Description: Ithaca [New York] : Cornell University Press, 2023. | Series: Police/Worlds: studies in security, crime, and governance | Includes bibliographical references and index.
Identifiers: LCCN 2022053423 (print) | LCCN 2022053424 (ebook) | ISBN 9781501769733 (hardcover) | ISBN 9781501769740 (paperback) | ISBN 9781501769757 (pdf) | ISBN 9781501769764 (epub)
Subjects: LCSH: Private security services—Brazil—Sociological aspects. | Private security services—Brazil—Employees. | Public safety—Brazil. | Human security—Brazil. | Racism against Black people—Brazil. | Urban violence—Social aspects—Brazil.
Classification: LCC HV8291.B6 R633 2023 (print) | LCC HV8291.B6 (ebook) | DDC 363.2890981—dc23/eng/20230124
LC record available at https://lccn.loc.gov/2022053423
LC ebook record available at https://lccn.loc.gov/2022053424

Contents

Acknowledgments	vii
Introduction: Private Guards and Social Order	1
The 12 por 36	29
1. The *Carreira das Armas*	35
The Anger of Other Men	57
2. Hospitality Security	63
Small Thefts	83
3. Securing Affective Landscapes of Leisure and Consumption	87
Routine Suffering	111
4. Emotional Labor in the Security Command Center	117
Securing Life	137
Epilogue: Selling the Sensation of Security	141
The Post of the Future	155
Notes	161
References	171
Index	183

Acknowledgments

The research and writing of this book were supported by funding from the San Diego State University's Behner Stiefel Center for Brazilian Studies, College of Arts and Letters, and the Division of Research and Innovation. Early fieldwork was also made possible by a Drugs, Security, and Democracy fellowship from the Social Science Research Council.

A great number of people in Rio graciously taught me about the security universe that I write about. They answered my one million clarifying questions with patience and good humor and shared their interpretations and insights with me. The book would not have been possible without their help. I gratefully acknowledge Guilherme, Daniel, Waldinei, Renan, Fernanda, Arthur, Palloma, Denise, Maria, Marisa, Angela, Henrique, Luis, Marina, Dani, Robson, Ben, Ludmila, Malu, Alexandre, Igor, Serginho, Gabriela, Reinaldo, Bianca, Mila, Wagner, Christopher, Wanderley, Margit, Marta, Richard, and Jaime. Vítor, my first teacher, supported this project from the start all the way to the last page and deserves a special shout out here. During our time(s) in the field, my family was lovingly supported by Mara, Andreia, Inga, Daniela, Suzette, Caren, John, Karen, Thalles, and Cida. Flavio and Helena saved our lives, quite literally. I am especially grateful for the friendship of Rogerio and Iris. Thank you for being family to me, Michael, and the kids.

I am beyond lucky to find myself in a community of brilliant colleagues who inspire me with their incredible work. Each of them gave encouragement during hard times in the field, listened to my doubts and concerns about the project, read drafts, and just generally supported me. My deepest gratitude to Fabio de Sa e Silva, Michelle Morais de Sa e Silva, Dan Mains, Noah Theriault, Andreana Pritchard, Derek Pardue, Tessa Diphoorn, Jaime Alves, Vijayanka Nair, Jessica Graham, Tom-Zé Bacelar da Silva, David Kamper, Kathryn Sanchez, Abner Sótenos, and Ben Cowen. Rosana Pinheiro-Machado and Jennifer Roth Gordon offered critical insight and greatly improved the text with their comments. Kim Marshall and Rebecca Bartel read every word, sometimes twice. I could not have finished without their encouragement or friendship. My mom, Anna Joyce, told me when I wasn't making sense—not to mention lowered my blood pressure at many critical moments. Love you, *mamãe*.

I owe an enormous debt to three people in particular—the geniuses Susana Durão, Meg Stalcup, and Tomas Salem—companheir@s in thinking about police and security in Brazil. I am so grateful for our ongoing conversations and for all the ways in which you have helped me to fine-tune and improve this text. At SDSU, I have amazing colleagues in the Department of Anthropology and count on the daily support and friendship of the incredible humans at the Behner Stiefel Center for Brazilian Studies, all of whom helped in various ways. Thank you to Flavia Soares, Cassia de Abreu, Isabelle de Lima Vargas Simoes, Brooke Dollabella, Amethyst Sanchez, and Kristal Bivona.

Kathleen Kelly and Grey Bivens believed in this book when I was convinced it was hopeless and taught me to be a better writer. The Garage Band Writing Group held me accountable on the bleakest of pandemic mornings. Tilly Wookie Cookie kept my feet warm. Cassie Galentine dragged me kicking and screaming across the finish line. And Guito Moreto took the most stunning photos. Thank you to all of you! At Cornell University Press, I am grateful to Kevin Karpiak for believing in the book from the get-go and to Jim Lance, Clare Jones, Jennifer Savran Kelly, Ellen Douglas, and others for their support.

On a more personal note, dearest friends Jerusha Ogden, Estee Fletter, Jen Hecht, Emilia Sumelius-Buescher, and Jamie Kohanyi kept me nourished and reminded me of the bigger picture. Dawn Meader McCausland provided the chocolate.

Nothing that I have ever achieved professionally would be possible without Michael, who supports me unconditionally and who has always understood the importance of the time and space needed to do this work. He made this book possible, even with babies and small children in the mix. I am beyond grateful. Thank you to D and A for the perspective you bring, for keeping it light, for reminding me to slow down. All shortcomings are, of course, my own.

Introduction

PRIVATE GUARDS AND SOCIAL ORDER

On the first day of every basic training course he teaches, Mauro sails on autopilot, giving the same speech. "*Olha*," he says to the young men. "I want to start by talking about my mother." Surprise is followed by spontaneous laughter erupting from the aspiring guards assembled in the training facility classroom. Mauro takes his time, waits a few beats, lets our curiosity build. A natural born showman.

"My mother, fifty-two years old. A nurse by profession. Resident of a modest, gated condominium on Ilha de Governador." He continues: "She goes to work. Tuesday to Saturday. She passes through the front guardhouse of the condominium. The guardhouse is staffed by who? Private security." Walking out from behind the table, he paces at the front of the room. "She takes the bus to Vincente de Carvalho, where she gets on the *metrô*, which is guarded by who? Private security." He picks up the tempo: "At work, access to the hospital is controlled by . . . ?" "Private security," an eager student sitting next to me pipes up. Mauro snaps his fingers and points to him with a smile. "At lunch, she meets her friends for a meal in Barra Shopping, a business guarded by . . . . that's right . . . . private security. Now, my *mamãe*, she is a Vasco fan . . ." He pauses expectantly to accommodate the jesting boos from the back of the classroom from those who support a rival soccer team. "On Saturdays, she goes to games guarded by who? That's right, private security. Everything, gentlemen, everything my blessed mother does, depends on the professionalism and capacity of who?"

"Private security," shouts the class in unison.

"And who is private security?" Mauro asks. "*You*. You."

As Mauro aptly illustrates, private security guards, known as *vigilantes* in Portuguese, are a visible, permanent fixture of everyday life in the Brazilian city of Rio de Janeiro, significantly outnumbering police officers.[1] Yet their presence is not distributed uniformly; instead, it mirrors the wider racial and socioeconomic inequality present across the city's landscape. Rio is famous for the way its gleaming beach front condominiums stand alongside the simple self-built brick houses of the city's low-income citizens. Sprawling gated condominium complexes, with manicured gardens and tennis courts, abut open sewage and improvised cardboard shelters. Such contrast also shows up on bodies, with the majority of the city's darker-skinned residents living in favelas or urban peripheries and working in a service industry that cares for the homes, well-being, and leisure of the city's lighter-skinned residents. Social class, education level, and economic mobility are indisputably linked to skin color, with race acting as the structuring dynamic that determines life chances (Nascimento 1989).

Within this context, private security, which draws on the labor of low-income Black workers to protect elite spaces of leisure and consumption, plays a key role in maintaining inequality and upholding white supremacy; it both reflects and reproduces the wider Brazilian social order.[2] Drawing on long-term ethnographic research with entry-level guards, managers, company owners, and elite global consultants, this book examines the performative, emotionally laden provision of security in Rio from the perspective of those charged with providing it. The pages that follow offer a fine-grained portrait of the logics that underpin the always-unfinished work of securing the contemporary city and maintaining the unequal status quo.

Nearly every person I interacted with during my research told me that the real work of security was not to provide absolute safety, a goal seen as so lofty and unattainable as to be laughable. Rather, they insisted, the objective of security work was to communicate a *sensação de segurança* (a sensation of security) to clients, customers, and the general public. This sensation of security, however, is not designed to be obtainable by everyone. Like other commodities on the global market, it is available only to those who have the capital to pay for it.

I explore how this sensation is cultivated through resonant performances by security laborers across scales and how it takes both spectacular and mundane forms. As a subjective feeling, the sensation of security is a set of culturally shaped impressions related to danger, safety, order, well-being, and cleanliness. Its presence signifies enjoyable safety, its absence peril. Furthermore, the *sensação de segurança*, and its counterpart, the sensation of insecurity, are routine elements of everyday life in Rio. While much academic attention has been paid to the overall experience of insecurity, danger, and fear of crime in Brazil and to the role of the state in enacting violence, less often have researchers considered the way in which security is constantly performed for the city's residents.

As I have noted in previous work, state violence in Rio is as spectacular as it is deadly, and the spectacular nature of security often occludes quieter and less flashy ways of maintaining the social order. Police cars and armored tanks, machine guns slung over the shoulders of beat cops, police invasions that resemble a scene out of a war film, are all commonplace (Robb Larkins 2013; 2015). Such state terror, I argue, works as a constant backdrop against which more concierge forms of private security for elite consumers are performed. (Though these concierge forms of private security are no less spectacular!) The feeling of safety, well-being, and orderliness exists always in an implicit contrast with the terror, chaos, and death that is ever present for the city's low-income residents. The *sensação de segurança* is not designed to be for everyone.

Security logics are affective logics that filter through the larger Brazilian sociocultural context, reflecting existing racial, classed, and gendered hierarchies. Thus I understand and analyze private security from the perspective of how it is embedded in what philosopher Charles Mills calls "the racial contract," a foundational societal agreement and a political system that privileges whites at the expense of nonwhites and normalizes the exploitation of nonwhite bodies, labor, and lands for profit and economic dominance (1999, 11). White supremacy as a political system, therefore, depends on Black subordination and servitude, and in the case of private security, on the sacrifice of Black lives, or the use of Black laborers, as a buffer between urban violence and elites. While the precise terms of the racial contract change over time depending on evolving notions of what is socially acceptable, the underlying tenets of white supremacy and Black oppression are never truly interrogated (Mills 1999). When viewed in this frame, just as the sensation of security depends on the ongoing reality of violent spectacle, private security relies upon preserving antiblackness to protect racial capitalism.

As I observed it across a variety of security settings, the *sensação de segurança* refers to a logic that is both outward and inward facing. Security laborers at all levels must produce safe, comfortable, and clean spaces for leisure and consumption by mitigating threats and maintaining calm. They must make patrons and corporate sponsors alike *feel* safe. Such feelings are not merely cerebral but embodied. As Rivke Jaffe writes of the aesthetics of security in Jamaica, "Safety is something that is felt in a corporeal way as people move through urban space: security and insecurity, apprehension and reassurance, are bodily sensations produced in response to a range of aesthetic forms" (2020, 137). In secured spaces, my interlocutors explained, people feel free to just enjoy themselves. They don't have to be vigilant, constantly scanning the environment for potential danger.

They don't have to clutch their purse or look around before taking out their wallet. The *sensação de segurança*, one guard explained to me, is pleasurable.

But the *sensação de segurança* is not only about the embodied experiences of the clients served by the industry. It directly depends on the embodied performances of security workers. Low-level guards, for example, are themselves a crucial part of the environment of guarded spaces. Effectively creating the sensation of security requires them to manage their own racially marked bodies in ways that signal care and hospitality for the clients and guests they serve, a topic which I take up in more depth in the second chapter. Thus, while the *sensação de segurança* indexes an outward facing task of allaying fear of crime and maintaining order in elite spaces, it also refers to emotional labor and to the inner affective and embodied worlds that security workers must navigate.

In the first part of the book, I draw upon fieldwork with low-level guards working in a variety of hard and soft security settings, examining how guard bodies and behaviors contribute to the sensation and to the logics that underpin its production.[3] Next, I turn to the mid-range managers, who work to elicit and coordinate performances that produce the *sensação de segurança* in elite spaces like shopping malls and stadiums. In the last part of the book, I employ research with elite actors—the choreographers of security—during Rio's 2016 Olympics to examine how a specifically Brazilian sensation of security functions when put into practice in the context of a global megaevent and how it intersects with global repertoires of planning and preparedness.

Selling the *Sensação de Segurança*

"There is something that I like to tell my students," Mauro tells me, standing up from the lunch table and bending to tie the laces of his combat boots. He runs his hands though hair slicked back from heat. "It goes like this," he intones, adopting what I recognize as his classroom voice, an even, Socratic tone. "First, I say, 'I am going to start this class with an extremely stupid question.' They love this, especially when they are still trying to figure me out as a teacher. My question is this, I say: 'What is the goal of a private security company?' They think this is a joke and they look at me with this kind of 'what the hell' look. So, I repeat it, right, and then there is always this one student, who says something like, '*Fazer a segurança*,' (to provide security). He rolls his eyes at me and I smile expectantly for the punch line that is slow in coming. *Fazer a segurança. Porra nenhuma.* Fuck no! The objective of a private security company is to make money—*gerar lucro*, generate profit! No one opens a company of any kind unless it's to make money. Who needs to be worried about security, that is *you*." I say to them. "Who is going to take a bullet is *you* and who is on the front lines to learn about security, it's *you*. The company is worried about administration and numbers. The company thinks about security—oh yes, they think about *making money* from your security service. I repeat: the objective of the private security company is to make money." Mauro's lecture here, intended to disabuse guards of any notion that private security exists for some greater good beyond the generation of profits, points to the capitalist logics that define the provision of security.[4] Private security, he reminds us, is not about citizen safety or rights. It is a profit-driven business that depends on selling the sensation of security.

The first use of formal private security guards in Brazil was in the banking sector in 1969 (Zanetic 2013; Durão, Robb Larkins, and Fischmann 2021). Guards were first hired in response to a rise in bank robberies orchestrated by the political opponents of the country's military dictatorship, who stole cash to fund the resistance (Cardoso 2018; Lopes 2018). Postdemocratization, the sector began to grow substantially, still maintaining a strong presence in banking, but also expanding to other areas. The boom in the industry reflected the wider context of life in Brazil's cities, where violence rose dramatically in the 1980s and where that violence began to be mediated in ways that augmented feelings of insecurity within the population. By the 1990s, what Caldeira (2002) has called the "talk of crime"—the constant circulation of narratives about crime or stories about assaults and home invasions that keep fear in circulation—was fully cemented in the public consciousness and continues today to operate as a core cultural logic that structures Brazilian social relations, especially in Rio and São Paulo (Robb Larkins 2015).

In addition to the ongoing spectacle of urban violence, changes in the spatial organization of cities also fueled private security's expansion (Zanetic 2013; 2009; Cardoso 2018; Lopes 2018; Quintella and Carvalho 2017). Tall metal gates went up at the front of apartments, segregating the public space of the sidewalk from private residential space. Condominiums became gated condominiums. And the proliferation of a wide range of semipublic spaces such as shopping centers, sports clubs, business parks, government buildings, and corporate offices all necessitated new forms of protection. A new gentrified police force suitable to protecting these gentrified places was suddenly in demand.

Such changes in urban space were not, of course, restricted to Brazil but reflected the larger restructuring of global cities driven by the privatization and commodification of urban space (Sassen 1991; 2015; Smith 1982; Harvey 2008). As Quintella and Carvalho note in the Brazilian case, private security's growth was linked to "the advent of global capitalism, the hypervalorization of the sense of security and the protection of space for the free market, where security is rendered a good that the consumer should be able to obtain with their own buying power" (2017, 5; my translation). Thus, while a neoliberal wave was commodifying urban spaces in novel ways, security itself was also becoming an attractive consumer good.[5] No longer were guards employed merely to protect property but were increasingly called upon to guard an intangible sensation, part of which hinged on keeping "undesirables" out of these new semipublic spaces (Quintella and Carvalho 2017, 6). Performances of security therefore also naturalize the right of global capital to use the city as a staging ground for profit-driven enterprise.

As the sector grew, it also drew the attention of regulators, who sought to bring the industry under tighter government control (Huggins 2000, 122). In the first decade of the 2000s, new governing statutes were passed. The most important of these, Portaria 3.233 (2012), called the "bible of private security" by those in the industry, established the scope of work for private companies and subjected them and their guards to oversight by the Federal Police.[6] In addition to making it very clear that private security was limited in its jurisdiction and therefore not in competition with police forces, regulation had the collateral effect of creating new revenue streams for the government, which now collected lucrative licensing fees from what had previously been a vast informal labor market.

Expanded government oversight also birthed another important pillar of the private security sector. By mandating certain training for guards, the state—together with the insurance companies which begin to require the presence of private guards to pay out policies—opened the space for a proliferation of new training facilities, like the one where Mauro taught. These schools offered the training and credentialing necessary for guards to obtain a work permit from the Federal Police, but the quality of training remained of dubious quality from the outset.

In fact, many security experts that I spoke to told me that education at for-profit training facilities did not significantly improve guards' job performances or their life expectancy. Like Mauro, they insisted that the training process was so broken that guards were not given the most basic tools for survival when entering the job market, a factor which was especially concerning for those working in high-conflict settings such as the armored car, where they face high levels of assault from armed robbers. "Look, Erika," Mauro explained, his voice crackling over the WhatsApp audio. "For the company, they don't care if a guard is capable. They care that he has his paperwork in order. They care that he has a diploma from a school. That he is registered with the Polícia Federal. For the private security company, that is a *vigilante apto*. *Apto*, or 'suitable,' is sufficient for any company to put the guard in the street. But as you know, suitable doesn't mean that he is actually competent to work. It doesn't mean he has the skills to survive."

Regulation of the sector, including mandates around training and certification, therefore, has always functioned more as a rubber stamp or box check. It conveniently generates tuition revenue for powerful security company owners, many of whom are also financial stakeholders in security schools, but does little to improve working conditions for guards. In this way, the organizational structures of the industry reliably direct profit upward, toward company owners, who historically were (and still are) often high-ranking police officers, military officials, and globally connected businessmen. This group differs considerably from the majority of private security's foot soldiers. Thus private security's internal power dynamics reflect wider social, racial, and economic hierarchies (cf. Jaffe and Diphoorn 2019).[7]

In order to work legally in the industry, guards are required to complete a basic training course plus at least one area of specialization, such as personal security, *escolta armada*, *transporte de valores*, and electronic surveillance. Specialized courses in management and nonlethal weapons training are also available, and schools often allow guards to purchase "bundled" classes for a discounted price. Guards must also complete continuing education credits (referred to as recycling) every two years in order to keep their license active, a requirement which ensures that a steady stream of students moves through the schools.

In 2011, with Brazil selected as a host for both the World Cup (2014) and Olympics (2016) and, as a result of aggressive lobbying from industry leaders, additional laws created a new specialization in *grandes eventos* or "megaevents." While the rationale from company owners and unions was that guarding these high-profile sporting events necessitated special training, many instructors, including Mauro, felt that they were simply a mechanism to direct more profit to the schools, since everyone working in relation to the World Cup and Olympics was required by law to pay to get this new certification regardless of work experience or years in the industry.

Even with the move toward more oversight, it bears noting that most experts believe that the clandestine private security field absolutely dwarfs the formal one (Costa, Chaves, and Potter 2018; Durão and Paes 2021). Accordingly, guards have an abundance of opportunities to take up clandestine security work, which can be more flexible and even pay more.[8] However, these two forms of work—formal and informal—are viewed quite differently by many security guards and by low-wage workers in general (cf. Araújo and Lombardi 2013; Hirata 2021). Work in the formal market, whatever its type, certainly confers valuable material benefits, like the right to labor protections and unemployment. But it also carries symbolic capital that is attractive to low-wage workers. Formal work was generally framed by the guards I spoke with as morally superior to informal labor which was often associated with illegality. Furthermore, the idea of *vigilante* as a professional identity, composed of like-minded security professionals, is entangled with the push toward accepting (and even aspiring to) low-paying formalized work. Put differently, having a work permit or a *carteira de vigilante* is unequivocally linked to an imagined status as a "security professional." Discourses to this effect are very common at the security schools, where guards were not only receiving technical training but are also being socialized into the profession. Thus, just as guards themselves are hired to supply the *sensação de segurança* to clients, they are also experiencing their own kind of "sensation of security"—aspiring to or experiencing a sense of social mobility through security work and being part of a larger community of imagined like-minded workers.[9]

Traditionally, semipublic spaces such as shopping malls had their own teams of guards, who were referred to as "organics," meaning that they were directly employed by the companies they were charged with protecting. But increasingly in the 1990s and first decade of the 2000s, these same corporations began outsourcing. They employed a smaller set of in-house managers and got the majority of labor directly from a private security company who hired and managed its own guards. Outsourcing wasn't just happening in private security but across a range of low-wage jobs. The same companies began to provide both security and cleaning services. These two kinds of highly gendered and racialized labor, both of which "cleaned spaces," were now bundled together for lower prices if the same company carried the contract for both. If privatization changed the face of the city, turning public spaces to guarded ones, outsourcing of private security jobs transformed the labor landscape for those working in low-wage service jobs.

Outsourcing facilitated interchangeability and replaceability, making it far simpler to just change company contracts than it had been to terminate organic employees under restrictive Brazilian labor laws. This trend, in turn, drove prices for security services even lower as competition for contracts grew. The interchangeability and the ease with which corporations could replace companies and their subcontracted guards is now a core structural element of the industry, a dynamic which extends beyond Brazil. As Dickins notes of private security in Guatemala: "The security guard industry thrives on the flexible workforce that neoliberal policies intend to create and that translates into periodic unemployment and low wages for workers. Implicit in the idea of a limitless and flexible labor pool is the conceptualization of guards as replaceable bodies, a view that is held by contracting agencies as well as their 'clients' (the individuals and businesses that hire guards)" (2011, 114). Outsourcing had not only financial but symbolic advantages as well. With third-party contractors providing the majority of security labor, clients could place the blame for security incidents at the feet of others, thereby protecting their own brands from reputational damage.

As should be obvious by now, the *sensação de segurança* entails far more than just the simple protection of bodies in secured spaces. It protects the wealth and power of corporate brands. If the principal objective of private security is to create a sensation of security in order to facilitate the movement of capital, a place's reputation as either safe or not safe establishes the baseline for guard work. For example, as Susana Durão, Carolina Fischmann, and I have noted in regard to maintaining the space of the shopping mall as one that is associated with safety, "breaches in the unspoken agreement that the mall be preserved as a peaceful place impact not only the shopping where a particular episode took place, but extend to all others" (Durão, Robb Larkins, and Fischmann 2021, 147). As one security consultant explained to us: "There is no competitiveness between malls in terms of security. If something bad happens in a mall and the news gets out, for example, about let's say, a case where the guards get overly aggressive, we all lose. The entire sector. It is the mall, any mall, that is no longer seen as a peaceful place." Therefore, there is great pressure from the mall industry to provide top-notch security in order to protect the branded image of the shopping mall as a place.

The heightened focus on securing the corporate brand increased with the arrival of the World Cup (2014) and Olympics (2016), events which depended on large private security forces. The object of protection in the megaevent context is not merely the athletes or even the fans that pack stadiums. Rather, the highest priority for protection are the brands of the events themselves—the brand of the Olympics or the FIFA World Cup—and those of their powerful corporate sponsors, such as Visa, Sony, or Coca-Cola. Thus, from the private security perspective, a potential incident at the opening ceremonies does not just pose a risk to human lives in the venue; more importantly, it threatens the long-term viability of an Olympic brand and all brands associated with it that can continue to generate wealth and corporate sponsorship in the future.

But the importance of security to brand protection was not the sole privilege of well-known global corporations. It was mentioned by every shopping mall or stadium security team that I interviewed, all of whom understood their work as fundamentally about securing brand viability though the management of more garden-variety security risks like theft, infrastructural collapse, or terrorism. The branding framework also trickled down to conversations about individual guards' aspirations. At security schools, for example, I observed instructors talking to guards about the cultivation of their own professional brand as individuals, embracing a kind of entrepreneurial discourse that was presented as a pathway to mobility.[10] Crucially, this discourse does not acknowledge the structural constraints that guards face, as they work within racialized and classed hierarchical systems. Rather, as I will discuss more in chapters 1 and 2, guards are taught to adhere to a neoliberal, bootstrapping narrative that claims that the responsibility for professionalization and success is firmly within their grasp if they work hard and behave as moral subjects.

The *Sensação de (In)segurança* in Brazil's Antiblack Democracy

The way private security reflects the larger social environment in which it operates while simultaneously reproducing elements of that environment is especially apparent in its connection to antiblackness. In Rio, Black men are both direct targets of violence and used as a disposable labor force, deployed to protect elite capital from (often racialized) threats. Thus many Brazilians, including many of the guards with whom I worked, live in what Christina Sharpe describes as "the wake"—an existential state related to "the continuous and changing present of slavery's as yet unresolved unfolding" (2016, 14) and shaped by "living with the immanence of death" (2016, 15). In the specific context of the security world, living in the wake means navigating the governance of death and governance *through* death, where death can be social and political as well as bodily (Mbembe 2003).

As an industry which relies predominately on the low-paid, devalued labor of Black men, private security reflects and extends the antiblackness of the "Brazilian necropolis" or the "anti-black city" as Jaime Alves alternately describes it (Alves 2018). In his work, Alves shows how Black men are constructed as acceptable targets of state-sanctioned violence, in a country with some of the highest murder rates in the world.[11] In 2020, even with the early pandemic Supreme Court ruling essentially halting police raids in low-income communities in most of Brazil's major cities, the police killed over 6,000 people, 1,245 of them in Rio de Janeiro alone (*Atlas da Violência 2020*). The vast majority of those who die at the hands of police are young Black men. Police killings typically go uninvestigated and very rarely are officers held accountable for their actions, so it is not an exaggeration to say that Rio police kill Black Brazilians with an absolute and undeniable impunity. This long-standing practice has only been exacerbated by President Bolsonaro, who has consistently expressed enthusiastic support for violent police and who has offered increased legal protections for police who kill civilians in the line of duty (Pinheiro Machado and Scalco 2020; Ribeiro and Diniz 2020).[12]

Private security as an industry relies on the ongoing underlying antiblackness which allows for the normalization of death and suffering and directly benefits from existing necropolitical norms that allow for ongoing high rates of death for

Black Brazilians.[13] As Mauro cynically noted, guards are "prepared and trained to die." One of the most deadly working environments in private security, and one in which guards are predominately dark-skinned, is *escolta armada*, a form of security in which armed guards protect valuable cargo trucks as they move from port to warehouse to market. Cargo theft is quite common in Rio and working in *escolta* was described to me by many guards as a "death wish." Guards are under constant attack from the heavily armed gangs that target the cargo and who have far superior weapons. There are scant statistics on guard deaths, as companies protect their brand and hide the body count. But during the part of my fieldwork when I was interacting the most with escolta guards, it was estimated that in Rio and São Paulo a cargo truck was hijacked at gunpoint every nine minutes.[14] Thus the conditions of escolta labor attest to the way that low-income Black security workers are sacrificed—maimed and killed—in order to keep goods in circulation for companies and consumers.[15] That Black security guards are targets and casualities of deadly violence—via truck hijackings or armed robberies while working to protect corporate property—is an essential part of the underlying antiblack ideologies in circulation in Brazilian society and illustrative of Charles Mills' assertion that the Black body is "subproletarianized," and compelled to perform "the most menial of the menial" labor (2001, 83). The system of racial capitalism uses race as the central factor in deciding who is deemed appropriate for such menial and hazardous labor. In sum, necropolitics is one of, if not *the*, central premise on which the industry's business model of racial capitalism rests (Gilmore 2020).[16]

Routine Antiblack Discourses

Alongside this more overtly necropolitical reality, a second employment path for guards is in what I call the "hospitality security" sector. Characteristic of gated condominiums, shopping malls, country clubs, private schools, corporate office buildings, stadiums, and the like, hospitality security requires guards to provide safety and customer service, contributing to the overall sense of well-being for the patrons of elite spaces. Service oriented, and always smiling, hospitality guards signal the safety and cleanliness of a place. Security, in this iteration, is a part of a larger suite of racialized labor including maids, nannies, gardeners, and drivers, that caters to elite comfort. Whereas the armed work of escolta necessitates the performance of security as ostentatious spectacle, hospitality work requires gentrified guards, catering to gentrified spaces. But just as with escolta, these performances of security are wrapped up with guards' racially marked bodies and their behavior which must be carefully calibrated to the preferences of the clients and guests they serve. This is true of both low-level guards and more elite ones, as they interact with the global security market where contractors and corporate clients bring different culturally shaped expectations to the security encounter.

So while the normalization of Black death is one side of antiblackness, the expectations of Black hospitality workers in white spaces represents another.[17] High-end shopping malls, luxury corporate office buildings, elite sports clubs, and pricey megaevent sporting competitions were (and are) predominantly white spaces, where Black workers are required to perform whiteness as hospitality workers. Acting as helpful, polite professionals, guards can neutralize white fear of Black men, who are often seen as a potential source of the *sensação de (in) segurança*. This ambivalent logic—which casts Black men as threats while denying the way in which they themselves are victims of state violence, prejudicial security practices and everyday forms of suffering and exclusion—is at the paradoxical center of much private security work (Sharpe 2016).[18] As a result, Black security guards occupy an incredibly ambiguous position where their imagined proximity to criminals requires them to constantly and cordially perform as upstanding, law-abiding professional citizens who are maintaining the racial contract and accepting their subordinate role in it.

Whether the spectacular security of escolta or the more nuanced fine-grained work of learning to act hospitably, guards are required to *perform security* as a form of public-facing work while showing that they embrace it as a kind of inner work, molding their bodies, selves, and professional identities to reflect elite preferences and the racialized social hierarchy. As I discuss in more detail in chapter 2, particularly in hospitality security, guards are taught that they must adhere to a certain standard of grooming. For example, by wearing their hair a certain way, standing up straight, and speaking in grammatically correct fashion, avoiding slang at all times, guards are taught to display white acceptability.[19]

Professionals: Striving within the System

Even with all of its contradictions, private security labor was seen by many guards as an opportunity for self-betterment and as a potential path to professional growth. This narrative, which was widespread among low-level guards and those that trained them, ignored structural racism, focusing instead on individual responsibility and the importance of guard's inner work—having discipline, developing a strong moral compass. This was discussed in a general sense as related to the idea of being a "security professional."

In every security setting that I encountered, security laborers at all levels were being encouraged to act as "professionals" and to take responsibility for their own professionalization. Professionalism for low-level guards was linked to the cultivation of moral discourses that differentiated them from other demographically similar but morally suspect subjects. During training, guards are lauded for being on the "right side of the law," and for choosing righteous work instead of what Mauro referred to as *"vagabundeando na rua,"* (thugging around). Security schools thus work to launder "blackness and badness" through the security apparatus. The industry renders suspect subjects virtuous in order to exploit and profit from them.

In the last year of Mauro's teaching, before he left the school where he taught to work as a manager for one of Brazil's largest private security companies and study for the police entrance exam, he focused his attentions on cultivating a moral sensibility in the classroom. "Remember that story I always tell about my mom—how if something happens to my mom it will be *segurança privada* that will get there first, not the police?" he asks. "When I tell them this, their perception changes. It's like I just showed them a path to respect, *um caminho*. Then I always say, 'On your way here, did you see anyone that was still at the bar drinking since 10 p.m. the night before? But not YOU, you are here! *You* are in a class on Saturday morning at 8 a.m.' In my vision, the shift in their thinking, this is what can maybe change something. Maybe a guy leaves the class feeling that he can do something more, that he isn't a *guardinha* (the derogatory feminized term used by police to describe *vigilantes*) but a professional."[20] Motivational discourses like this one also work because they tap into larger Brazilian cultural repertoires around "the myth of racial democracy," or the idea that race is irrelevant to achieving success. In this very widespread way of thinking, structural issues are not as determinative to success as is personal dedication and hard work.

For higher-level security workers, who were predominately white and middle class, professionalism was also important, but performances took on different dimensions. Professionalism was tied to breaking with a perceived inferiority related to being a postcolonial subject and being accepted into a global security community that was dominated and controlled by "first world" actors, the most respected of whom were those from the United States, United Kingdom, and Israel. As I discuss in chapter 4, while high-level security workers were racial elites in Brazil, when entering the more globalized sphere of security for the World Cup or Olympics, they were often cast as lesser than their Global North counterparts. This hierarchy manifested when global contractors spoke of their Brazilian colleagues as corrupt, late, or unprepared, all of which indexed stereotypes about Latin America. For their part, the Brazilians sought to counter this subordination by their foreign counterparts by performing to the standards of global professionalism. Their performances—focused primarily on emphasizing their planning and their possession of cutting-edge technology—put yet another layer of *sensação de segurança* in circulation.

The sensation of security is not just about convincing Black workers to protect the status quo but also involves (at times spectacular) performances of whiteness. One particular example stands out in this regard. A few months before the opening of the Rio Olympics, I found myself role-playing the part of the state of Rio de Janeiro's governor, Sergio Cabral, in a citywide security simulation that transported high-level foreign dignitaries and heads of state from a posh dinner at the governor's mansion to the famous Maracanã stadium to attend the opening ceremonies. Sitting in the back of the governor's armored minivan accompanied by his private bodyguards and drivers, we mimicked the governor's trip across the city.[21] The minivan led a motorcade of limousines and black SUVs full of other faux dignitaries, played by other members of the local organizing committee for the Games. Rio is a city of traffic so fierce that one can show up an hour late to nearly anything without issuing an apology. But the "governor's" motorcade covered what would normally take forty minutes in a mere eight. In front of the caravan, motorcycle police teams clad in full body armor opened the streets like a gift. Careening at over a hundred miles per hour, I hung on for dear life while my "spouse," simulated by an aging grandmother, told me that the experience made her nostalgic for her childhood. As the daughter of a leading general during Brazil's military regime, she had the frequent privilege of traveling with an armed police escort.

Sitting inside the air-conditioned vehicle, we passed throngs of people waiting for the bus in the hot sun. Some, obviously unhappy with the massive security performance, made lewd hand gestures at our motorcade, but this, said my spouse, was to be expected. Pulling my seat belt tighter, I thought about the feeling of power generated by moving through roads closed just for you. While sometimes we had to practice things multiple times to get them right, this particular simulation went off without a hitch. The spectacle was flawless. Security actions like this unequivocally performed security's power for the wider city—as residents were, quite literally, stopped in their tracks. While ostensibly enacted to practice the anticipated need for protection of elite white bodies, this spectacular exercise also performed whiteness and was indicative of the way in which security across scales is bound up with mobility and racial and class hierarchies.

In these more elite security spaces, where the decisions about how to mobilize the mass of workers were made and where most of the personnel were light-skinned, security performances still worked through affect, and security workers were still working on generating the *sensação de segurança*, albeit in a slightly different manner. One particularly salient way in which this occurred was through the cultivation of "preparedness thinking" which prized emotional detachment as a valued form of professionalism. Preparedness rationalities, popular in security circles for the last several decades, do not seek to prevent disaster but rather to shape security workers' response to crisis (Anderson 2010, Collier 2008, Collier and Lakoff 2008a, Lakoff 2012). In my experience conducting research on security teams, preparedness exercises such as simulations tested our response to potential bombs, chemical spills, doping, or fan riots. It also tested our ability to secure VIP bodies, and to ensure the bodily surveillance around drug testing of athletes was intact. Through simulations, we learned to practice muting our emotional reaction to crisis and to produce records that could be used as evidence of our efficacy, an efficacy which in turn was seen as germane to producing the sensation of security for a global audience.

Furthermore, as I explore in greater detail in chapter 4, preparedness mentalities also required learning to classify the world according to the norms established by the company providing the security. As workers intended to protect private property and corporate interests, security laborers were taught to assess risk to the value of brands and to guard commercial goods, and not necessarily to concern themselves with human lives. In this way, the scope of much security work is not focused on life and limb but rather on logistics and flows (Cowen 2014). Such a framing of the emotional labor demanded by the private security industry brings us full circle to the way that commodification and the preeminence of capital permeate all corners of the industry.

Ethnography of Private Security

A great deal of the existing anthropological scholarship on security has centered on how police, military, or other nonstate security actors create heightened conditions of *in*security for urban populations, especially for low-income, socially excluded citizens. While I acknowledge the crucial ways Rio's security actors contribute to and enact violence (a topic which I have explored in previous work), this book takes a different approach. By detailing the mechanisms, beliefs, actions, and streams of capital of the security industry and of its laborers, my objective is to write an ethnography of *security itself*, thereby adding much-needed complexity to the existing literature. My approach responds to Samimian-Darash and Stalcup's call to focus on "security assemblages," a strategy for the study of security that is "oriented toward capturing how these forms of action work and what types of security they produce" (2017, 60). This method, rooted in Deleuze and Guattari's concept of assemblage, allows for ethnographic consideration of a variety of security objects, logics, and actions without reducing security to insecurity.[22] Furthermore, security assemblages allow a "move away from focusing on security formations per se, and how much violence or insecurity they yield, to identifying and studying security forms of action in all of their heterogeneity, whether or not they are part of the nation-state" (Samimian-Darash and Stalcup 2017, 61).

In this way, the assemblage framework is also useful for overcoming the dichotomy that is often set up between public and private security actors. As Abrahamsen and Williams explain it, such an approach "does not frame private, non-state security actors in opposition to state authority." Rather, "it focuses on a multiplicity of actors, the different forms of power and resources available to them, and the manner in which they come together in a contingent whole to exercise powerful effects on specific sites" (2017, 15). Thus, a focus on security action, not on singular formations or institutions, such as "the police" or "the military," helps transcend simplistic public/private dichotomies and better reflects the lived reality of security work.[23]

In Rio, as elsewhere in the world, security actors are configured in highly ambiguous relationship to one another. Tessa Diphoorn, in her work on private security assemblages in South Africa captures the blurry conceptual territory between public and private forms of policing (2016b; Diphoorn and Grassiani 2019). Building on her research, I take a similar approach, focusing on private security as an overlapping performative space composed of law enforcement, active and former military, private security company owners, aspiring politicians, "organic" (in-house, rather than outsourced) security teams, training facility owners, instructors, supervisors, rank-and-file guards working for third-party contractors, and "fixers" who work with organized crime to control theft. I learned during fieldwork that it was not uncommon for actors to occupy multiple roles and to shift between them when strategically advantageous.[24]

This book is the result of research stretched over seven years, including two distinct one-year fieldwork periods from 2013–2014 and 2015–2016, followed by shorter trips between 2017 and early 2020. As a result of this timing, I was able to capture the expansion of private security in the period immediately leading up to and during the World Cup (2014) and Olympics (2016), which was generally described by my interlocutors as a pivotal moment for the industry as it both grew in size and in profile as a result of global attention. In a general sense, I view the Olympics and the World Cup moment as offering a privileged window into ongoing large-scale urban processes. As has been well-documented, megaevents often act as a Trojan horse, compelling draconian urban change, rapid gentrification, removals, and the implantation of monolithic security regimes (Gaffney 2010). Given that Rio hosted the world's two largest sporting events within a two-year period and that the security budgets for these events were the largest in their history, the expectation of nearly all observers was that hosting would fundamentally transform Brazil's security apparatus.

However, as became rather quickly apparent in the post-Olympic period, the events were not the bellwethers of change that industry leaders and low-level guards had expected them to be. The sector remained largely the same, with relatively few of the people that I knew experiencing real mobility within the field as a result of their work during the events. But what had changed in the post-megaevents period was the wider political context. If at the start of my fieldwork, leftist President Dilma Rousseff was in general continuing the policies of Lula's Worker's Party, by the end of it, Brazil was two years into the term of radical far-right President Jair Bolsonaro, who was elected on a number of hardline positions, including promises to crack down on crime and provide security personnel with carte blanche to kill. While this book is not explicitly focused on politics, the ethnography provided here offers clues to the shape of some of the emergent far-right subjectivities that would later crystallize around Bolsonaro. This is particularly evident in specific conservative moral positions that were cultivated as part of guard training, a topic that I will take up in more detail in chapters 1 and 2. In this way, the ethnographic setting described here provides us with an entrée into understanding how ideas about security intersect with an emergent far-right world view and how they reflect rising authoritarian sentiment.

The majority of my research collaborators had been Bolsonaro supporters from the start of his role as a congressman, and many had been talking about him in praiseworthy tones as early as 2014, when I first met them. He was described to me as "the one politician who shared their views"; who knew what it meant to fight crime in Rio. Others suggested that I really ought to talk to him myself since he "was very knowledgeable on how police and security work" and offered to introduce me. Even these passing comments suggest that part of what made Bolsonaro so appealing in the contexts that I studied was the way in which his leadership style engaged with and drew upon an authoritarian world view, particularly as related to security and the fight against crime (Costa 2021; Schwarcz 2019).

Studying across the Hierarchy

My research was organized to capture private security across the hierarchy, from the humblest of guards to the powerful company owners and global contractors. In order to understand the logics at play in the formation of guards as security subjects, I trained to be a guard at two different Brazilian security schools, taking multiple versions of the basic training as well as accompanying specialty classes in megaevents, armed escort of cargo, personal security, the armored car, non-lethal weapons, and security management. Participating in these formal trainings gave me firsthand knowledge of the messaging that guards get about their profession. Although there are certain core materials that must be taught in the classes, each instructor brought his (for they were all men) own particular style and illustrative examples to the classroom. I became particularly close to Mauro, who served as a key interpreter, and to several other company managers, who will be introduced over the course of the text. These long-term research relationships have allowed me to track changes and continuities in the field that have resulted from the shifting political terrain and the COVID-19 pandemic.

Over the course of this part of my fieldwork, I interacted with approximately two hundred low-level guards and aspiring guards and eighteen different instructors. While training alongside these people, I participated in countless hours of collective banter and storytelling about the experience of working in security. Informal exchanges in the classroom setting often helped me to understand elements of the profession that I could later address more fully in formalized interviews.

Each class had both a classroom component and an applied or practical component. As a result, I also engaged in tactical training, learning personal security techniques like how to disarm an assailant with a knife. I did a lot of pushups and burpees. I did a lot of sweating on the hot rooftops of the security school building or in the courtyards where most of the tactical trainings were held. While this sort of immersive fieldwork was educational for me in terms of getting a sense of some of the embodied elements of performing security, I do not claim to have experienced training or security work in a way that was equivalent to that of my interlocuters. Rather, I had the privilege to choose to experience this sort of labor for a specific window of time in order to produce research about it; I was not choosing it as my life's work within a narrow range of opportunities available to me because of my skin color, education level, or gender. Even as an outsider in training settings—I encountered only a few other women, no other middle-class women, no other white women, and no other foreigners—I was warmly welcomed by those I interacted with at the schools, who generally thought that it was interesting that I wanted to learn about their work, saw it as validating that private security was the object of academic inquiry, and hoped that perhaps I might somehow be useful to their future employment opportunities since it was assumed that I "knew" people in the industry, a notion that I did my best to disabuse them of.

In order to capture the range of private security labor in Rio, in addition to spending time with low-level guards, I also "studied up" the chains of power in the sector. I met with managers at some of the most prominent companies, talked with and shadowed "organic" security personnel at several of the largest shopping center chains in Brazil, interviewed union leaders, as well as a handful of company owners, insurance industry representatives, police officers, and consultants that provided security for multinational companies working in Rio and in the larger country. I attended professional events in the sector, including conferences and equipment fairs. Throughout the process, I looked for ways to participate daily in the private security world. In sum, I wanted to learn to think and to perceive the world as my interlocutors did by "working" in the industry. Eventually, as a result of my relationship with some of the police that I had interviewed for my first book, who were now employed as security contractors and as consultants for the corporate sponsors that bankrolled the megaevents, I was able to accompany the security-related planning for the games and participate in trainings.[25]

My interlocutors at the Olympics, who by the opening ceremonies were short both on budget and on staff, appointed me as a volunteer "security analyst" so that I could continue my research and observe security processes from the point of view of the main operations command center. I could also, they determined, be useful in answering the phone when English speaking callers rang to report incidents and could help with any communication issues that might arise with the largely English speaking leads of other sectors of the organizing committee. Along with a handful of other Brazilian analysts, I worked fifteen-hour shifts, logging and routing security incidents occurring across all of Rio—which allowed me to experience more directly the finer details and emotional landscape of performing security. My time doing fieldwork in this capacity taught me a great deal about security from the inside. This vantage point gave me unique access to high-level security actors. Nonetheless, in this setting, I was the outsider par excellence: one of the only women in a male world, the only foreigner, not a career security worker, and an observer with decidedly different ideological views. I also, admittedly, struggled with feeling complicit in processes that I did not personally agree with. While talking with low-level guards about their world views was one thing, translating a security manual or a software interface into English felt more like providing a service to a system with which I fundamentally disagreed—even if it was the price of access.

Furthermore, navigating my relationships with these more powerful security personnel was far from simple, given the very different ways we viewed the world. As Didier Fassin notes, while ethnographers of police often struggle with a tension around feeling enmeshed with or implicated in potentially troubling police behavior, such unease "is similarly experienced by researchers who study groups and professions with which they feel little sympathy or even profound antipathy, be it because of their political affinities, ideological stances, or social practices" (2017, 5; see also Jauregui 2013b). As anyone who interacted with me during the study-up phase of fieldwork can attest, I was miserable and paranoid most of the time.

Nonetheless, as articulated by some of the pioneers in the anthropology of violence, we must necessarily focus our attention on "perpetrators," not because we agree with them or because we seek to glamorize or validate their world view, but because we urgently need to examine the logics which underpin systems of violence and oppression from their perspective (Whitehead 2004). In this case, my own political commitment to understanding the security-cum-far-right project as it sees itself—as it articulates its own logics and subjectivities—outweighed the challenges of the research. In addition, I also draw inspiration from Susan Harding's critique of anthropology's struggle to engage with what she calls its "repugnant cultural other," conservative fundamentalists of varying stripes who are not politically aligned with the discipline. As other anthropologists have more recently noted, Harding's insights have yet to be widely taken up by scholars, leading to a general disciplinary tendency to produce flat and unnuanced portraits of repugnant cultural others while also continuing to view those who study them through a lens of suspicion or skepticism (Carey 2019, n.p.). Furthermore, humanization and complexification of these subjects through ethnography need not and should not be equated with complicity with fundamentalist positions. Rather, as Harding contends, a better politics of opposition can emerge precisely from ethnographies of these challenging subjects which offer "more nuanced, complicated, partial and local readings of who they are and what they are doing and therefore design effective political strategy to oppose directly the specific positions and policies they advocate" (1991, 393). Representing security worlds and actors, with all of their messy nuance, does not foreclose political engagement either (Alves 2021).

One step toward this work is to think critically about how ethnography can contribute to documenting security's logics so that they can be dismantled. My experiences as an ethnographer in security settings reinforces the relevance of adopting an approach that focuses on understanding security logics, rather than simply focusing on documenting abuses or critiquing how specific actors create insecurity. Interactions with two retired police *coronels* who were then working in private security serves to illustrate my point. One day, we were heading across town to a meeting and the commander had asked them to give me a ride. "We read your book," one of them said suddenly, referring to my first book on violence in Rio's favelas. While I tried to regroup from the shock of the fact that one of them was saying that he had bought my book on Amazon Kindle and read it in English, the other said something like, "We don't think you really understand police very well." "Well, that is why I am here with you now," I said hastily, knowing full well that I had previously limited my engagement with police to strongly critiquing their violence against favela residents. "I am here with you now to try and understand better than I could at that time." What was at play in their comments was both a critique of academic elitism and a frustration with scholarship that only framed security in its relation to insecurity without properly attending to the motivations that informed security action. While direct criticism of these men would be easy, it is also not very interesting, nor does it add anything new to current scholarship. To focus only on individuals would also unproductively trap the project in a cycle of neoliberal individualism, eliding the structural and systemic critiques which are more, to my mind, relevant and urgent. Instead, I argue, we need critical ethnography on the logics of security and how security actors understand themselves and their work. In the specific context of Brazil, we need to examine police and security world views without always turning to insecurity or only to the easy, knee-jerk critique. Rosana Pinheiro-Machado and Lucia Scalco, writing of their work with far-right subjects, characterize this endeavor as part of practicing "nuance as an anthropological responsibility" where "humanizing fascists" "does not imply transforming them into adorable subjects but intelligible ones" (2021, 330).

On the eve of the Olympics, nearly nine months after our initial conversation in the car, I encountered one of these same *coronels* at a party intended to build staff morale before the kickoff of the event. He started in on a rant about "leftist" academics and journalists who were, at the time, producing lots of critical pieces about the Olympics and the monolithic security project it entailed. I decided that rather than just nod in a quiet gesture that could be mistaken for sympathy, I would see what happened if I went a different route. "Well, I am a leftist academic too," I said. "You?" he replied, throwing his arm around my shoulder. "Ha! You are totally not." "But I am," I protested. "Okay, okay querida," he acquiesced, "Even if you are maybe a leftist, if you say bad things about us, well I guess you have the right to say them because you have spent all this time here, with us," he gestured to the room full of security personnel. "What I hate are the people that do one interview and then think they understand enough to portray us as terrible people." While perhaps this coronel might have preferred a celebratory text that championed his efforts to defend Rio from terrorism, I have written from my own deliberately stated point of view about the security worlds we coinhabited, and have chosen an account which quite intentionally focuses on structures, performances, and power dynamics rather than individuals.

Organization of the Book

The book is structured to guide the reader through the logics of the world of private security in Rio across its hierarchy and to show the different ways that the *sensação de segurança* is cultivated. Chapter 1, "The *Carreira das Armas*," presents ethnography with armed guards working in *escolta armada* and with the security instructors who train them for work. I analyze guards' formation as security subjects to show how they come to understand their work through related frameworks of masculinity and professionalism, which, when considered together, form a moral economy that helps guards accept and excuse the dangers of their working environments. In chapter 2, "Hospitality Security," I turn my focus to guards working in what I call the "hospitality security" industry—in shopping malls, hotels, stadiums, and so forth. Security laborers in these settings are taught to perform the sensation of security by managing their bodies and performing whiteness for the elite clientele they will interact with and protect. Based on participant observation in classes at a handful of security schools, this chapter shows how the hospitality security protects white supremacy and deploys antiblackness in order to generate profit. Chapter 3, "Securing Affective Landscapes of Leisure and Consumption," draws on interviews and participant observation with middle managers at several different private security companies to analyze how the sensation of security is created in two settings—the high-end shopping mall and the leisure-based sporting venue. I demonstrate how managers draw upon a multifaceted security infrastructure to cultivate a *sensação de segurança* for clients and consumers. Chapter 4, "Emotional Labor in the Security Command Center," employs participant observation with high-level security laborers leading up to and during the Olympics to examine the workings of preparedness logics and their relationship to cultivating the sensation of security. Security workers performed preparedness in two main overlapping realms, using simulations and through engagement with technology. Both of these modalities worked to control emotional responses while performing capability for outsiders, offering insight into the emotional labor at work in creating the sensation of security. Last, in the epilogue, "Selling the Sensation of Security," I explore current events in the security field in the time since fieldwork. Recent high-profile incidents involving violence on the part of private security guards has put guards, and the industry more generally, under the microscope, calling attention to ongoing issues at the nexus of security, race, and inequality. Despite this, I argue, guards themselves continue to find meaning and belonging in what my interlocutors called "the security family," the patriarchal, racialized hierarchical networks that compose the security world detailed in the book.

In addition to the traditional ethnographic chapters of the text, the book includes two other kinds of ethnographic representation: one textual, one visual. The textual sections are made up of five interludes, placed between the chapters. They center stand-alone stories from approximately twenty-five different low-level guards. Collectively, the narratives give the reader a sense for the routine, quotidian elements of the private security field, as guards connect their work to life experience in a raw, testimonial form. While loosely organized around themes, some of which also feature peripherally in the ethnographic chapters, these pieces are meant to convey both the affective and practical elements of guards' experiences on the job.

In the first interlude, "The 12 *por* 36"—a reference to the standard shift, twelve hours in a thirty-six-hour period—guards describe the mundane rituals of labor, calling attention to the exhausting rhythm of work and to the ways in which they are often juggling multiple jobs at once in order to make ends meet. In the second interlude, "The Anger of Other Men," we hear details of the sorts of conflicts with other men that define guard work and about the strategies they employ to defuse precarious situations, often by attempting to command the respect necessary to deescalate violent situations on the job. In the third interlude, "Small Thefts," guards narrate their work protecting property from theft, describing challenges with petty crime and communicating the startlingly low economic stakes of much of security work. Their testimonies signal how guards often find themselves policing poverty, hunger, and the ever-evolving ingenuity of thieves. In the fourth interlude, "Routine Suffering," the stories shift from the suffering of others to focus on how guards themselves regularly experience violence and injury on the job. Their plain-spoken narratives address the ongoing scars of security work and the lack of industry support for dealing with trauma. In the fifth interlude, "Securing Life," guards describe their experiences as first responders, attending to medical and psychological emergencies on the job. While this element of security work is underemphasized both in the literature and in the field itself, guards cite it as some of the most impactful and lasting work they are asked to do. They also describe emergency work as an area in which they experience rare praise and appreciation, scant commodities in a context where guards are generally held in low regard. The sixth and final interlude, "The Post of the Future," features guards' reflections on the future of the field, especially in the context of the COVID-19 pandemic. Including these interludes between chapters is intended to underscore that while the reader is finished and the arguments are tidily concluded, the low-income laborers who do the vast majority of security work continue to go to work each day.

Also complementing the chapters are a series of photos taken by Rio-based photographer Guito Moreto, organized around the theme of "security infrastructure." As with the testimonial interludes, the idea here is to allow readers to encounter security through a different sensorial access point, the visual.[26] While the images can be read in multiple ways, I chose the theme of security infrastructure for several reasons. First, it is hard to convey in writing how completely ubiquitous security architecture is in the city of Rio. Yet the built environment supports and gives shape to the spaces that guards come to occupy. Using the images, I invite the reader to contemplate the role of built spaces while capturing the centrality of security infrastructure in the urban space of the city. The photos are a visual device that threads through the entire book, bringing the material worlds of cameras, fences, and checkpoints as actors on the scene.[27]

Additionally, as I have suggested above in my discussion of the inclusion of guards' narratives, the collection of images also invites reflection on the cumulative power of the mundane and its role in creating the sensation of security. The very routine, unnotable or uninteresting, can be occluded in ethnography, particularly in ethnography on security, which tends toward the collection and interpretation of emblematic and spectacular moments. These photos, in contrast, are repetitive, conveying how security permeates the city's space and its quotidian. Most of the time, the photos suggest, it presents as tedium rather than spectacle. I hope they compel readers, especially those who do not encounter such constant, visible security presence in their everyday lives, to imagine Rio's dramatically securitized cityscape while thinking about what it would mean to encounter this sort of infrastructure in everyday life. What are the cumulative embodied effects of experiencing gates, surveillance cameras, and other such checkpoints every day?

In sum, I see these different modes of representing anthropological knowing as opening the possibility for readers to experience the security worlds under examination in a multisensorial manner. The book invites engagement not just through theory and ethnography but also through storytelling and aesthetics. While each of the chapters takes lived experience and scales it up in order to build an argument about the logics which underpin private security in a general way (as is typical of ethnography), the storytelling and visual elements operate at a smaller scale. I purposely do not seek to make these narratives or images into evidence for statements about the nature of security work writ large, instead encouraging readers to contemplate them on their own terms. Their aesthetic qualities as short narrative and visual windows into security worlds are maintained by not integrating them into larger explanatory passages in the text. As anthropologists, we do not usually privilege messy snippets of people's lived experiences. If ethnographies teach readers about the worlds under study, the vignettes and images included here intentionally give space to more open-ended narrative.

FIGURE 1. Guard inside a restaurant. March 2021. Photo: Guito Moreto.

FIGURE 2. Security guard checks delivery driver's credentials outside a gated condominium. February 2021. Photo: Guito Moreto.

FIGURE 3. Guard desk in condominium. April 2021. Photo: Guito Moreto.

THE 12 POR 36

Right now? Well right now, I am "freelance." A freelance security guard. Most days I wake up early and go to work. I own a *peixaria* (fish stand) and so I work in the fish stand. I do that most of the day. Then I leave the neighborhood at 8:00 p.m. to work night shifts with security. I have three children. Two live with me. The other lives with my ex-wife. I have to support all three. So, it's like this: I get up early. I go to work. I eat lunch when it's possible to have a lunch break and don't eat if it's busy. And then when the weekend comes, there is more work. I leave on Friday at 7:30 in the morning, a little before then sometimes, and I go to my security job. Then Saturday morning I get home after working all night, take a shower. Sleep a little. Return to security work. Usually finish in the *madrugada*, 2:00 a.m. or 3:00 a.m. Sometimes there are jobs that end at 4 a.m. and I don't get home until 5:00 a.m., you know. And then I go back to the *peixaria*. I have to be there at 9:00 a.m. On Sundays, I only work at the fish stand until 1:00 p.m. I clean the stand, close it up. I take a shower and then start another security shift around 5:00 p.m. That one always goes until 2:00 a.m. My routine these days is about like this.
—Bruno, thirty-six years old. Ten years in the security field.

During this time, my day-to-day life was really complicated. I was trying to work on my spiritual self. Because of this, I needed to attend worship services at least two or three times a week. And then I would attend church on Sundays too. Sunday was usually my day off. I worked a 12 por 36. I would wake up at two or three in the morning, take a bus to a train to another bus. I would get to the (security) company locker room, put on my uniform, get my *colete* (bulletproof vest) and my *armas* (guns), and then wait for the company to tell me what my route and function would be on that particular day. You see, we had to wait for our assignment to come down from the operational wing of the *empresa* (company). After this, we would be assigned to a team and told what our work would be.

There was a lot of *tensão*. Nervous tension. Because sometimes we would leave on our route and we could get a call and be told that there had already been a hijacking. Another team had been assaulted, you know? We would get reports of incidents with other *carros fortes*, (armored cars), *tentativas* at banks (attempted bank robberies), other stuff. And we would hear about these *sinistros* (lit. sinisters, incidents) and we would know that we would then be spending our whole day picking up and dropping off money in banks, *mercados*, shoppings, other stores and that we would be transporting the contents of ATM machines, all of it. And so, the *medo*, the fear, the nervousness, the *pânico* was *constante*. There was this huge pressure, this huge pressure on our lives.

It didn't help that we could barely eat. It wasn't just that we couldn't eat because we didn't have a fixed lunch break, but also because there wasn't any structure for eating. Sometimes, we would ask to use the microwave at a bank, to *esquentar marmita*, (heat up food brought from home in a lunch box) and then we would eat on the road, in the *carro forte*. So, our days were full of pressure, just totally *cheia de pressão*. There was internal pressure from the company just as much as external pressure from *correndo risco de vida*, running the risk of losing our lives. All because we had to deal with all this money, money which, you know, really attracts *bandidos*, it draws the energy, the attention of *bandidos*. They will do both the possible and the *im*possible, even take your life, if it allows them to meet their goal, which is to take the money. So even with all this pressure, I worked in the area for a while. For five years. Eventually, I was let go because the company lost its contract. There is so much corruption inside of these companies, even more than normal because of the money. Now I work in a different area. As an exterminator. *Dedetização*. Pest Control. Fumigation. The transport of dangerous chemicals.

—Reginaldo, fifty years old. Thirty years in the security field.

My very first *posto de serviço*. Shopping El Dorado. I can guarantee you that working in the shopping is not one of the best assignments. Twelve hours on your feet. You have your lunch but by the time you get to the breakroom to warm up your food, eat it, there is no time for rest. So, it's twelve rushed hours. I worked in this shopping for one year and seven months. Let's just say that I left there laden with the baggage of experience or that the job gave me an appreciation for some of my later assignments, which I hoped would be less strenuous.

My shift there was 12 *por* 36. I worked from 10:00 p.m. to 10:00 a.m. The night shift would leave and the day shift would arrive, and I overlapped between the two. And even after the shopping closed, we had to do patrol upon patrol. Upon patrol. Upon patrol. Because as soon as the shopping closed, the window opened for maintenance, for fixing things, for rearranging decorations or store windows in the main areas and inside the stores. So, us guards, we had to check all the stores, make sure they were closed and that all was well with no signs of disturbance. If there was to be someone there working in the stores, we had to make sure that they had proper authorization.

All night, our job was to patrol the stores, check workers' information and send the information to Central (the central command of the shopping), and then wait. If for any reason, we didn't call in the authorization information right away, like if it took longer than fifteen minutes, Central would send an inspector to make sure there wasn't something bad happening to us and the inspector would demand to know why things were taking so long. Then we had to wait for Central to approve the authorization information before we could leave the maintenance people alone in the store. Guards were doing this same process all over the mall and so there might be two or three other guards in front of you, checking on other stores, and you had to wait. We couldn't leave the service workers alone without getting authorization. I heard of colleagues of mine that waited so long that they *chegaram até fazer necessidades em pé no lugar de serviço* (peed their pants while waiting). They nearly died of shame. *É complicado*. It's a complicated job.

—João, thirty-four years old. Twelve years in the security field.

Oh, I have some things to say about the day-to-day of someone who works in security. Some time back, like in 2006, 2007, 2008, the cost of living was more reasonable in Brazil. And security paid pretty well. But the profession began to deteriorate. Why? Because of *má prestação de serviço*. Bad work, poor management. Lots of companies, new ones, that flooded the market and started underbidding the jobs, getting the contracts, and then cheapening the whole profession by using really poor labor (*mão de obra.*) What happened then, my friend? What was our day-to-day then? It was spent on the bus, maybe a ride to work if we were lucky. (He yawns loudly.) Working 12 *por* 36, but we used our time off to pick up extra work to make a little more income, to supplement the lower salary. (Yawns again.) We would work for Uber, work a different side job. Some worked in construction, anything to bring in more income. And so, what happened? Well, the norm became to always be eleven or twelve hours away from home, working. We work at night. Then there is the commute. If you take the bus, you are talking about fifteen hours. (Yawns.) You sleep maybe six hours a night. Maybe.

You can't ever get rested when you have two jobs. And so, it is a hard life, where the security worker sacrifices time with their families, their spouse and children and in this profession, a lot of people end up going the way of drugs or drinking. Because they feel an emptiness inside. Because, well, listen when you work in security, even the *porteiro* (doorman) to a certain extent, you are alone, right? You are just there in the guard house. You have more contact with people from outside your family than with those in your family. This is the reality. You see, you know about all of the things that happen with resident that lives in X condominium, in Y *apartamento* in the Z block. You know this guy, you know this family, you know his wife, you know all about him. His whole life. Like how he wants to have his mail delivered. You know all these little particulars working in the *portaria* (guardhouse or a reception desk depending on work context). But about your own family? You are totally distant. You don't see your kids grow up. You don't see your son or your daughter. Because when you arrive from work at dawn, they are still sleeping or maybe they have already left for school. And when they get home from school, who is sleeping is you. And then your wife has already gone to work. Because generally who is working in security, both the parents are working outside the home, né? It's hectic.

And you know, it is interesting, because we have various unions. *Para que serve* these unions? What are these unions for? For nothing. *Nada!* Nothing! They negotiate terrible contracts, they get some money, some dirty gratitude money because they made crappy deal for the sector, you know? They treat us like *miseráveis* (poor, wretched). *Vigilantes* don't even get dental plans now. You used to be able to go to the union there in the center of the city and get your hair cut for free, but then they started raising the prices, making it more and more expensive. *Jesus, que isso?* No one looks out for us. *NINGUÉM. Ninguém.* It used to be if you worked in the *portaria*, you had to be a responsible person, a decent person, but this doesn't have merit now because you are going to work and you don't have even the basic conditions to do a good job—you work alone, all alone on a night shift inside the *guarita* (guard house) all alone. (Yawns). And so, if you have to leave to go to use the bathroom even, and something happens, then you are totally humiliated. It's hard. The day-to-day is like this. It's work, return home in the morning, sleep, and then leave at two or three in the afternoon for your side job, then back to the main job at night. Sometimes I am twenty-four or thirty-six hours away from home working. Leave at 7:00 p.m. at night and then not arrive home until 2:00 p.m. the next day. Day after day. This life. For what is this life? *Para nada, querida.* For nothing, dear.

—Clovis, fifty-two years old. Twelve years in the security field.

I worked in the bank for five years. A bank guard's hours are a little different from the 12 *por* 36, banking hours. I liked working there. Thanks be to God, I never suffered a holdup during this time. When you work the bank, your whole focus, your whole life, is the door. Because the door is where everyone has to pass. The electronic door. The person has to empty their pockets and their purse and put any metal in the container to the side of the door for us to check. Cards, keys, umbrellas. Then the client passes through the revolving door, which is a metal detector. The door is a stress. Because when someone goes through it and it locks, they think it's bad. They think it's an insult. That the guard did something, that the guard didn't like their face (didn't like the way they looked). It's not that at all. The door is automatic. The door doesn't see faces. When this happens, when the door locks people have to go out, go back to a line on the ground *(faixa amarela)* and then repeat the process. If it locks again, maybe it's the belt buckle. But they just don't understand this. People start fights all the time. They start to curse at us, swear at us. They scream that they want to talk to the *gerente*, the manager. And so, this is our constant struggle. The guard in the bank has to be so attentive. Watch the door, watch the tellers. All of this so as not to encounter any surprises. Lunch is only thirty minutes and that's all you get to sit down. It's a *serviço puxado*, your day is just all about being really attentive and dealing with the door. Monday through Friday.

—Jorge, forty-four years old. Twenty years in the security field.

I always say that security has to be one day ahead of any situation that might arise. I train a lot. I walk, I bike, I keep fit because any security guard that wants to be competitive on the job market today needs to be in excellent physical shape. I always study firearms. I practice shooting so that I am prepared. This is not to say that using the weapon is the end goal. But you have to be able to shoot if you need to. You shouldn't be thinking twice, you know? But shooting, it's the *último recurso, não o primeiro*. (It's the last resort, not the first resort.) Today, you need to have your mind prepared, you need to do some psychological work, you know, so that if you are in a situation, you can react without needing your weapon. I have always done martial arts and so I am always ready to fight because we have to always be ready, *prontidão*. Martial arts give us a mental doctrine, help us to find a kind of mental presence. And of course, nutrition. A good guard, a good bodyguard, a good escolta guard, has to have one thing at the front of his thoughts: I have family. *Vou fazer o certo para não promover o errado.*

As a bodyguard, I always arrive in the location where I am going to work at least one hour before the job starts. Every place has its weaknesses. You want to get to know the place, explore the dynamics of the job, and to see what the expectations are so that you can understand exactly who you are protecting, what the person needs you to be doing. You need to show up early so that you can get the information to do a good job. So always be early.

I prepare my clothes one day in advance. *Roupa*, I always iron it before. So, it's all laid out. Clothing, tie, firearm, verifying that it's all *certinho*. I check with the client what kind of clothes I am supposed to wear because they don't always want you in a tie, sometimes they want you more plainclothes, sports casual, and other times they want you all spiffed up in a tie because it's a more formal situation where you're accompanying them. It's relative.

I usually work somewhere between six and twelve hours. It can go longer. There are clients who say I am leaving (this contracted event) and going to another place. I will pay. Can you accompany me? As a bodyguard, you have a start time, but you don't have an end time. You can be just getting back home and the guy might call you and say come back because I want to go out now. Or you might be on the job, already super tired, *quebrado* (broken) and the guy will be like, "Hey I want to go to the club." And you have to be like, "Okay then, let's go." You can't say anything else to him. And one other thing. *Sempre*. The client is never your friend. He is a client. Don't ever forget that because that is the original sin. The first mistake you will make is thinking that the client is your *amigo*. *Entendeu*? You need to treat him like "*O Senhor*," never as "*Você*." (Meaning that you always address him formally, never as an equal.)

I am lucky that I have had the privilege of working with the *alta escalão* (high society.) I am not embarrassed at all to mention that I have protected people like the top executives at TV Globo. (He recites a litany of famous actors and musicians.) I know how to work with really important people. I know how to do this well.

Is there a start time? Yes. Is there an end time? No. Is there lunch hour? No. Will you eat well when you do it? Sometimes you eat like a king. Other times you are going to eat crackers you brought from home. Bodyguards are soldiers. Like soldiers, they might have to stay awake all night. Be cold. But standing up straight, always saying "Yes, sir." This is the function of the bodyguard.

—Francislei, thirty-eight years old. Thirteen years in the security field.

1
THE *CARREIRA DAS ARMAS*

My *escolta armada* (armed escort of cargo) classmates were not much older than twenty-five, though the fatigue on their faces aged them. On our first day of class, it was an uncharacteristically cold morning in Rio. Guards shifted from side to side to generate heat, blowing on their hands to warm them outside the school's still-closed steel door, a door that remained shut until the official starting time. At the end of the block, a *boca de fumo* (a drug-selling point) run by traffickers from the adjacent favela, was already doing a brisk business peddling small packets of cocaine and pot to passing motorists.

At 8:00 a.m., the door swung open on rusty hinges, and we shuffled inside the dilapidated courtyard. We walked up the metal stairs that swayed and clanged under our weight to sit in a tiny, poorly ventilated classroom. I was the only one that seemed to fit in the furniture that looked like it was made in miniature and half of which was broken, probably from accommodating the guards' typically colossal, bulky bodies. The security school was run by three aging men with bellies of improbable girth. They chain-smoked and looked unwell. The most talkative one, an instructor named Antonio, showed me a long scar hidden under his hairline, a souvenir from when he was shot during a freeway heist.

The class was there to "recycle," the term for continuing education classes required for periodic license renewal by the government. Recycling consisted of a psychological evaluation (we all failed the first time), an endless reading of legal statutes, and cursory weapons training. Class also fostered a sense of shared social space. While we waited for Antonio to finish his cigarette, the group of guards began to trace a genealogy of shared acquaintances; figuring out who they knew in common, who was still alive, and who was now dead. I learned that a man named Ricardo had died from a bullet that came through the front window of his car. Vinicius had taken one to the leg and limped but was still on the job. Rodrigo owed his life to a bulletproof vest his wife had ordered off the internet. Paulo had crashed the car during a high-speed chase. The glass forever stuck in his face made his smile lopsided. Though most of this was delivered with limited emotion—guards merely shook their heads regretfully at the accounts of others' plights—escolta classes were largely somber and sobering. It was clear that the guards understood themselves to be part of something very, very broken and dysfunctional.

The oldest in the group, thirty-year-old Marcos, a stocky, dark-skinned man who wore a pink-and-green shirt from the Mangueira samba school, where he had once played in the *bateria*, had been working escolta since he was twenty-one. He told me in no uncertain terms that escolta was a death wish. "I am completely disposable (*descartável*)—*igual lixo*—like trash. If I die, there are twenty guys to take my place." I nodded, asking him to say more. "See," he said, gesturing at the room full of guards making small talk: "Any one of them will take it. My job, I mean. And then when they are all dead, there will be more." His cousin Kleber, a quiet, dark-skinned man in his twenties who worked for the same company, reinforced Marcos' interpretation: "*Morre um, bota outro*. One dies, they (the company) put in another one. *Fila gigante* when they open positions. Long lines of people are always available." What both men described was a fundamentally necropolitical reality, where, as under plantation slavery, death is a dominant frame of being, and the labor force is disposable and interchangeable.

Starting in 2013, Brazil witnessed an enormous increase in armed cargo theft, with 80 percent of the crimes occurring in Rio de Janeiro, São Paulo, and the highway corridor that connects them.[1] Truck hijackings spiked due to changes in the configuration of organized crime in Rio. As criminal factions diversified from the simple sale of drugs into new markets, including service provision (cooking gas, transportation) in low-income communities, cargo emerged as a lucrative and relatively easy way to supplement drug revenue. Even with absolute numbers in slight decline in the pandemic years, theft and subsequent resale of cargo has remained an important part of Rio's criminal activity—with targeted cargos ranging from the spectacular goods like iPhones and imported whisky to more mundane ones like cream cheese and traffic cones.[2] As Antonio explained it to the class, "Rio doesn't *have* 'hot spots' (*lugares vermelhos*). It *is* a hot spot. The whole damn place is an area of risk." The veteran guards nodded in affirmation.

In response to increased risk, the *escolta armada*, or the armed escort of cargo, grew to meet market demand.[3] As I detail it in this chapter, the cargo security field reflects the dire condition of Brazilian urban life under late-stage capitalism, where perverse market logics dominate, and guards' injury, and even death, has

FIGURE 4. Armored car transporting valuables on the highway in the North Zone. December 2020. Photo: Guito Moreto.

become socially and politically acceptable. While the backdrop of the neoliberal city informs the context under analysis here, I am primarily interested in the mechanisms through which people—the laborers in these trades that demand bodily sacrifice—understand the work they are doing in providing the sensation of security in this sector of the industry. How and why do people like Antonio, Marcos, and Kleber choose to work within a field which places so little value on their lives and well-being? In exploring answers to this question, I highlight the processes that contribute to the creation of security subjects in Rio and explore how security workers themselves are trained to come to accept the fraught task of performing the *sensação de segurança*. The task of providing the sensation of security is framed as honorable and status-imbuing, and it is often experienced by guards in that way. Yet guards' experiences of this honor and status are often in open tension with their critiques of the industry as operating according to necropolitical logics.

In what follows, I analyze how escolta guards understand their work and how they circulate their understandings within the shared social world of security schools, the training centers that prepare them to enter the labor force.[4] I argue that, in this particular part of the security world, guards' subject formation is negotiated through two main interlocking mechanisms, which when taken together, form a moral economy that can help us to understand why guards would choose to work in such a dangerous context.

The first of the two mechanisms is related to the cultivation of a certain form of masculinity. Escolta offers a pathway to a type of manhood wherein working with guns leads to financial solvency. The "hazard pay" guards are awarded for putting themselves in the line of fire is far more than they can earn doing nearly any other kind of work, given their skills and educational level, and the widespread racial- and class-based discrimination many suffer.[5] Thus guards experience an affirmation of their masculinity within a social context of devaluation and demasculinization, which is affirmed through both the income generated by the hazard pay and through engaging in the traditional masculine work of militarized gun-toting, what my interlocutors call the "*carreira das armas*," careers which involve the use of weapons and which hold the potential for the use of force.

Second, *escolta armada*, like other forms of guarding, offers workers a route to become "professionals." The recent formalization and regulation of the private security industry is leveraged to sell guards on the idea that they are doing professional work, replete with a uniform, regular paycheck, and a coveted *carteira assinada* (a signed work contract). Many, if not most, laborers in guards' social class work in informal markets, performing work which is not seen as skilled, prestigious, or professional. By contrast, employment in the formal sector is status-imbuing not only because it is associated with training and education but also because it is often performed in contexts that are occupied by middle-class and elite actors. Furthermore, the professional work of escolta is constructed as moral work, where guards see themselves on the "right side" of the conflict, the side of the law. Given the range of illegal options available to guards, escolta was framed as a way to be an upstanding citizen in the world and part of a righteous moral crusade against *bandidos*, corrupt cops, and *marginalidade* in general.[6]

All of these logics give value to security work while also engaging with questions of capital, gender, class, race, and morality, and are central to the subject formation not just of escolta guards but the wider group of men (and a very few women) who choose to work in the *carreira das armas*. In sum, escolta offers guards a path through which to envision themselves as well-compensated, armed professionals on the right side of the law, an image of their work which attempts to invisibilize, or at the very least to make livable, the dire reality of being subject to routine danger and death. I do not present these mechanisms to say that they worked effectively to dupe guards into self-sacrifice for the protection of cargo. This was not the case. Instead, what I learned in interacting with those in the industry is that these elements of subject formation were almost always in tension with and coexisted alongside the necropolitics of the profession. In this way, providing the *sensação de segurança*, was for escolta guards nearly always fraught, ambiguous, and paradoxical work.

FIGURE 5. Private security school training facilities. January 2021. Photo: Guito Moreto.

Learning to Guard

After Antonio spent the morning drolly reading the legal statutes that govern escolta verbatim, we spent a few hours on practical training. We were told to assemble ourselves into small groups of four and proceed to the courtyard to sit around a series of blue picnic tables emblazoned with the logo of the Antarctica beer company. Feeling very awkward at the prospect of finding a group, I was relieved when Marcos waved me over to join him and Kleber. Our fourth was a baby-faced man with dimples named Carlos who was just out of the army, and who I had met in basic guard training.

We made small talk while lounging on the plastic chairs and for a moment it felt more like an afternoon at the neighborhood *boteco*, until one of the instructors came in and unceremoniously dumped a .12-gauge shotgun, an ancient-looking handgun, and a pile of ammunition on the table in front of us. Because ammo is so expensive, escolta guards are allowed to shoot only a handful of bullets at each training session.[7] Due to this restriction, one common training tactic at the schools was simply to have escolta guards spend countless hours holding, cleaning, unloading, and loading firearms in an attempt to create muscle memory. The lack of real tactical training was not a major issue for this particular group, who as veterans with at least three years in the field, were there to recycle, or, as was the case with Carlos, had a few years of work with weapons in the military. They were thus accustomed to daily use of weapons. That said, many people in the sector expressed their general horror at how little experience guards were mandated to have before carrying firearms every day. Accordingly, my group spent most of the time bemusedly teaching me how to load and unload while good-naturedly answering my questions about their work. If at first my hands shook with nervousness, after a while, I, too, felt the effects of repetition. The loading and unloading made an almost musical rhythm as Marcos, Kleber, Carlos, and I stood around the table, since we could not load the .12-gauge while sitting down. The slide of the bullet into the chamber, the clack of pumping it into place, reversing, and handing the weapon out, handle first, to the person next to you. Around we went, like a deadly minipercussion ensemble.

Just as this exercise was intended as a simulation for real training, our group of four was also an intentional mockup of an idealized team configuration.[8] According to the Brazilian legal statute Portaria 3.233, aka the "bible" of private security, that was painstakingly read out loud in its entirety at trainings, *escolta armada* entails the hire of four armed security guards who escort the cargo truck, which is usually driven by a civilian truck driver who does not possess any security-related training.[9] Sometimes, the guards and the driver have to move the cargo from distribution warehouses located in the poor suburbs of Rio (or any other city, as this is replicated in other urban centers) to retail outlets located in the city center and in affluent areas. At other times, their destination might itself be located within an "area of risk," at a commercial center at the edge of a favela,

FIGURE 6. Escolta guards practice technical skills during a training session. December 2020. Photo: Guito Moreto.

for example. Either way, they must traverse highways surrounded on both sides by large complexes of low-income communities, where organized crime factions who conduct heists are often based.

Neither the guards nor the truck driver are aware of precisely what kind of cargo they are transporting, as this information is not shared with them, supposedly to deter their temptation to steal it. Additionally, the caravan does not have the latitude to chart their own route through the city but is required to take the one predetermined by the client.[10] Private security company owners underscored to me that this is because the details of the route influence the premium the client pays for insurance on the cargo. Critically, the guards themselves also factor into the insurance calculation. Depending on the value of the cargo, their presence is necessary for the policy to pay out in the case of theft. This means that guards, dead or alive, ensure policy compliance and minimize financial loss for the client if the truck is hijacked. They are not actually there to stop the hijacking (even if they might deter it). For the private security company, as well, their presence is pecuniary, not protective. Kleber put it this way: "For the company, they only care about whether or not they will carry any liability in whatever happens. We are just upholding the contract (*segurando contrato*)." Escolta is, therefore, quite indicative of how security works as a performative modality. Guards, company owners, and actuaries all readily admit that moving cargo across the city is a high-risk activity, whose danger can only be thinly mitigated through the sacrifice of guards. Yet the performance of security—the cultivation of a sensation of security—is valuable to the overall endeavor.

Guards understand the protection of cargo as extremely fraught—not because they doubt their own inability to fight and do the work—but because they believe that the structural conditions of Rio's urban warfare do not support a favorable outcome. Armed with old, poorly made, and often defective weapons, like the ones we used at the school, provided by their companies and limited by law in the weapons they can wield, cargo guards are radically outgunned, compared with the arsenals purchased with drug money.[11] When I brought this up to Antonio, he agreed, explaining that despite the fact that under the law, guards have a right to weapons in "perfect working condition," their service guns are in fact "totally unmaintained with old or expired ammunition. If they have to shoot, the weapon will probably fail." Further complicating the politics of responding to an assault is the fact that most truck hijackings happen on well-traveled roads where an open gun battle could produce civilian casualties. Kleber and Marcos told Carlos and me a cautionary tale about a man who worked with them who discharged his weapon wildly in traffic, and one of the bullets had grazed, but not killed, an elderly woman in a nearby car. Not only did the man lose his job, but he was being sued by the woman's family. Kleber noted with disgust, that as third-party or outsourced laborers, guards have far fewer legal protections than police, who are rarely, if ever, held accountable for killing or maiming civilians.

When trucks are hijacked, guards are usually confronted by one to two cars of armed criminals, who signal the robbery with a gesture of their guns to direct the truck and escort car to follow them to a nearby location where the cargo is plundered. Sometimes it is unloaded onto the ground by community residents employed to help with the theft. In other cases, refrigerated items such as meat (a popular cargo) are loaded directly into another refrigerated truck provided by the thieves. Until late 2017, when the number of assaults skyrocketed and changing configurations of organized crime appeared to alter the conventional behavioral standards for cargo assaults, escolta guards usually reported being treated cordially by the gangs. For example, talking over a coffee break one day, two of the guards in my training class came to the realization that they were held up by the same *quadrilha* (gang) who, on separate occasions, invited them to enjoy an all-you-can-eat *churrascaria* (BBQ) in a nearby favela while their cargo was unloaded. But even if escolta guards suggested that they could generally count on the *bandidos*' benevolence as long as they didn't impinge on efforts to steal, guards still framed their work as extremely high risk and reported that their colleagues were killed and injured during heists at alarming rates.[12]

FIGURE 7. Guards practicing escolta formation using the instructor's personal car. January 2021. Photo: Guito Moreto.

Marcos, the veteran on my mock escolta team, remarked on a notable shift in the dynamics of assaults over the course of his career. He claimed that increasingly, *bandidos* needed to *feel* like *bandidos* (*se sentem como bandidos*) and so they barreled down onto the freeway, shooting. "The criminal doesn't understand that if they don't come in shooting then the guards won't either. Criminals don't have this operational understanding (*Marginalidade não tem esse conhecimento técnico*). They think they have to eliminate the guards' capacity to stop them from stealing the cargo." Nodding his head in agreement, Kleber explained his understanding in this way: "Not all *marginais* (marginals) have the expertise and experience to assault a truck without killing someone. Maybe some of them, but lots just have the guns and they wake up one morning all '*tudo nós*' (slang expression suggesting that they feel powerful) like they like to say, and so they are going to go down the hill to the freeway and try it. This *bandido* is less predictable. In like 80 percent of the cases they are going to be lethal because they don't know enough to know that we aren't going to react. And knowing all of this about them, then we *are* going to have to react because we figure that if they shoot people on the sidewalk over a cell phone, why wouldn't they shoot us?" Finding a way to chime in, aspiring guard Carlos added, for emphasis, "Yay, fucking *marginais*." At stake here, both in the real world encounter the guards described and in the discursive way they built it out for me, are claims about the restrained violence of rational *bandidos* and guards versus uncontrolled violence of those who want to feel powerful by assaulting trucks and killing, a contrast which is also racialized and gendered. By distinguishing themselves as trained and professional members of the *carreira de armas*, guards were able to usefully distance themselves from marginal identities and lay claims to societal belonging or rights by *not* being *marginais*.

In addition, I would again like to underscore the way in which the dynamics described here suggest security's spectacular and performative sides. No matter how well-trained guards are (and they aren't), actually defending the cargo (as in shooting) is often a death sentence. This contradiction completely defines guard's work. They have to protect the cargo, or they must perform the sensation of security, even if their chances of success are diminished by subpar working conditions; guards have to defend themselves so they can go home alive, but they have no chance against the *bandidos* who are attacking them. The unpredictability of the nature of the *bandidos* who will confront them, the precarious condition of their working materials (poor quality guns, cars that are not bulletproof), and the sharp rise in the number of cargo assaults means that escolta has become extremely high-risk work with questionable results in terms of reducing risk but with more apparent value in terms of performing the sensation of security for clients, *bandidos*, and the general public who encounter cargo trucks (and their assault) on their daily commute.

Masculinity and Violent Labor

As the most militarized form of private security work, escolta is directly linked to expressions of masculinity. In hypermasculine security settings, doing high-risk work is explicitly understood as a way to gain status and respect. Henrique, a former weapons instructor for the military who worked at a training facility that drew a large veteran population, explained that many escolta guards want to earn a living through what he called the *carreira das armas*, careers related to authority, guns, and the use of violence. He identified people who choose this kind of work as those who like the "operational or tactical" side—which when pressed, he clarified that they "like the guns and the action." Henrique, who was more middle-class and lighter-skinned than his guard-students, observed that his students also opted for escolta because they believed that the *carreira das armas* would bring them status, however limited. "They don't have the education for anything else," he explained with thinly veiled pity. "They think this is the right path—working with guns—to gain status. It's kind of like the *bandido* who thinks he will be someone in this world (*ser alguém na vida*)."

Guards, in contrast, characterized their aptitude for escolta as an innate ability and natural outgrowth of their inner selves; they were born for this career. For example, Carlos explained why he wanted to work in escolta: "I have a vocation for this. I do it because I like to. A vocation comes from the cradle." The reference to the cradle here underscores the sense of genealogy often found in policing families. Marcos chimed in claiming, validating Carlos' feelings: "I feel better doing this than being in a *lugar tranquilo e ar condicionado* (a relaxed and air-conditioned place). I feel good." In this way, guards see the private security field as an arena for the expression of an imagined innate masculinity that lies within—one they were born with, one they embody. Envisioning escolta work as an outlet for the expression of one's true self goes a long way toward mitigating or obscuring the more necropolitical or structural deficiencies that are also laid bare by the dynamics of the sector.

Another arena where it is possible to observe the salience of masculinity as a trope that informed escolta and added value to the work for guards was when trainees failed to live up to expectations of toughness. Indeed, some of the most poignant moments that I observed at the security school were those in which aspiring guards could not convincingly perform the masculine scripts that dominated the environment, particularly in situations of simulated combat. This nearly always came during the tactical training sessions at the shooting range.

At one such training session, the bullets were carefully counted out and registered on a sheet by the instructor. We were not supposed to shoot at anything in particular. The paper target with the outline of the "bad guy" had long since

FIGURE 8. Shooting range. January 2021. Photo: Guito Moreto.

been blown to shreds by other classes and was usually but a mere scrap of paper hanging from a piece of string. The point did not seem to be about being accurate but about conditioning new guards to react in measured fashion while under pressure. We were instructed to drop the ammo straight into the chamber, pump the shotgun, and simultaneously fire as Antonio screamed "*vai, vai, vai!*" (go, go go!) and clapped his hands loudly, simulating bullets whizzing by as the armored car came under attack.

In one class, a new guard looked green in the face as he stood up to shoot. Hands fluttering, he could barely load the weapon. He seemed to become even more nervous as his anxiety drew the attention of the audience of guards waiting for their turn. Antonio began repeatedly screaming: "You would already be dead!" Unable to handle the pressure, the guard dropped his gun on the floor. We all jumped, afraid it might go off. The room shuddered with disapproval. Changing tones, Antonio said, somewhat kindly, "Son, you are just not made for this." The guard finished out the remainder of the day by avoiding eye contact with everyone. This wasn't hard, as his failure to perform under pressure made him an instant pariah and everyone else avoided him too. "Better that he doesn't come back tomorrow," said Kleber. "No one would want to be his partner." Marcos noted, "Even you, Erika, would do better on the job than him." (An ironic commentary on my potential for performing masculine scripts despite my gender when compared to this sad emasculated dude.) The guard did not return to the training course. In this case, his failure to live up to the expected and prescribed conduct of masculine behavior in simulated combat rendered him subordinate to the school's and Brazil's gendered hierarchy. This guard's failure, then, demonstrates how adhering to traditional conventional masculine scripts of toughness and detachment are part of what it means to successfully perform the sensation of security as an escolta guard.

Yet, as with other elements of the profession, where ambiguity and contradictions govern guard experience, expressions of masculinity are similarly complex and fraught. On the one hand, guards' expressions of masculinity are believed to deter assailants, and on the other, they must exercise restraint because unbridled violence is not sanctioned by an industry that only needs their bodies for insurance compliance. This means that guards are asked to perform militarized masculinity while simultaneously subduing expressions that are too conflict seeking. Tomas Salem and I (2021) describe a similar dynamic for Brazilian police, where "wild" or "unrestrained" violence is strategically deployed in certain settings but in other moments can be discouraged in favor of more controlled and rational modes of violence.

In private security, uncontrolled violent masculinity is embodied by the figure of the "*vigi-lícia*," a slang term used to denote a cop wannabe (combining the words *vigilante* [guard] with *polícia* [police]). Henrique, the weapons instructor, described this figure to me in this way: "It's the guy who likes to use military accessories, like tactical belts, knives, big flashlights, military badges. . . . And he will act like a cop, or even better, like a very violent cop." In the classroom at the security school, the *vigi-lícia* was a pedagogical tool for shaping guard behavior. Instructors frequently made these guards the butt of the joke and presented their pumped up, confrontational attitude as the antithesis of what good guard behavior should resemble. Guards explain to me that the *vigil-lícia* can't just do his job. When I asked Marcos about this figure, he said: "A *vigil-lícia* has to feel like he's on the front lines of a war. He is the guy who looks for problems." Most guards that I interviewed, however, saw the performative masculine figure of the *vigi-lícia* more as a buffoon than as a someone worthy of emulation. They viewed the *vigi-lícia* as undisciplined, unmeasured, attention-seeking, and unable to control himself—attributions which were also racialized and linked to wild or savage male violence. Guards far preferred another kind of (white) masculinity, one that favored training, logistics, competence, and keeping one's cool (Salem and Robb Larkins 2021). Thus the sensation of security was also bound up with distinct microperformances and embodiments of masculinity, violence, and race. If guards were overzealous in their enactment of the *carreira das armas* as a vocation, they would evoke feelings of insecurity rather than impart those of security.

Hazard Pay

Guards tolerated the need for this delicate balance of masculinity and security often because of the pay. The most frequent reason that guards gave for choosing escolta over some other form of security work was that it pays considerably more. According to the 2022 salary scale for the state of Rio (it varies by state), guards working in the most basic private security function, merchandise protection done in retail settings, earn R$2,160.88 (US$410) per month. Escolta guards earn R$2,809.14 (US$534) per month.[13] Marcos explained the motivation in this way: "I think there are just a lot of unemployed people these days, people that can't get jobs. They come to private security and to escolta because there are job openings. They might consider the risk, they might even consider it seriously, but they just want to *ganhar pão*, to earn bread." When I asked him about the motivation of his students, Antonio agreed with Marcos and said he believed that the pay was the number one reason that people worked in the field. For those who had recently left the military, it was pay and a sense of vocation.

The logic behind the higher renumeration scale is that escolta workers have a right to hazard pay, an additional form of compensation earned by exposing themselves to injury and death. In other words, hazard pay becomes a way for guards to accumulate extra capital through the potential sacrifice of their own bodies, bodies that are already deemed "appropriate" for hazardous work. Within the necropolitical landscape, guards' deaths are socially acceptable ones; society allows them to die and to die violently.[14]

As I have explained previously, private security work is considered to be the lowest form of security labor, and security labor itself is already a symbolically laden form of "dirty work," to be undertaken only by poor, nonwhite subjects (French 2013; Jauregui 2013b). In order to understand how this choice is a logical one for guards, we have to consider the wider social landscape in which guards reside. This differs considerably from the North American setting, where policing is constructed as a noble and heroic profession. In Brazil, as elsewhere, those who choose to become police officers do so either because they are part of police families or because they are attracted to the militarized worlds of the profession (Salem and Robb Larkins 2021).

If we understand that policing in Brazil is symbolically dirty, as well as corrupt, since police are responsible for cleaning up the dregs of society, roughing people up, killing, and taking bribes, private security is considered to be an even lower form of work, where guards are viewed as the repugnant detritus of society by the upper echelons of Brazil's corporations, police, its political class, and so forth (French 2013; Jauregui 2013b). Even more so in the case of the dangerous, disposable work of escolta. When I was doing research on Olympic security in

Rio and mentioned to the high-ranking police that I was also working with *vigilantes*, they were nothing short of horrified, a sentiment which seemed less about the job itself than about the kind of people they imagined to be filling these positions. One officer said, "I can't even understand their Portuguese. I have no idea how you can. They can't speak at all." Not being able to properly "speak" was a veiled reference to guards' imagined lack of education, while notions of guards' dirtiness or dangerousness are linked to racist paradigms that connect violence and hygiene with skin color. Others chimed in, saying of guards: "They are rude." "They are pitiful." "They are not reliable. They are dangerous." These comments catalogue the speakers' ideas about guards' race and class status in crucial ways, which reflects how low-status security work is connected to the wider discriminatory frameworks in which guards find themselves trying to earn a living.

Hazard pay, and the risky labor it rewards, also contributes to the temporality of escolta work. Unlike the hospitality guards, who I will discuss in the next chapter, and who see themselves working hard in order to slowly rise in status and secure incrementally better positions, thereby accessing more consumer goods and symbolic capital over the course of a career, the escolta is much less future-oriented; hazard pay itself suggests a short high-risk payout in the context of an uncertain future.

Professionalizing Security

One of the most crucial and valuable things that private security work offers guards is a chance to view themselves as "professionals," a term which was consistently deployed by guards, instructors, and company owners and which encapsulated both the stability of a job with good pay and reflected a version of masculinity that most guards sought to embody and which they perceived as status-imbuing. Being a professional was, of course, also not being a *marginal* or a *bandido*. All of these things meant that the term floated around constantly in discourse. In fact, Marcos and Kleber preferred *"profissionais de segurança,"* to the more common term, *vigilante*. Professionalism took on mythic proportions, as a kind of symbolic capital used to compensate for both structural and hierarchical deficiencies. Professionalism was this precious thing, located within their control, which appeared akin to something like pride. For example, Henrique regularly experienced what he perceived as a lack of respect for the private security sector as a personal insult to his own professionalism as an instructor. "I am trying to train professionals but they (the school) don't give me even the minimal conditions or resources to do so. For example, for the tactical training.... It would cost like nothing for the company to get us an armored car to train with or even to get us a regular car to use to do the escolta with. I mean, it's obvious, right? Guards should receive training that approximates their under-fire conditions, right? But no, the company is so cheap that they tell me to just put four chairs together and to tell the *vigilantes* that they should imagine they are riding in a car." I think of sitting around the courtyard on plastic tables instead of working with a real car. "Ridiculous!" Henrique continues, "This is why I can't teach these classes anymore. I am a professional and I am being asked to work without a modicum of respect."

Guards were similarly offended at how companies and training facilities did not respect their attempts to be professional. Kleber noted that they only got "better training from the (private security) company when there is some kind of incident, some *sinistro no posto* (incident on the job) and even then, it's only because the client demands it. It is never preventative, only reactive. '*Casa cai, bota tronco*' (colloquial expression meaning that it's only when the house collapses, they think about putting up its frame and support beams)." The sentiment is that they (authority figures, whoever they may be) only consider something essential when it affects them.

Yet discourses around professionalism also sometimes functioned as a rebuttal. When guards were confronted by dire situations that revealed the flawed and unequal hierarchies that underpinned the industry, many would default immediately to statements that acknowledged the issues but that positioned their own professionalism as the answer or as something with agency to counter their overall societal devaluation.

Guards are taught to internalize an entrepreneurial, neoliberal logic that says that they are responsible for their own professional development. Instead of limiting themselves to leveling critiques of the system for devaluing them or underlining how it prohibits them from realizing their professional potential, they focus instead on personal initiatives on their path to professionalism; on bootstrapping situations in which they display initiative and assert control. Marcos explained: "As for the company, they don't care that much about qualifications. We are just *alvo fixo—uniformizado e armado*. A mainstay, with a uniform and a gun. But for us, we can't wait for the company to dole out better conditions, we have to be attentive, ever vigilant. For us to be *alive*, we have to take steps to be better. We have to qualify ourselves." Kleber chimed in, "We have to be afraid of dying. This leads us to do excellent work."

Another guard in the class, who overheard our conversation, joined in, lamenting about the poor state of equipment, and explaining to me how he began to stay after work to organize the gun locker and clean and maintain guns because he was too scared to work without having some measure of control over the functioning of the weapons. Through his efforts, he improved the condition of guns for everyone at the company and, earning the respect of his superior, was eventually promoted for taking initiative. His initiative attests to the way the attempt to ensure survival is outsourced to the guards and that duty is removed altogether from the company itself. But it also suggests an internalization of a late capitalist discourse of entrepreneurship, where self-betterment and personal initiative are shifted to the individual security worker, who has the responsibility to become a more "valued professional" laboring to impart the *sensação de segurança*.

The Moral Universe of the *Carreira das Armas*

Guards frequently explained their decision to do the work of escolta through an understanding of themselves as part of a moral universe, where they are working legally, according to terms laid out in a legal contract, and working to protect merchandise from illegal and immoral theft by armed criminals. They routinely asserted a kind of moral superiority over other figures working in the *carreira das armas*, one which helps us to better understand how they choose to do their work and how they understand themselves as (perhaps low-ranked but morally just) figures in the security hierarchy.

One of the central ways that this emerged at the security school was through the open and constant criticism of police officers, who are simultaneously idealized and hated. Many guards are themselves failed police officers, who would have preferred to work in law enforcement but due to their low level of schooling, were ineligible for the entrance examination that required a high school diploma. Both Marcos and Kleber described themselves as having dreamed of careers in law enforcement but explained to me that "life" had not allowed for that opportunity. One form of reckoning with this disappointment head-on was to reconcile their lower position in the security hierarchy by drawing constant attention to the corrupt ineptitude of the police. For example, Kleber blamed the growth of private security on the police, explaining: "Our field is growing because of the 'failures of public security.' We grow because they don't do their job. And yet when police look at private security—the guard, *não é nada pra ele*. He is nothing and nobody. They see him as ill-prepared. They think he doesn't have the balls to be there. How he speaks, how he walks, how he doesn't take care of his equipment."

The humiliation of the *vigilante* as experienced through dismissal and disdain by the police is further countered by the adoption of a moral discourse where guards present themselves as morally superior to police officers. It is not the guards themselves that create their miserable conditions, Marcos claimed: "We follow the laws. I mean we don't have the minimum conditions for victory. Our *governantes* (politicians) don't give us the right to use the guns we need. But the police, they get them ... and they steal, they kill, they are dishonest."

Even stronger and more strident moral overtones inform the division between private security guards and drug traffickers, perhaps due to how they are diametrically positioned as enemies, but also because of their social proximity. If becoming a police officer is a foreclosed option for most guards, becoming a trafficker is not. Such an opportunity is much closer to the realm of possibility. Maintaining boundaries between the ethically sound, legal work of escolta and the illegal work of drug trafficking requires constant vigilance and polarization. It was all about being on the "right side of the law," with "the law" being a construction which was not challenged by escolta guards or by the criminals that targeted the cargo. Rather, the difference between engaging in the legal work of private security and the extralegal work of *bandidagem* was one of a moral imperative. Henrique claimed that some (problematic) "less committed" or "opportunistically oriented" guards do security work not because of a "true and actual" passion for the operational side of the work, as was his case, but due to a "passion for a supposed power," as was also the case of *bandidos*. Indeed, the split between working because of the satisfaction of the work and working for power, was one of the central moral framings that I heard leveled at security labor. For example, Henrique related to me that if he didn't have the character he did, he wouldn't do the work he did now. He had been recruited by both the traffickers and the *milícia* and had refused both because "I have character." And "I want to live." "Some of our colleagues, you know, they go to the other side. They are weak. They take the easy way out." When I ask how come some people end up on the side of the traffickers, he answers, "*Simples: falta de caráter.*" (They don't have a moral compass; they lack character.)

In this chapter, I have explored how social interactions at security schools and in the workplace come to shape guard subjectivity in key ways which can help us to understand why these men opt to labor under such extreme conditions of risk. In the field of escolta, long-standing, racially charged inequalities are being negotiated in the context of highly divided urban spaces and against the backdrop of the ongoing advance of late capitalism and the political polarization of contemporary Brazil. For dark-skinned, economically and socially marginalized men like Kleber and Marcos, security work becomes a way to "be someone in this world," as Carlos described his aspirations. The private security industry understands the desire of these marginalized guards and, thus, takes advantage of those desires to convince them to do dangerous labor in service to selling the *sensação de segurança*.

Guard training processes, as well as the shared sociality of the security schools themselves, create a space for the development of a specific guarding identity and mentality, where extreme risk is recast in terms of masculinity, economic solvency, professionalism, and moral righteousness. These elements focus guards' attention on factors within their control, strategically diverting attention from the ways in which the industry treats them as cannon fodder.

From guards' perspective, escolta offers multiple paths to achieve societal respect and to accumulate capital. Additionally, guards understand their work in strongly pronounced moral tones. The moral capital of being on the right side of the law and demonstrating that one has overcome possible temptations to bear arms for the narcotraffic is both powerful and desirable. And yet, while these discourses attest to the mechanisms through which escolta work is rendered appealing by the industry and by guards themselves, these motivators do not ever completely elide the fact that escolta work is dangerous, precarious labor. Yet the guards I interacted with frequently recast risk as a natural consequence of their vocation, rather than demanding better working conditions from the security companies that sacrifice their bodies and lives in the name of corporate wealth. Understanding guards' labor subjectivity is especially significant then because it helps us to understand how private security polices the urban population from within. Importantly, it signals some of security's central logics—as connected to race, crime and morality, neoliberalism, and masculinity—logics which play on wider cultural discourses in order to both appeal to and appease urban subjects.

FIGURE 9. Eye of the camera outside a condominium in Recreio, Rio de Janeiro. January 2021. Photo: Guito Moreto.

FIGURE 10. Low-tech equipment improves the view for guards. January 2021. Photo: Guito Moreto.

FIGURE 11. The guardhouse or *guarita* is a fixture of the residential enclosure. January 2021. Photo: Guito Moreto.

THE ANGER OF OTHER MEN

Listen, here is how it is. I am security. I am the *disciplina*, the bouncer, for Salgeiro (one of Rio's samba schools, which during carnival season holds large parties). The *disciplina*, he is there to minimize *confronto*. So like, a guy comes up and is like "Security, man, I was just here with my girlfriend and this *cara* (guy) came over, dude, and *passa mão na minha namorada*, groping her, getting too close to her. The *cara* is trying to start some shit with me. Can you come over and check it out?"

So I go over there I find the guy and tell him that to *passar mão*, like touching other people's wives, can cause a problem, you know? "If you continue to do this," I say, "I am going to have to throw you out." Basically, I tell him that there is going to be consequences if he keeps it up. I let him know. I give him the information. I make it real clear. I tell him that I am going to be watching him. And I am going to be really watching.

If the guy tries to be pervy with the woman again, I am going to go over there, I am going to call him "*amigo*" (friend), and say "You need to leave the event. I have to ask you to leave the event." But now, let's say this was the situation. Let's say that I get there and the fight is already underway. This is what I do. I work to immobilize both of them. Call for backup. Get them outside immediately. This all happens every single week. Both of these situations.

—Zé Carlos, thirty years old. Five years in the security field.

I am going to tell you a story about when I was working as a *vigilante*. I was working at *bailes*, late-night parties, on Fridays and Saturdays and Sundays too. I was totally negligent as an employee. I didn't understand *anything* about security. I. didn't. understand. anything. Not about security, not about how to frisk people. Nothing about controlling a situation, nothing about people, how they should or should not be approached.

And so, this is where my story starts. I was unemployed and broke. I got an invite from my friend to come and work with him. As a matter of fact, this friend, Celso, just died this week, from COVID. *O Senhor o levou* (God took him). *O Senhor tenha, possa ter, misericórdia da alma dele* (and may God have mercy on his soul). Back in the day, we had just met and were chatting, and he asked if I worked, and I told him I was unemployed and he said, "God is going to help you." And I said, "Yes, Amen. *Logo, logo,* He is going to *arrumar um serviço para mim*" (Soon, God is going to provide me with a job).

And then, one day, Celso and I ran into each other at the barber shop, at Jorge's barber shop, where we both got our hair cut, you know? And he said something like "I need a security guard to work for me on the weekends. *Sexta, sábado, domingo. Você topa?* Are you in?" I said, seriously? I knew nothing. Like nothing about security. But I had worked with the public before, so I guess that counted for something. So, we sat down and talked about it and he said, "Okay, you are hired." "What should I wear when I show up?" I said. *Calça social, camisa social,* and a black tie. And so, like that I started working. He asked me if I could bring another friend, someone who I thought would work well with me. The friend I recruited was a huge strong guy. He could beat up anyone. And I thought he was perfect because he was going to protect *me.* I told Celso all about the advantages of him being my partner, because he could chase a guy, and do this or that, and he had experience in the military too. So, he got hired too.

Celso, because he was a smart old dude, what did he do? To test us out as security, he called some people, some people that were from the *malandragem* (criminal life), the local *malandragem,* and he said, "Listen, you are going to enter *armada* in the place so that I can see how my security interacts with you." Me and my friend didn't know about any of this, of course. Celso's instructions to us were to not let any outside alcohol or guns in. Those things can't come in, *de qualquer forma.* So, you have to perform your work to make sure they don't. If something comes up, you can call me.

So, the night went on, we frisked and searched everyone, kept the line organized, and when it was between 1 a.m. and 2 a.m., two guys showed up and when it was their turn to be *revistado,* they said no, we aren't going to be searched. We said, listen, amigo, we are just here doing our job and so if you want to enter the *clube,* well, you will have to let us frisk you. When I said this, one of the guys, he just lifted his shirt (in a pseudo kind of allowance to be searched) and said, we are going to enter as we please. When I looked behind me, my friend who I thought was going to be the one protecting me, he looked at me and said, "Uh, I am going to go and get a drink of water," and left me all alone. (Laughs)

Long story short, the one guy kept saying he was going to enter however he pleased. So, I said, "Listen, brother, can I talk with you?" "*Olha*, I know you want to enter, but I want to keep my job. I just want to say, I am not going to get in your way of having a good time once you enter, but I also don't want you to take the bread out of my children's mouths. If I let you in, I am going to lose my job. And if I don't let you in, you might do something against me. But I want to be able to return at the end of my workday, to take the Lord's daily bread to my children. And I want you to please try and understand why I am asking you to comply." In the end, the *bandido* or *maluco*, or whatever he was, he was one of the ones who had been contracted by the *dono de baile*, he just turned around and left without another word. He went to get the *dono*, who came back with him, with Celso. So Celso, you know, he asked me what was going on? And I said, "This man wants to come in but he is armed I think, and you told me no guns, no booze. So because I am the security, I told him that he can't enter. I was *sutil* and polite with him. But I told him that I was acting on my own behalf, that I needed to do my job."

Celso, looked at the guy and said, "See, what did I tell you? Did I or did I not finally find myself a real security guard?" And so, the *bandido*, who was who was in charge of the region where the *baile* was said, "Here, you are free to search whoever you want. And if anyone gives you a hard time, you call me. Because who commands everything in this area is me. What you did right now, *isso foi papel de homem, foi papel de segurança*. And no one messes with an honest, *fiel* (loyal, faithful, reliable) security guard."

Oh, and my partner, my friend that I thought was going to protect me? He only came back from his water break after it all calmed down.

—Alexandre, forty-two years old. Fifteen years in the security field.

It all started on a normal day. We got to work. We got ready. Me and my team. We followed our regular rhythms of preparation. We were given our route. Like all our routes, it was a fixed route. We were sent this time to transport the cash from a McDonalds. This was done in the *carro forte* (armored car). We were just arriving at the place and we checked in with the manager that it was clear to proceed when we were alerted by the McDonalds employees that there were two "*elementos suspeitos*" who were threatening the workers. They wanted a free burger and said if they didn't get it, they were going to *dar tiro* (shoot up the place). They had caused a panic inside the restaurant, including saying they were going to kill some of the other customers. We were just arriving right then, so we decided to circle around and park the *carro forte* on the road behind the restaurant. We got out and went on foot to the locale, with the idea of finding out what was going on, if there had been a holdup or what. Basically, we had to figure out what was going on so that we could get the cash we were supposed to and do the work we were given, *tranquilo* and *em paz*. When we got there, the employees told us the suspects were in the bathroom. So, my colleague and I went into the bathroom, guns drawn. We told the two guys to lay down on the ground and proceeded to search them. We frisked them to see if they had an *arma de fogo* or *uma arma branca* (lit. white weapon, meaning knives or other potentially deadly weapons that are not firearms). We didn't find anything on them. We gave them a talking to and told them to get out of the restaurant and to not come back or else we would detain them and call a squad car to take them to the *delegacia*. We reminded them that they couldn't do this kind of thing and that it put us—as guards—at risk. Because our job was to get out of the armored car, *retirar* the money and they were in there saying they were going to rob and shoot up the place. They apologized and left *com o rabo entre as pernas*, their tail between their legs.

—Carlos, forty-five years old. Twenty-five years in the security field.

One of the first rules of security is "*Nunca agrida ninguém.*" Never attack anyone. Because you don't know who the person is and you don't know who *com quem eles andam* (who they walk with). Twenty years ago, a security guard would earn fifty *reais* to work a *balada*, a party. No snacks, no juice, no water. You had to work with nothing for fifty. And us guards, we were young. My partner back at the beginning, one of the other guards that I worked with, he was so young. He didn't know anything. He confronted a guy inside the *balada*. The guy was causing some issues, so the idea was to immobilize him and boot him out of the party. But how was this done? Smacking him around, punching him, even kicking him in the ass and then saying, I am throwing you out of here, son of a bitch. (Sorry for using a swear word, *professora*.) The guy said, "I will be back for you."

Now, I don't know what my partner was thinking, but we were really young you know. But he left the *balada* at 4:30 in the morning, walked out onto the dark road, and the guy said to him, out of the darkness: "Hello, I told you I'd come back" and shot him twice in the head. My partner was twenty-three years old. "*Bonito*," the ladies said. *Jovem*, with a whole life in front of him that he didn't get to live because of his action, his incorrect action.

After that, well anytime I went to work at any event, even now whenever I do any type of work like this, I remember: *you cannot act better than anyone.*

Whether you are armed or unarmed, you need to be the same person, with the same conduct. The same posture. Because the door that you open correctly, *ele nunca se fecha. Nunca.* The door you open correctly doesn't slam shut. So, if you want to be a security guard, *a vigilante, o porteiro, a escolta*, remember this: Never think that you are immortal. Because you are so not. Knives kill, forks can kill. Today, there are people that even kill each other with a pen! And when a guy wants to do a *maldade* (bad thing) he waits for the *hora certa, momento certo* (right moment, right time). Is your life worth that R$50 you'd get paid? Is your respect worth R$50? *Não*. Respect your life, protect your life, and remember that there is always someone waiting for you at home. If you don't make it back home, you will leave someone crying.

—Francisco, thirty-eight years old. Fifteen years in the security field.

Logo, logo after I started this job, here at the condominium, I worked the night shift. I encountered a problem. A few days before, you see, there was this car parked nearby. It was a Ford, a white Ford. What happened was that some of the condominium residents passing by noticed that there were guys in the car and that these guys were armed. They got nervous and came to the *guarita* (guardhouse) and they asked the *vigilantes* who were working that day to go and check it out. But when they did, the car was pulling out. They filed a report, as is customary, but nothing came of it. The guys didn't come back that day or any other day that week.

When they did come back, it just so happened that it was the day of my first day of work at the *posto* (post). I had arrived at 22:30h and the guys pulled up driving the same white Ford. *Placa* (license plate) was from out of state. I think it was from Paraná. When I saw that the plates were from out of state, I watched a little closer. The car drove in, made a loop, and then came out past my *portaria* to leave. And the driver asked me where *fulano* (so and so), one of the other guards who worked there was, if he was working, because according to him, they were friends. Which was obviously not true. He asked me if I could look at the schedule and tell him when his "friend" was working, which shift, so he could meet up with him. When I asked him his name, he didn't want to tell me and I started to be suspicious, wondering if he was looking for the other guard to cause him some harm. I asked a few more questions. He didn't answer me and drove off.

In the following days, he started coming by all the time. Circling around. We reported the activity to the police, who apparently went to his house and questioned him. He said he was an Uber driver and that that was his reason for coming around the condominium all the time and they let him go.

After that, he came back again. It was Dia dos Pais (Father's Day) 2018. He pulled in front of my guardhouse, me *chamando de "irmão."* Calling me brother. *Quero falar com você, irmão*. And I didn't reply because I didn't know him at all. *Não, eh?* Plus, I didn't like the "brother," you know, the implication of that. I wasn't going to talk with him if he didn't speak respectfully to me. And my colleague who was working with me—it was Lima, my manager, that day—he zeroed in on the guy. He started questioning him. "Why are you here provoking our *vigilantes*? He's just here being quiet." The guy started swearing at Lima, real *agressivo*. "Why are you swearing at us?," we said to him. And at that point, I said "What is it you want with me?" And he started telling me that he was mad that the police had come to his house. That he had been sleeping in his bed with his wife and he started going on and on about how they had pulled him out of his bed and asked him if he had a gun and tore apart his car searching it. They made a huge mess saying they were looking for a revolver. And then he said, this happened because of a *vigilante* that works with you. I want to find him so that I can *resolver com ele,* settle things with him. You know who he is. And I said, listen, he isn't here. And plus, the *vigilante* just did his job filing a report based on what the residents who walked by saw. They saw your car and you and your colleagues with guns. The report said it was you and two more people in the car, all of you armed. And the residents were scared and so they asked the *vigilante* to make a report, as is the procedure. The *vigilante* is here to help and to execute these kinds of requests. But if you come back, if you keep coming back, well, you are going to find what you are looking for. If you come in peace, you will find peace but if you are coming looking for war, this is what you are going to find.

    Well then after I said all that, he got real quiet and finally said "Sorry, man." And I said no, you should apologize to my supervisor because you swore at him. And he said, sorry man, to him as well. I am just feeling extra emotional because it's Father's Day, he said, emotional about the situation that he had experienced. He said sorry a few more times and that he was going to bring the "*disciplina*" to resolve the situation. With this he meant his own security person. In the *linguagem do crime*, we understand this term to mean the guy who resolves things, the "cleaner." The guy *que vem para resolver,* who comes to settle scores. And then I realized that he really wasn't anyone. He didn't have any power to settle scores himself. That he was coming by all the time just to terrorize us. He drove away and never came back.

    —Nascimento, thirty-seven years old. Five years in the security field.

2

HOSPITALITY SECURITY

"Star Shine Security" has a well-heeled address in an upscale neighborhood that boasts one of the most expensive prices per square foot in all of Brazil. I look up to greet the security camera as I buzz the building's entry gate, a practice which is routine in Rio, where residents often live behind tall bars in security enclaves. It has taken me several months to get an interview with the head of this particular fast-growing private security company. I have only heard praise for the firm, which was unusual in a field where almost everyone has a complaint about their employer, or their competitor. The success of the company was often attributed to the specific leadership skills of its executives, a high-powered couple. The male partner was a veteran police *coronel* who worked in the mayor's office. The female partner, an American whom I call Vivian, was an anomaly in the security world due to her gender. Her company's success was often attributed to her business savvy and worldliness in securing sought-after international contracts. Yet the mere fact that she was an acceptable and even desirable figurehead for a security company—a field which is absolutely dominated by militarized men—is indicative of key contemporary changes in the field of private security, particularly in what I call "hospitality security," where a poised, beautiful, and globally connected woman is actually a well-positioned leader.

I waited for Vivian in her office. The furniture was tasteful and high-end. I could hear the crashing of the waves from the sea. She came in late, more dressed up than me; Louis Vuitton handbag dangling from outstretched hand. She quickly explained, as if sensing my question, that this was the office that they use for hosting prominent clients who don't want to have to travel to the peripheries where most companies are headquartered. (I wondered how I qualified as prominent.) Indeed, everything about the space functioned to distance our encounter from the bodily, fleshly, potentially violent or dirty work of security. The space itself performed its own sensation of security, imparting an overall sense of well-being and confidence.

We sat. The office maid turned up the air conditioner and brought us small cups of espresso. I asked Vivian about the growth of the private security industry, grateful to count on our shared cultural bluntness. Who are the thousands of *vigilantes* that work for your company? Where do they come from and what do they look like? "If you had asked me a few years ago, I would have shown you this." Vivian pointed to a photo in the company's brochure that she has given me, part of the ritual gifting of company swag that occurs at the start of most of these visits. I looked at the picture she indicated. There are three dark-skinned male guards and one dark-skinned woman. All are smiling widely, except the one she points to. He is bulky and muscular, dressed in a military-style uniform, gun on his hip, arms authoritatively crossed over a barrel chest. "A few years ago, I would have said that *this* is the typical guard. But now, I would probably tell you that it is *this*." A lacquered nail taps another dark-skinned guard wearing a coat and tie, eyes hidden behind aviators, the company emblem glowing gold on his lapel. "This is the kind of guard that we see more of."

What Vivian indicated, with a tap of her finger from one image to the other, is the way in which private security in Rio relies on the labor of two different kinds of dark-skinned bodies, which perform two varieties of security behavior. While a militarized hypermasculinity typical of *escolta* has long been the norm in the industry, it is now complemented by what I call a "hospitality security" model which works to impart the *sensação de segurança* to clients, customers, and guests.[1] Hospitality security is aimed at providing a different form of service to Brazilian and global elites in secured spaces of leisure and consumption on multiple scales: smaller scale shopping malls, concert venues, hotels, and global scale World Cup or Olympic stadiums.

Hospitality security, as I have written elsewhere with Susana Durão, is "a material, social and symbolic apparatus that should signal care for the spaces and consideration for clients, visitors, and customers. Hospitality security in Brazil is set up precisely to confuse and mix security with care. It operates as part of the larger grammar shaping everyday urban life, complementing both the 'tougher' forms of security more typically studied in the field (policing and militarism) and the broad realm of services (maids, nannies, gardeners, doormen, drivers) that provide for the well-being of the affluent" (Durão, Robb Larkins, and Fischmann 2021). If hospitality security has its roots in Brazil's colonial and slave systems, where security was a form of labor vital to servicing the needs of the white elite, it has expanded in prevalence considerably in the past decade, for a myriad of reasons including city planning models that emphasize semiprivate, access-controlled space; and the arrival of the World Cup and Olympics, enormous hospitality-oriented events which demanded that Brazil, and Rio in particular, adhere to models of security that were more palatable, more acceptable globally. As one foreign security consultant explained to me: "No one wants to watch a soccer match with some guy toting a machine gun next to them."

Hospitality security exists in places that have already been "secured" by other kinds of urban processes, like spatial exclusion or gentrification, topics which I take up in more detail in chapters 3 and 4 (Davis 2006; Graham 2011). Once these processes have achieved their desired goal of clearing urban spaces of "undesirables" then hospitality security is what is expected *inside* such spaces. Outside, the old and outdated model of "harder" security still exists in spades (Robb Larkins 2013). The rise in hospitality security is therefore connected to the rise in the number of secured elite enclaves being produced around the city of Rio, intensified as a result of megaevent-led city planning (Gaffney 2010; Carvalho, Cavalcanti, and Venuturupalli Rao 2016).[2]

Social class, geographic place of residence, and skin color all mark *vigilantes* as potentially dangerous, violent actors in the places they work.[3] Donna Goldstein has noted for Brazilian domestic employees that, "the domestic worker, no matter her skin color, is symbolically associated with the dirty work to be done in the household. Palpable in the racial commentaries across classes is a recognizable discourse that associates domestic work with dark skin, and dark skin with slavery, dirty, ugliness, and low social standing" (2003, 73; see also Pinho 2015). Similarly, security is conceived of as racialized "dirty work" and guards' profession further entrenches their place in wider class and racial hierarchies (Hughes 1958) both because the industry rests on ongoing exploitation, expendability, and replaceability of workers and because, in some cases, certain guards can be trained to shape their bodies and behavior in such a way as to signal protection, care, and safety to the clients that frequent elite spaces.

Paradoxically, at the same time that guards face racial discrimination in their everyday lives, precisely because they are seen as threatening, the security world values these racial and class markers. Training is viewed as critical to refining these inherently threatening guard bodies, making them more acceptable to middle- and upper-class consumers. As Amanda Chisholm and Saskia Stachowitsch have observed in their work on military contractors elsewhere in the global south, security workers are believed to have a "'natural' or 'raw' talent that needs to be 'sanitized' through western training" (2016, 820). In the present case, the guards I studied learned to perform acceptable or sanitized versions of what Loïc Wacquant (1995) calls "bodily capital" at the security school. Writing in the

FIGURE 12. Guard filling out registration forms. January 2021. Photo: Guito Moreto.

context of the boxing gym where he did his early fieldwork, Wacquant claims that the gym itself functions as a form of "social machinery" where "abstract talent" he calls "bodily capital" is transformed into boxing/professional capital through training and socialization (1995, 66. Cf. Diphoorn 2015). In this chapter, I ask how guards learned to refine their bodily capital at the security school in order to be effective hospitality workers and to be pleasing tools for the generation of the *sensação de segurança*. I draw primarily on data from the basic training and megaevent course, which are more hospitality-oriented than the "hard" security practices of the armored car or armed cargo escort.[4]

Security schools maintain relationships with various companies, who in turn provide guard-students for these continuing education classes and then also hire from the schools' pool of graduates. The school that I focus on in this chapter was a feeder school for Vivian's company, and thus, I believe reflects the firm's aspirations to fill a growing market niche in—or even establish a monopoly over—hospitality security in elite spaces.

Learning to Be Hospitable

At the security school, Eduardo was my first instructor. He seemed to have a hard time controlling his exuberance in class. He delivered lectures at a breakneck yell, often pausing to crack jokes and laugh uproariously. In conveying such enthusiasm for training, he was not only passing on information about the security worlds that guards aspired to enter, he was the embodiment of the dream they hoped to achieve. Dark-skinned with a short, military-style haircut, he dressed in designer label jeans and colorful Ralph Lauren polo. Eduardo had almost a decade of experience working as a lead guard on the city metro, a coveted stable position. In his off hours, he taught at the school, where he had developed and written most of the curriculum. His industry experience combined with the authority derived from being an instructor gave him instant street cred with his students, nearly all of whom were in their early twenties and who saw Eduardo as their future.

A good part of Eduardo's lectures seemed aimed at selling a hospitality security career based on his own experience, peddling a platform like a politician during an election year. "I am proof, living proof that hard work bears fruit and that you can get ahead in this profession!" he proclaimed, welcoming a new cohort, of which I was part, to the school. He continued to talk about being a father of six, and how he had worked his way up at the metro so that he could provide his family with a nice house in a far-flung suburb. He talked about his twin daughters, of aspirations for their private schooling, and of being respected by peers on the job. He also related to the class his ongoing battle with exhaustion. He would get off from a night shift at the metro, sleep a few hours, and come back to work. Was this hard? "Sure it is," he said. "But when we love our work, it is not so hard." Indeed, many of his classes followed a theme of fulfillment through labor. Moreover, his lectures were populated by inspirational quotes on PowerPoint slides

FIGURE 13. An instructor in front of class. January 2021. Photo: Guito Moreto.

and clips from self-help videos. For Eduardo, private security was not a profession, it was a way of life, a transformative way of life that was sure to benefit his students just as it had transformed him and his family's circumstances.

Yet there was another ingredient to success that complicated his "self-made" story. The "hard work pays" theme was periodically complemented by bursts of pandering praise for the security school's owner, a light-skinned, middle-class former military officer. The school owner, he said, preening, saw his "promise" and gave him a chance to teach. This didn't seem to detract from his claims of being a self-made guard; growing a network of more powerful allies was also work. Patronage was a natural outgrowth of his own dignity and work performance and a strategy aspiring guards should also consider as they started out in the security field, which he likened to a "big family." In lectures, he bound the two together like a recipe: work hard and you will be noticed and rewarded by the establishment for your composure and poise. If you are known as someone who offers *um serviço diferenciado* (exceptional service), you will get special opportunities. His job was to show the students what such services might entail and to teach them how to best promote their specialized expertise. On their part, students needed to develop their skill set through diligence and hard work. This also included how to best mask their socioeconomic "baggage" to seamlessly morph into a more palatable part of the hospitality security enterprise.

Performing Professionalism

Providing good service centered on balancing two seemingly contradictory interpretations of guards' bodies. On the one hand, their typically muscular, bulky, and dark-skinned physiques were valued for emitting signals about intimidation and the potential for violence. Guards' physical fitness was a given. I heard the statement: "You need to learn to fight. You have to learn. Period," on the first day of every class. It was also assumed that guards already had fighting identities—that they already were engaged in those worlds—or else they wouldn't even be in class to begin with. Combat classes often got quite heated. During one session, we ended early after someone got his arm broken. Some security managers and owners told me that they recruited their labor straight from the boxing or martial arts gym, since guards would come already trained to fight. Military training was a bonus; former soldiers entering the profession were frequently touted by instructors as more qualified and disciplined than others. But while fitness was desirable, militarization was not since it would clash with the tranquil and secure environment of luxury spaces. Overmilitarization could even have the deleterious effect of making patrons feel *in*secure. Thus, the best guards would be fit, signaling pride and self-care, but not too buff. Someone that could convincingly run after a perpetrator but not someone who looked like they were on steroids, Eduardo explained to me with a chuckle over lunch one day. Someone who could fight but who looked like they would prefer to resolve things with words. "That's right! You are diplomats, guys!" he yelled out enthusiastically to the guards within earshot.

At the same time that guards were expected to cultivate a desirable physique, they were also required to demonstrate, through bodily performances, that they would put their potential for aggression to work on the side of "good," for the protection of property and clients (Monaghan 2002; Hobbs et al. 2002). Yet guards were required to make their bodies docile through a set of behavioral and performative markers. This was talked about in general terms as presenting oneself as a "professional." Professionalism meant managing the ways in which guard's bodies sent signals about race, class, and criminality, while still allowing these markers to function in the background, where they could be activated if necessary. Developing their "professionalism" also placed them in a more advantageous position in gendered hierarchies of violence workers (Higate 2012b; 2012c), above the escolta guards discussed in the last chapter, who were talked about as rougher, unpolished, and generally unsuited to hospitality work.

Body Management

Discourses around professionalism for hospitality guards governed both physical flesh and its clothing, as well as attributes like speech, posture, and nonverbal communication. In class, I learned that bodies must be, first and foremost, meticulously clean. Guards should bathe, at minimum, three times a day. Once before going to work, in order to arrive appearing well kept and smelling fresh.[5] Once when leaving work to go home, if their work provided a bathroom with a shower, and then again upon arriving home. When I asked about why anyone would take a shower before getting on hot public transportation, I was told that the motivation was to "clean oneself up after work," to remove the signs of labor before moving out into the city off-shift. Long rides on packed buses made this step critical. "If you don't shower or clean yourself up, everyone will notice, especially the people who have to stand by you," Eduardo reminded the group. In addition to bulletproof vests and billy clubs, a good cologne was added to the list of tools of the trade that guards would need to acquire in order to work effectively. The cleanliness imperative taught at the school reflects older Brazilian ideas of *boa aparência* or "good appearance," in which racial markers are negotiated through social performance and taps into ideas about hygiene as related to race and class standing (Damasceno 1998; Sansone 2003; Pinho 2015; Roth Gordon 2017).

Beginning classes spent considerable time discussing personal grooming habits in even greater detail. Nails should be clipped short, preferably manicured. "Your hands should be extremely clean at all times," Eduardo lectured, showing his own filed nails to the students in the front row. Hair should be kept short and sideburns trimmed. Getting a haircut was a matter of "self-respect," which would "show you take care of yourself and care about your appearance." In one class, there was a heated debate about whether beards, which were currently in fashion, were acceptable or not. Eduardo, who was generationally distant from the beard-wearers in the group, felt that being clean-shaven was preferable and admonished participants that shaving conveyed important signals about cleanliness to others. Upon noting five o'clock shadows on several students, he "tsk-tsked" and did a finger wag. The one woman in the class and I were instructed to tie our hair back in a bun and wear light but tasteful makeup, in order to "soften the uniform" a little, as Eduardo put it, grinning suggestively.

Tessa Diphoorn argues for a conceptualization of bodily capital that "does not only concern the actual flesh of bodies but includes particular embodied objects" (2015, 337). Similarly, I observed that clothing and uniforms were viewed as part of guards' bodily capital and the maintenance of uniforms—symbols of belonging—keeping them neat and clean, was discussed as part of looking the part of a hospitality guard and commanding respect as a result. Proper attire was discussed as an extension of grooming, including attire at the training facilities themselves. Students should arrive demonstrating their seriousness. Clean jeans and close-toed shoes, ironed T-shirts. At one of the schools I attended, this was rigorously emphasized and one student was even removed for sporting a soccer jersey. The school's proprietor disciplined him in front of the class, equating fandom with favela residence and illegality: "I don't like your shirt, not because it's not my team, but because it makes you look like a *marginal*."[6]

On the job, the uniform itself was an important part of the body and a source of pride for both company owners, who liked to talk incessantly about the various symbols or color schemes of their company logos, and for guards. "The uniform is a thing of respect," Eduardo said, which needed to be kept clean at all times. Boots should be spotless and polished. Owning "one good suit" was a necessity for those working as bodyguards or drivers.

The well cared for uniform worked as a form of social capital, a visual device which signaled a moral commitment to law-abiding, hard work. The pride of wearing it was later evident in social media posts from my cohort of guards: almost daily, security workers post images of themselves, picture perfect examples of Eduardo's sartorial guidelines, with captions like "off to work another day," "with pride and faith," and "go and conquer." In this manner, guards show evidence of having correctly learned bodily techniques at school through photos.

Performing a personal moral identity through clean uniforms is linked directly to performing a sensation of security for consumers.

Furthermore, the uniform functioned as both a resource to denote professionalism and a concretization of identity; it was part of a guard's image. This was particularly notable when, in interviews, guards talked about how being uniformed signaled that they belonged in elite spaces—it underscored that they were employees, not patrons or potential assailants. But when guards took off their uniforms to move from the workplace to the bus stop, the once-in-uniform body that was perceived as a source of professional protection became a threat when traversing the sidewalks of upscale neighborhoods. One guard confided to me that once the same rich old lady who had given him a nod of approval inside a bank, later crossed to the other side of the street with her poodle to avoid him when he was dressed in his street clothes.

While guards were taught to manage the presentation of their bodies to others, they had to also focus on how to keep their bodies internally subdued given their terrible working conditions. Individual hygiene worked as neoliberal fix that put the onus on the individual worker rather than the employer or state to mitigate poor working conditions or environmental injustice. In classes, I often heard how bodies were instruments to be managed—bodies that suffered from twelve-hour shifts standing in hot and uncomfortable clothing. Bodies with blisters from the chafing of stiff uniforms. Thus, security instruction was concerned with the guard managing and maintaining his own body, a body apt to rebel from the unnatural conditions of long service hours. Eduardo offered lots of tips and tricks in this regard and guards took careful notes on the best brands of compression socks for pesky veins, undershirts and specific types of underwear to protect the skin. Other tools of the trade included heartburn medication to quell an upset stomach after wolfing down enormous plates of food in the standard thirty-minute window allotted for lunch. Instructors advised the benefits of a coffee-flavored candy or the Brazilian equivalent of a "five-hour energy drink" followed by a crisp mint piece of gum to not only maintain hygiene on the job, keeping breath fresh for dialoguing with clients, but also to wake tired bodies sleepy from long stretches of inactivity. Guards' bodies were things to be tamed and quieted, a strange parallel with the way that offending bodies of others were also to be tamed and quieted by the guards themselves.[7]

The Dangers of Overperformance

Hospitality security guards were instructed to adopt bodily habits that demarcated them as "workers" not "*marginais*," but they had to be wary of overperformance that marked them as too militarized or as parts of security forces. They also had to be able to shift their presentation of self according to the needs of the context, performing a kind of mental and bodily gymnastics. At work, they had to distance themselves from the social markers that suggested they could be drug traffickers or "undesirables" from the favela, but it was also dangerous to be overzealous in embracing a police or military aesthetic. Since many guards reside in communities controlled by drug traffickers, they ran a risk of being accused of being *alemão* or "x-9" spying on the criminal activities inside the favela. This was an offense commonly punished by death.

During one particular training session, a student arrived late with a swollen black eye. The instructor stopped the class and stared. Beat-up security guards are obviously not appropriate in hospitality settings. When everyone looked at him expectantly for an explanation, he said simply: "The guys looked in my backpack." With no further comment or clarification, the class continued. By this time, I had been around long enough to understand that the "guys" meant the criminal gang that controlled his neighborhood. They had been searching people for some reason—perhaps as part of their own rituals of performance intended to cultivate the *sensação de segurança* in the communities they control—and had looked in his backpack, which contained his security school T-shirt and instructional manual. Because of the school's close affiliation with the police and the military, they interrogated him to ensure he wasn't reporting on their illegal activities.[8]

No one in the room seemed particularly surprised by this as reconciling the potential dangers of undertaking security work while living under the tacit rule of criminal gangs is a generally shared experience for guards. Denyer Willis (2015), for example, describes the common practice of Brazilian cops drying their uniforms behind the refrigerator and not on the veranda, where it is a visible and dangerous marker of identity likely to trigger repercussions. That people must conceal their security identities from traffickers is accepted knowledge. Thus, while guards must perform an identity that marks them as different from these law-breaking actors in their professional lives, they must be careful not to reveal it on their bodies or in their demeanor when at home.[9] Within these spaces, traffickers themselves own the sensation of security.

Posture

Guards need to curate their outer appearances in ways beyond just clothing and grooming. Training also entailed learning how to hold and move one's body. Even if a guards' fighting skills were suboptimal, he could still adopt a posture which suggested to the world that he was ready to take on potential threats. On the first day of hands-on training, Eduardo taught techniques to convey this. "Look professional. Look serious. Stand with your chin up high, with squared off shoulders, chest puffed out. Put your arms behind your back, periodically move them to cross in the front to communicate authority." We practiced the posture of prohibiting access, chins high for hours—for this was the posture that guards had to hold for the duration of their twelve-hour shifts. The idea here was to be authoritative but welcoming at the same time. Just hospitable enough that those approaching to ask for directions to a store or for the location of the bathroom would feel welcome while also communicating that one was a capable and trained professional, signaling care and protection for clients and spaces.

Posture extended to speech as well. Eduardo liked to make fun of how favela residents are believed to speak (Roth Gordon 2009). Relaxing his posture, with his arms flailing, he'd let out a litany of slang which produced a chorus of laughter. "This is not going to get you anywhere, guys. You need to stand up straight and say yes sir, no sir." As Susana Durão, Carolina Fischmann and I explore in our analysis of hospitality practices in an elite mall in São Paulo, guards are instructed to approach and speak in very specific ways to clients. They must confront while not being confrontational, diffusing situations that could attract public attention (2021). Remembering that the whole point here is to impart a *sensação de segurança* to the population of the establishment, any open conflict would raise immediate red flags, working against the policies and norms of hospitality security and the perception of elite and guarded spaces as attractive and secure. Guards, therefore, are instructed to approach suspects with a helpful and polite stance, saying things like, "How can I help you?" or "Did you forget something?" to those who have shoplifted. Such a focus on the microinteraction between suspect and hospitality security guard is shaped by the fact that hospitality security is security on stage, where even the vague awareness of a security-related issue can detract from the overall climate of well-being of a place and hurt business.

Our class was constantly reminded that what we do will always be observed—by clients, or in the case of those doing megaevents, by a television audience of millions. How would we subdue offenders with everyone watching? Here, Eduardo painstakingly offered a long typology of field invaders who would run onto the green disrupting the game: naked guys, politically motivated people and the *beijoqueiro*, a well-known crazy who just wanted to kiss famous people. "Listen, how you do this will impact the entire profession," implored Eduardo. Before we practiced, he showed us a number of "blooper" videos of bad stadium arrests, pointing out the slouchy posture he had just modeled. In the videos, there were packs of cops kicking offenders senseless, or dragging off an offender by one leg and getting attacked from behind by a mob of angry fans. We laughed a lot at their botched and unseemly efforts. Overzealous violent behavior was presented as inferior to the adoption of cool professionalism.

Trudging up the stairs to the school's rooftop for our practical training, we were instantly sweating in the 105-degree summer heat. First, we lined up to practice our formation on how to approach an offender, we planned on who would grab his legs and who would grab his arms. The idea, explained Eduardo, was not only to make the profession look competent, but to *not* draw the focus of the cameras or the crowd. "You have to remove the problem from the center of attention as quickly as possible. Deescalate and remove the offending person from view. Once you're out-of-sight, then, you can kick them," said Eduardo.

He explained that this might be very awkward. "Sometimes, people are yelling and screaming. Sometimes they might be foreigners." Everyone looked at me. Inevitably, I would then have to play the role of the foreigner invading the soccer field that didn't understand the verbal commands of the guards. This was intensely uncomfortable, though, because since I am a woman, they also felt weird about manhandling me/touching me. More nervous laughter. Eduardo started to yell at me, "Come on!" I thought about fieldwork reciprocity, the idea in anthropology that we are supposed to give back to the communities we study. This was my chance; I had to be useful. I hammed it up. I threw myself into it and acted the part. Lying down on the dirty floor, I hurled obscenities at them in English and kicked my legs while they deftly practiced removing me from the imaginary field of play.[10]

Elite Offenders

As evidenced by the role-playing I was asked to do, in hospitality security, which takes place in middle- and upper-class spaces, many of the offenders that guards encounter are elite and light-skinned. When taken with the fact that a primary objective of hospitality security was to maintain a calm and peaceful environment in order to nurture the sensation of security, dealing effectively with elite offenders was critical to guards' success. Consequently, significant class time was devoted to talking about how to take care of problems and manage emotions when confronted by disrespectful, privileged people.[11] Eduardo detailed how guards would have daily interaction with those who didn't think security regulations or metal detectors applied to them. They would need to use all the body techniques he had taught them to command respect.

The worst, everyone agreed, tended to be what were referred to as "playboys," young light-skinned men, who adopted positions of class and racial superiority to ignore the instructions of guards by trying to get into a venue without a ticket or using drugs in the venue, for example. This same group drew on stereotypical claims of their fathers' status and position—like "my dad owns this club" or "my dad is a judge"—thus indexing the privilege their bodies were seen to signify to demand exemption from the rules which hospitality guards were there to enforce. When denied entrance by guards, their tempers would flair and they would become increasingly irate.

Perhaps part of the reason that the "playboys" would get so upset about not being allowed entrance was because they saw the barriers to entry as constructed for other kinds of people, for "undesirables," not for them. Their class and skin color were what allowed them the right to pass. When denied by guards who, by virtue of their class and skin color were not seen as legitimate authorities let alone as arbiters of spatial class privilege, things got ugly. For their part, guards had to learn how to enforce discipline without disrupting the experience for the majority of participants, people who perhaps didn't want to be confronted by the fact that it was classed, light-skinned bodies like their own that were, in fact, the source of the security problem.

Guards worked through simulations in order to mentally prepare themselves for gate-keeping work. The training exercise Eduardo used was for guards to practice maintaining posture and authority when being insulted and sworn at, in highly explicit ways. Eduardo proceeded to play the role of a client and gestured to a guard to approach him. His voice rose immediately as he set about creating a general scandal, oscillating between saying things like "Do you know who you are talking to?" "Who do you think you are?" and hurling insults that pushed on sensitive class differences between the client and guard. At Eduardo's urging, the rest of the class gathered around, emulating shoppers or fans in a stadium. Taking turns enacting this scenario, guards were required to politely attempt to deescalate the situation, even while Eduardo's tirades against them droned on for five minutes, timed with a stopwatch. Responding appropriately to this abuse asked the guards to work to control their emotions and body language even as Eduardo's insults grew more heated. When their turns finished, one by one the guards let out yells and high-fived one another. "We did it!" said one guard to another. "Men in Black!" (in reference to the film), said the other. There was a power, a victory in that forced politeness, in resisting anger, and not becoming the person their pretend abuser was trying to evoke. In this way—even while guards were well aware of the inherent contradictions and inequalities informing their performances as hospitality guards—they also saw a chance for self-respect and empowerment in these performances as well. Self-respect was directly linked to notions of professionalism, which in this context meant keeping emotion at bay in order to perform respectability on the job. "*Missão dada é missão cumprida*" ([akin to] "mission accomplished"), said Eduardo, patting the guards on the back.

After completing training, guards from Eduardo's class typically went to interview for coveted positions at Vivian's company. When I asked her and her hiring manager, a similarly elegant and affluent-seeming woman, about their hiring criteria, she offered vague answers that made more sense to me only after my time in Eduardo's class. "You can just tell who will be good by how they present themselves, how they talk and how they smile. You should come to one of our interview days to see how it is. You can just *feel* who will be a good guard and who is too rough, you know?" What Vivian was referring to was precisely the combination of skin color, speech, clothing, and posture that make up *boa aparência* and which were the building blocks of Eduardo's project of subject-making in classes. The ability to "feel" who would be a fit reflects the ephemeral qualities (of white supremacy?) that contribute to the sensation of security, where a guard's body and demeanor is evaluated for whether it can seamlessly contribute to the aesthetic of the mall itself. Vivian, and her team of managers, all light-skinned middle- and upper-class women, were an excellent litmus test for the impressions and feelings of the clients who inhabit hospitality spaces and for whom the sensation of security is constructed.

Private security companies have become a fixture in elite spaces, offering a distinct form of hospitality in the service of securing corporate property and making patrons feel comfortable and safe. Security bodies are intended to generate the sensation of security in order to deter perpetrators and reassure patrons. The overall ambiguity of guards' physical appearances in the elite settings typical to hospitality work means that performances of self must be mastered by guards if they are to succeed in communicating the *sensação de segurança*; they must mold their bodily capital to conform to the expectations of their employers and clients.

Hospitality guards learn to do this in the security school environment, where instructors like Eduardo emphasize hygiene and clothing choices that they believe convey guards' professionalism and which they see as necessary to communicating the sensation of security. Beyond appearances, guards also learn how to adopt a posture that reflects on the entire profession, a posture that was particularly critical in the context of the World Cup and Olympics and the attention they brought to the sector. In these settings, security is not a top-down, one-size-fits-all endeavor. Rather, the efficacy of security is based largely on its performance and that performance depends on the very complex and often contradictory bodily training that I have described here.

Furthermore, security as hospitality and guard training must be understood in the wider social context of race relations in Brazil. Livio Sansone notes that for dark-skinned Brazilians, part of performing *boa aparência* (a good appearance) is about cultivating a visual appearance that involves, "speaking intelligently, being polite, looking attentive, and showing off status symbols" (2003, 67). Guard training thus produces whiteness, naturalizing and defending it as a desirable quality linked to status. The relationship between hospitality and security is deeply historical; the project to refine dark-skinned bodies in service to elite goals is not new, but rooted in Brazil's slaveholding history. The industry incentivizes the performance of whiteness as a means of Afro-Brazilian survival, thereby economically pushing the guards into reinforcing a racial hierarchy that is rooted in the country's colonial past, but which has evolved with the rise of global racial capitalism.

Security for hire also allows for a more direct exercise of the power of elites over urban space. When security is commodified, clients and company owners can decide what it looks like and how guards should act. They can also set prices that reflect what people will pay to feel more secure. This makes security available only to those who have the means to purchase it. However, despite its seemingly benign nature, hospitality security is key to producing the unequal status quo. It is only made possible through violent policing and through complementary practices of spatial exclusion embedded in Rio's city planning. This means that low-income, racialized communities continue to be on the receiving end of violent practices while the elite are treated in "hospitable" ways.

FIGURE 14. Guard and guardhouse, separating residents from visitors. January 2021. Photo: Guito Moreto.

FIGURE 15. Cameras under security lighting outside the lush landscaping of a luxury condominium. January 2021. Photo: Guito Moreto.

FIGURE 16. Walls and barbed wire outside a residence in Jardim Botânico, Rio de Janeiro. January 2021. Photo: Guito Moreto.

SMALL THEFTS

Us guards, we have to really pay attention. Taking care to watch the customers. Watching their gestures, their posture, their body language.
—Carlos, twenty-five years old. Five years in the security field.

I was working in Ipanema, in one of those big luxury hotels on the beach. You know the ones? Yay, I was one of the security guards there. A ton of big chunks of cheese—like those wheels of cheese, *queijo* brie, you know? Well, they started disappearing, along with *picanha*, steak, *picanha contra filé*, filet mignon. But because the hotel was full, it was really busy, full, it was hard to track how the merchandise, the food, I mean, was being stolen. But me and the manager started to watch it and do more inventory checks. And the *picanha* and the cheese were always coming up short. Three months we watched it, trying to figure it out because we weren't selling enough to account for what was missing. Finally, what we realized, is that it was the work of two cooks—the chef and the sous chef. What did they do? They took out the *picanha* and wrapped it in plastic wrap so it would stay clean. Wrap it up really good, in the *embalagem de plástico*. And then they wrapped that in aluminum foil. Then they would throw it away in a certain garbage bag. They would tie a blue string around the bag. The regular garbage bags all got a black string. So, with the blue string, they would mark it as the special bag. And they would put it out in the alley behind the hotel. They had an arrangement with the kid that picked up the recycling. So, he would grab the bags that they put out and get the one with the goods in it. They would sell the stuff and they would divide up the money. It took us like three months to figure this out. The employees themselves steal a lot of stuff. It happens. Like this time, the cooks would even plan their shifts—one covering the morning and the other one at night so they could steal more.

—Nabo, forty-five years old. Eighteen years in the security field.

I worked on this *obra*. On this construction site. The craziest incident I remember involved a *peixe grande*, a big fish. I was in the *portaria*, where the trucks went in and out with all the construction materials in them. Delivering materials like steel and cement. So, there was this engineer, this big fish, who ran the project. On the weekend, he would get the workers, like the *pedreiros* (builders) and electricians, and get them to work on his house out in Recreio! He took them off the job that was paying them and had them remodel *his* house! He was taking the construction materials from the job too. Now on the day that I realized what was up, it was Saturday, and there were trucks with materials coming and going and I thought it was weird. Because you know, Saturday, well normally there aren't deliveries of materials. But since he was the one that authorized this stuff, what could I do? *Peixe grande não pode denunciar.* You can't denounce a big fish. So, he was stealing stone, cement, rock, iron. All of it going straight to his house!

Eventually my bosses discovered it, but it was already too late. There wasn't really a way for them to take back the materials. I know he got fired. But people said that his house was already built and finished by then. I had written up the coming and going of trucks on Saturdays in my reports and said that it seemed weird. But what did they do when I did this? They just changed my post. They put me laaaaaaa ... (gestures) way over there at the cars-only entrance. I mean this was a big fish. When you mess with them either you get transferred or fired. The only reason I didn't get fired, I think, was because the head of security was a police officer, Marcos. We still work together to this day. He said if they fired me, he would report the whole thing. So, they just changed my *posto* and I stayed quiet. Big fish. Man, that guy. Big fish get away with everything.

—Alves, thirty-two years old. Four years in the security field.

I was working in the bookstore at the time. We had to deal with a group who would come into the store and steal. They would come in every single day with a slightly different strategy for shoplifting. At first, we couldn't figure it out but after a while, by watching the cameras really closely, observing, we began to understand. It was a ring. A ring of Chileans, in fact, that were living in Copacabana. And they were a big ring. Every day they would send out different men and women to the store. Their target was mostly games. Like video games for Play Station or Xbox. And even with all the security devices we had on these things, they were able to take them and somehow wrap them in an aluminum device that would block the signal so they wouldn't set off the alarm when they left the store. They could walk out without any sign, not a beep. And the women put the games inside their clothes. Sometimes even under their dresses. In their purses, backpacks. They had various methods. They would also use grocery bags. Like metal-lined grocery sacks. So, you would look from the outside and think they were just out shopping but inside they had a whole setup, some liner to block the signal.

We kept watching and finally we caught one of them in the act. We had already clued our police in to the thefts. So, they went outside and immediately they got caught. We can't ever *abordar* (stop and frisk) inside the store. That's a rule. So we always wait for them to leave to confront them. We let the lady walk like six meters away, thinking she had gotten away with it, and then our security stopped her and the police took her bag, and man had she bulletproofed the whole thing on the inside. It was full of video games! The *delegados* went to her house and they found a whole cache of stolen goods. Video games from the Lojas Americanas, stuff from the cell phone store, shoppings. They must have just spent their whole days stealing stuff!

—Charles, twenty-seven years old. Two years in the security field.

I was working in the shopping center and there was a robbery in a store, a store that sold phones, expensive phones. iPhones, smartphones. There was a *rapaz armado*, an armed guy. And a woman, who was carrying an *arma branca*, a less lethal weapon, a knife. And another woman had a .38. And even with them being armed, we were able to address the situation. I saw what was going on really clearly. I alerted the *Centro de Monitoramento* (Central Command) and they activated the Polícia Militar that were stationed right outside the store. We let them take the phones, right? And then when they went outside, the police stopped them, and we got our phones back. Around eighteen phones.

Listen, when there is an incident, you have to be really calm. You have to tell your partners what is going on, *com calma*. You tell them to call the police. One of you has to apprehend the person while the other one is calling the police, *com calma*. You immobilize the suspect. You stay calm. Did I say that already? That you have to stay calm? You follow the procedures from the manual. You have to be disciplined on this. Immobilize the suspect. We see conflicts and problems all the time. Just be calm.

—Lucas, forty-six years old. Six years in the security field.

When I worked in the supermarket there on Maria da Gloria, a ton of *leite ninho* (powdered milk, given to children) started going missing. Every single day, it seemed like a bunch would go missing. This was confirmed when we did inventory. Yep, a lot were unaccounted for. So, we checked all the camera footage and *nada*. Eventually, we figured it out. Women that came in, a group of them, wearing big skirts and dresses. They were sneaking these cans of condensed milk between their legs, securing them there, and somehow still managing to walk normally! No one realized it! I mean, they were walking normally, securing three or four cans under there. After months of this, out of sheer luck, one day one of them was leaving the store and all the sudden a can just fell out of her dress. We looked and she had four or five in there. Later we found out that she (and the other women) had been training to do this up in the community where they lived. Using bricks. Manguinhos and Mandela and Jacaré (names of favelas), all those places were really close by. It was so *bizarro*! How could those ladies secure so many cans between their legs and just keep walking about and acting normal? *Bizarro, mesmo!* But it's pretty normal that this kind of thing happens.

—Pedro, thirty-three years old. Eight years in the security field.

I work in a market inside a shopping mall. Patrolling. We are like the police of the shopping. We work armed. When people came to make trouble in the shopping, when they came to steal chocolate or to steal whiskey, we deal with it. If there is a dispute in the *caixa* (cashier/checkout) where they thought they were overcharged, it is our business to resolve. Basically, our job is to deal with these kinds of little disputes. One day last week, a customer got mad and threw a juice into a cashier's face. The other employees, well they are afraid to confront people in these small disputes, and so they call the *ronda* (patrol), since we have more influence, more weight. We are more prepared. The *ronda* is the one who is trained, physically, mentally, and also knows martial arts. He shows up in the place and confronts the person who is creating the problem. His job is to apprehend the perpetrator, take him to a small room at the back of the store, question him, and call the police.

In this case, the perpetrator committed a crime by throwing the juice, which then went up the nose of the employee. He attacked the cashier and even drew blood. We had to contain the perpetrator and put him into the room. This sort of situation happens quite often. We just wait with them until the police come to arrest them.

We have to show the other patrons that they can come to the shopping and can be comfortable to make their *compras* (purchases) with their families. So that's like our function. To transmit this security to the clients. I confess that it's not *fácil* because a lot of arrogant people show up that want to cause trouble. Don't want to pay, want to steal. People shoving merchandise in their clothes or bags. The *vigilante* has to be correct in everything. Vigilant and upstanding in everything we do.

—Rogerio, thirty-three years old. Six months in the security field.

3
SECURING AFFECTIVE LANDSCAPES OF LEISURE AND CONSUMPTION

"*Segurança em si não existe, é toda uma questão de promover uma sensação de segurança*" (Security in and of itself doesn't exist; it's just a matter of promoting the sensation of security), said Gomes, a middle manager at one of the largest private security firms in Rio, discreetly trying to wipe the sweat from his face with the back of his hand. An inbound train neared the platform, flooding the station with the bustle of the morning commute. We watch as the flux of people moves on and we are alone on the platform with three men, wearing neon green vests over black, hot-looking polyester pants and who I assume to be security guards. Gomes continues, emphasizing the performative work at the heart of private security provision: "The way to mitigate this potential negative security feeling is to manage the situation in such a way that you generate a *sensação positiva*, a positive sensation. That's exactly what we are doing here at the train station, even though there are no real security guards. We can't afford them. Just these people." He gesticulates and waves at the neon-vested men. "They have no training. They are just what we call '*orientadores de acesso*' (lit. 'access guides' but better translated as 'crowd control officers'). But if we dress them like guards, the public doesn't know the difference. They feel better just thinking there is a guard in every station. This is, of course, not the case, but it generates the right sensation. That is how it is done. Public or private security, rich neighborhood or poor one, that is how it is done. Sensations. Managing feelings on limited resources."

Gomes' comments confirm the way in which emotion and impression are entangled with perceptions of (in)security (Masco 2014). But he also suggests how security is not just a feeling nor is it merely performative or theater. Rather, the drive to impart the *sensação de segurança* mobilizes enormous resources. It erects fences, police and security checkpoints; influences urban design; employs masses; and navigates through specific, culturally laden mechanisms. This chapter draws on conversations and participant observation with middle managers like Gomes, to show how the sensation of security is produced in two different kinds of hospitality contexts—the high-end commercial shopping mall and the leisure-based global sporting venue—paradigmatic elite spaces which are coded white and linked to exclusion, containment, the flow of capital. Building on my exploration of hospitality guard training in the previous chapter, here I show how embodied performances of security fit within a broader landscape of security mechanisms and infrastructures, which coalesce around the production and protection of elite spaces and work to impart the sensation of security to their clients.

In the sporting stadium and the mall, the *sensação de segurança* depends on enacting measures aimed at curating who is present in a given space; security work in hospitality contexts entails managing populations through pervasive processes of gatekeeping and access control. As my interlocutors reminded me constantly, all security actions are shaped by the presence (or not) of a secure perimeter since the presence of a secured perimeter is directly determinative of who and what is guarded. Perimeters are created and maintained through what I have come to think of as processes of credentialing, mandating who can enter and who must be kept out. Credentialing might include a ticket, in the case of a sporting event, or proof of residency, in the case of a gated condominium, or a membership card for a country club. But in more fluid, semipublic environments like the shopping mall, access may entail the demonstration of more symbolic sorts of credentials, such as perceived class status, purchasing power, or whiteness. As I will show, much of the work of securing the perimeter is actually done far outside the perimeter—cultivating a desired public through exclusionary mechanisms like ticket price or other economic factors which function to deter certain groups of people from frequenting these spaces in the first place. However, semipublic spaces like a shopping mall, which has a more porous perimeter, require different, careful work. Here, security guards must interface with a more varied public, even if the presence of luxury stores and high-end products sends clear signals about who should be and who should not be shopping in the mall.

Security work inside the perimeter means quietly and discreetly ensuring that things and people are in their place. As is the case in all hospitality work, the goal is to effectively manage the space without spectacular displays or disruptions that call attention to security procedures or to security concerns, awareness of which might cause fissures in the sensation of security for clients. In sum, much of the work of creating the sensation of security is accomplished by establishing exclusionary mechanisms that encourage the presence of certain guests while deterring others and quietly removing undesirables when they do enter these spaces.

Notably, security in elite spaces of leisure and consumption does not merely protect people or commodities, but it performs the crucial work of securing corporate reputations as well. The sensation of security is directly related to the ideas in circulation about the kind of place being protected and whether or not it is known to be safe or risky. Brand protection is far from an afterthought in security work—it is often even described by security managers as the primary goal of security efforts because the reputation of urban spaces or commercial establishments is irrevocably linked to the *sensação de segurança*. The sensation of security, in turn, functions to sustain flows of capital for commercial establishments, global corporations, and even for cities whose economies rely on attracting tourists and investors. However, as I will show in this chapter, trying to balance the competing discourses and objectives surrounding the creation of the sensation of security and its relevance to corporate power can be complex, and at times paradoxical, for security workers.

Additionally important to understanding the functioning of security efforts in hospitality spaces is that the work of producing and maintaining the sensation of security is not merely the work of private guards. Rather, it draws on a whole security apparatus, what Susana Durão, Carolina Fischmann, and I call a "socio-technological security assemblage" (2021), or an effective combination of infrastructure, labor, and technology. Thus, the sensation of security is not only the product of private security guard efforts, even though they remain an important component of the endeavor, but instead includes a wider assemblage of (at times surprising) public and private actors, visible and invisible forms of policing, things like surveillance cameras, as well as low-tech technology like fences. This chapter shows how myriad actors and techniques come together to produce forms of exclusion and containment that contribute to the sensation of security in hospitality settings.

Finally, as Gomes suggested for the humbler context of the train station, it bears noting that security efforts in nearly all spaces are about providing the *minimum* conditions necessary for consumptive or leisure-based experiences to occur. I say minimum because nearly everyone I interacted with characterized this as the goal, referencing financial constraints and the impossibility of achieving total security. Put differently, the idea is to elicit the sensation of security with the most cost-effective configuration of men and equipment—security on a shoestring. Protecting capital without spending too much to do so.

Imagining Secured Spaces

Enclosed elite spaces have a long history. Enclaving as a form of security is as old as the hills. Fortresses and walled cities date from early times, with Latin American colonial cities relying heavily on the organization of space to reinforce hierarchy, restrict movement, and enforce spatial segregation. With increased urbanization in the twentieth century, new instances of enclaved living garnered attention from scholars noting increases in the privatization of public space (Harvey 2007; Soja 2000; Sorkin 1992). The closed, gated condominium in particular became the emblematic form of fraught urban spatial regimes in many places, especially in the Global South (Low 2001; Davis 2007).[1] In the Brazilian case, Caldeira (2002) famously analyzed the rise in such residential enclaves in São Paulo, noting how the condominium was a by-product of urban planning, private security initiatives, and exclusionary pricing.[2]

Duffield (2011) calls these urban enclaves "bunker spaces," highlighting how they foster maximum consumption, capital flow, and are locales for elite strategy making. But they are also demarcated as "bunkers" because of what is imagined to be happening outside of them. All over Brazil, closed condominiums with names like Ilha Pura (Pure Island), or Bela Vista (Beautiful View), promise a bucolic tranquility free from the chaos thought to reign outside their tall walls, walls that are, of course, guarded by private security. Here, however, I am less interested in these completely segregated spaces than I am in how dynamics of such enclaved spaces are replicated in more porous contexts. The spaces that I discuss here are especially interesting because they cannot be total self-contained enclaves. Therefore security must account for their complex flows of people and commodities while trying to approximate the same *sensação de segurança* as a fortified condominium.[3]

Such spaces can also be, as they were called by Olympic security planners, "bubble to bubble," meaning that people can move from one securitized space to another without ever really leaving the secure perimeter (like an airport.) In this way, urban enclaves do not exist purely in isolation, as enormous complexes that seek to provide everything residents need within their walls, erasing the necessity to venture out. Rather, in Rio, there is an effort to envision an entire city where people can move across fortified and exclusive spaces in bulletproof cars, to spaces guarded by one private security company to another with school, office, clubs, shopping, residence all connected as a securitized archipelago. Security workers are not the only laborers who make these enclaves run. Maids, nannies, gardeners, and cleaners all contribute to creating racialized spaces, are part of communicating care for elite bodies, and contribute to the production of a hospitality vibe that emits the sensation of security. They are part of the illusion too.

Shopping de Luxo: The High-End Shopping Mall

Insecurity, be it perceived or real, affects the organization of city space in myriad ways. Concerns about crime have evacuated many of Rio's public spaces, even in elite neighborhoods like Ipanema and Leblon. In response, the shopping mall has arisen as an oasis of secure consumption and social interaction. Malls are important social spaces in Brazil, as in many other parts of Latin America (Dávila 2016). The commercial success of the shopping mall is intertwined with the ability to attract a desired customer base. And part of what seems to be attractive about the *shopping*, as malls are called in Brazil, is that mall security has been so effective in imparting feelings of security to patrons.

Part of this success of the sociotechnical assemblage of the mall is that it is regionally and culturally shaped. Performances of security that resonate in one locale might not be useful in another. For example, in writing about the various intersections of security and the city in Beirut, anthropologists Fawaz, Harb, and Gharbieh (2012) argue that in high-end malls metal detectors and bag-screening procedures work effectively by "encouraging consumerism by reducing the psychological sense of 'threat'" (2012, 182). Such a militarized procedure, by contrast, would be out of place in Rio *shoppings* given the particular context but the logic of providing a baseline of culturally inflected psychological reassurance as a prerequisite for consumption is the same.

Mall security, then, is a given and one which depends on a perception of malls as safe spaces, necessarily replete with elaborate surveillance and monitoring systems and legions of hospitality guards. As Arlene Dávila wrote in her ethnography of malls in Colombia, and which is well reflected in my experience in Rio, security was "something the mall was assumed to have and embody, rather than something I saw enforced or acted upon" (2016, 102). Similarly, while much of the security in wider Rio functions through ostentation or spectacle, mall security works through more subtle registers. Hospitality measures are the most visible form of mall securitization and thread the needle between evoking protection and keeping out undesirables while also performing security as care work, signaling kindness and cordiality. The day-to-day work of mall security, then, is less about producing the sensation of security than it is about protecting the associations and presumptions about the mall as a place already seen as quintessentially defined by the sensation of security.

FIGURE 17. Guard at the entrance to a high-end shopping mall. December 2020. Photo: Guito Moreto.

Security Infrastructure

I met Guilherme, the in-house "organic" (the term for in-house, not third-party) security manager responsible for a nationwide chain of shopping malls at the "West Shopping" one afternoon. West Shopping was located in a neighborhood composed primarily of enclosed enclaves, serially arranged along the ocean front. Light-skinned and middle-class, Guilherme was in his late fifties and retired from a career as an intelligence officer for the *Agência Brasileira de Inteligência*, (Brazil's FBI), during the military dictatorship. Ever affable, he joked that the private security leadership in the country was now composed of people like him, "We ran the country, now we are old guys with beer bellies," he says, and laughs.[4]

As I walked the mall with Guilherme, he helped me to understand how its infrastructure itself both aided in securing the space and conveyed the sensation of security to clients. Guilherme insisted that, despite its seeming subtlety for patrons, security measures shaped the organization of the space and sociality of the mall in crucial ways. As he detailed, mall work is in large part focused on protecting consumer goods from theft. But all security decisions must take place in conjunction with commercial interests. That is, security plans must dovetail with interests of marketing experts and retail managers. Guilherme explained the tension between the mandate to secure the space and the need to maximize sales in this way: "No one just happens by and decides to buy a diamond or a

Rolex. Those stores are destination stores. So, from a security standpoint, what do I want to do with these stores? I want to put them in the back corner of the third floor. *Por quê*? That gives my guards more time to react, to see what is happening inside the shopping, and to apprehend a suspect before they get away with merchandise. Do you ever wonder why you have to walk around the whole floor to find the correct escalators to go up and down? Two reasons. Because some stores rely on this for business. Not the destination ones. The weaker [less exclusive] ones. But it is also for us, for security.[5] *Olha*, putting diamonds in the corner of the third floor might be okay for that store, but it might not work for a store that needs customers. I have to make concessions." So, it's a balance, I ask? "Yes, it's always a balance. Security is always a negotiation." In places like the shopping mall, the seemingly mundane infrastructure like a moving staircase secures capital while also negotiating its flow and maximization.

Outside the shopping, a parallel infrastructure of deterrence is also at work. Parking lots are built with only one exit, and loading docks are manned with extra security forces. Guilherme escorts me to the garage to show me instances of this negotiated space and its relationship to security. Outside the one entrance/exit is a man clad entirely in black astride a shiny yellow motorcycle with an illuminated flashing orange light. When he sees Guilherme, he wails his siren briefly in acknowledgment. He is a police officer from the battalion nearby, Guilherme explains, part of a group of officers that work for the mall while off-duty. "What exactly does he do for you?" I ask. "Well, if someone steals something . . . Listen, we had this case, with one of the jewelry stores. It was an inside job. Someone got to one of the employees. This girl. They threatened her family if she didn't cooperate. Followed her into work one day and demanded the codes for the safes. She gave them up but her colleague managed to activate the panic button, the alarm. You know, the one under the counter. So we knew something was going on." He pauses for dramatic effect. "Look, we weren't going to detain the thieves in the middle of the mall. There would be way too much risk. Imagine that. Bullets flying all over the place right across from the *praça de alimentação* (food court)? *Não*. We let them walk out. In this case, they used the loading dock exit. But by then our off-duty officer had already alerted the police, who were just arriving from the *delegacia* (precinct) when the jewelry thieves came down the elevator. This is why we have officers as part of our team. They can make things move a little faster when it counts." Off-duty police, in sum, provide private security companies and mall security managers with a concierge service: made-to-order, law enforcement contributes to the overall securitized infrastructure of the shopping and is part of the carefully orchestrated performance of the *sensação de segurança*.

Police can also, I learned from other mall security experts, make problems conveniently disappear by hushing up sensitive incidents like the one at the jewelry store. Such breeches in mall security, according to Guilherme, are rather commonplace. But they are rarely reported in the newspapers or covered on the television news. Negative news coverage is thus prevented from tarnishing the image of the shopping as a reliably safe and tranquil place. The power of both private guards and the police serves to protect private security's corporate image. Guilherme clarified the interplay between guarding and brand security: "I have to protect the merchandise. But I also have to protect the brand. Usually, the brand is more important." As Guilherme described it, securing the shopping draws both upon security-sensitive design that balances the strategic placement of expensive goods—jewelry and electronics—with the need to sell merchandise. But beyond the brick and mortar of the built environment, a quiet human infrastructure of police officers working second shift or on permanent retainer (indeed, in most of the shopping security command centers I visited, there was a direct line to the nearest police battalion)—at the ready to quietly solve problems in such a way as to preserve both the reputation of the shopping and clients' always-fragile sensation of security.

Gatekeeping and Racialized Surveillance

Security was not just reactive in the case of an incident, it was proactive in cultivating a population of patrons that were seen as desirable—low-risk, light-skinned, and cash flush. The "City Mall" is located in an upper-class haven for the nouveau riche—Barra de Tijuca—a neighborhood organized around residential enclosures and access to a motorized vehicle. At the entrances to the mall, there are armed guards wearing combat-ready uniforms, with high boots and bulletproof vests. But inside, security personnel wear business suits and earpieces to communicate with one another. Because the shopping has recently been remodeled and upgraded, its interior reflects the rise and hyperpresence of electronic surveillance. There are spherical ceiling cameras about every twenty-five feet. If the cameras appear state-of-the-art on the shopping side, far less modern are the command center facilities that house two tired-looking guards who monitor the surveillance images. Their command center is literally cave-like, a windowless room inside interior corridors behind the employee dining hall and is painted black to help the guards better see the monitors.

The City Mall is heinously ostentatious. Stores boast US$10,000 (approximately R$42,000 at that time) handbags and US$1,700 shorts. I even found a US$900 Speedo. Prices alone work as a security mechanism, sending a clear message that the establishment is only for those who can afford a thousand-dollar bathing suit. The mall contains none of the lower-priced chains, like Renner or

Lojas Americanas, that draw a more modest clientele; it is an elite enclave where nearly everyone is outpriced. Thus, gatekeeping isn't just a guard at the entrance but is also about establishing an (almost) unattainable price point.

"How do you keep the shopping secure?" I ask the mall's former security supervisor, a muscular man named Paulo, who worked for City Mall's family of shoppings for twenty years before he retired and opened a franchise of gyms specializing in boxing and MMA. "There are lots of strategies," he says. "We identify the *elementos suspeitos*—suspicious elements—when they enter the mall. This can mean a jacket in the summer, they look like they can't afford to be shopping here, or maybe they have a hat on that hides their face." Since the City Mall is hands-down the whitest place I have ever seen in Rio, I deduce that the identification of suspicious elements is linked to the politics of racist and classist exclusion. Indeed, such a highly racialized form of surveillance is precisely intended to curtail the mobility of certain suspicious elements before they can act. But it is also about deeming Black, "poor-looking" patrons as suspicious, a profiling behavior and apparatus that rests on the premise that the potential upward social mobility of these categories of people is suspect in itself. I should add that the large majority of the shopping's employees would fall into these racialized categories. From the security perspective, these are "acceptable" groups of people to be in the shopping as service providers, but not as patrons.

In addition to the people that are profiled as suspicious (i.e., they don't look wealthy or white enough to be "legitimate" patrons), suspects also include those who act suspiciously. Increasingly, high-end malls use surveillance software that flags unusual movement or activity in the flow of people in the shopping—and calls these suspicious movements to guards' attention for their immediate evaluation. This technique, one software vendor explained to me, was about ameliorating "observation fatigue" on the part of guards, since after a short time of monitoring a screen, it was difficult to keep attention focused. Furthermore, in discussions about the potential bias of defining "suspicious elements," Paulo mentioned that this was an advantage of the integration of technology into the profession. "The cameras only look at body language. They are more neutral than a guard," he insisted, echoing a common (yet fallible) idea that these systems are somehow so "modern" as to be color blind or not see social class.

Despite its poshness, the City Mall didn't have this level of technical sophistication and still depended on the interpretation of guards to determine what qualified as suspect or not. "If people are acting suspect, we track them on the cameras," Paulo explains. "You, for example, while you were waiting for me to come and meet you, might look like an *elemento suspeito* because you are taking pictures, watching us, and not buying anything. Most people just enjoy the mall, not look at all the cameras." He laughs. "But then again you look like maybe a tourist (a way of saying that I am white without directly addressing race) and you are dressed nice so we wouldn't worry about you. You wouldn't be a suspicious element." Carmen Rial, writing about a similar vagueness around identifying suspects in megaevent security in Brazil, has noted that while having a "suspicious attitude" will flag event-goers for surveillance and approach by security guards, what exactly such an attitude entails is left purposely vague. She notes that a similar dynamic exists in airports as well and that many other "public spaces have futuristic cameras with software that detects 'strange behavior,' determined by algorithms" (2019, 102). The whole idea here is that "suspect" is an open category, conveniently filled as needed. It's an empty signifier.

Most of this kind of profiling will happen beyond the conscious awareness of the mall's general public, with the most visible form of security being the hospitality-oriented guards who are stationed at different points throughout the shopping or who are roaming on Segways. Guilherme explains to me that this kind of guard is only possible in luxury establishments. "People who frequent these places are more aware, they know how to act in a nice mall. They are educated." (The discourse on "education" and proper behavior is again a common way of addressing race without openly doing so.) But when he is arranging guards and the security plans for malls located in less affluent areas or that house more middle-class shops, he has to use a different strategy. "There I would make sure I had some really big armed guards at the entrances, just to send a message, you know. The popular classes don't understand more subtle messages; they only respond to authority. They have to see a certain hardness to take it seriously." In these commercial contexts, the elements are *all* suspect, given that the clientele is understood by security personnel as "uneducated," a racist euphemism that constructs poor and dark-skinned citizens as automatically threatening to public order.

In sum, middle- and upper-class malls require subtle security which doesn't distract or alarm the client, while the malls of the masses have spectacular security, which is framed as necessary to control lower-class patrons. The distinction between subtle and overt falls along highly racialized lines.

Using the Networks

In the pursuit of the sensation of security in elite spaces, security managers always drew on wider networks of security actors, wider than those the public sees, such as the police I described previously. But sometimes they also deployed unlikely networks of connection among the popular classes, using them to control undesirables within the space of the mall. Paulo, the former security manager at the

Ocean Shopping turned MMA coach, explains a second strategy for securing the shopping with reference to his own biography: he had no formal background in security but was recruited to work at a mall in the late nineties by a military police *coronel* who also owned the mall's private security company. "I wasn't even in security, but I was the top *lutador* or fighter at the nearby boxing gym. The *coronel* came to the gym and invited me to the mall security command center at the Ocean Mall and showed me a clip of the mall being sacked the previous weekend. I knew a bunch of the people doing the sacking in the video from the gym. He asked me: "Can you control these guys? How much would you want to do that? I went back to the gym and announced: 'It's not that you aren't going to rob the shopping, you aren't going to rob MY shopping.' The next weekend, I put a champion athlete from each of the activities offered at the gym on duty. There was the prizefighter, the jiu jitsu guy, etc." That was the end of the looting. To rob the mall would have meant disrespecting powerful, localized networks of masculine authority.

Paulo's strategy is revealing of the way in which security also interacts with organized crime and how the same young men who are in one instance seen as threatening to the sense of security, can be quietly marshalled to ensure its protection under Paulo's guidance in the next instance. All of this operates below the radar, as to reveal the partnerships between security and crime would be damaging to the *sensação de segurança*.

Guilherme, the manager at the West Shopping used a similar tactic in his network of shoppings. He employed an upper-level manager whom he hired on the qualification that the man had certain *redes*, or connections. "Connections?" I ask. "He can negotiate with the criminal groups. If we have an issue, he goes to them and they discuss it and resolve it." Other security managers told me that resolution might sometimes involve a trade—organized crime would agree to crack down on assaults at the mall, for example, in exchange for several guaranteed job openings in security for their people. "I would never go and talk to these guys myself," Guilherme explained to me, a disgusted expression crossing his face. "Me! A former intelligence officer! I would never do that. It would be against my nature. But that is why I have a *despachante*—a fixer—who does that kind of negotiation."[6]

In sum, securing the shopping means cultivating the perception of safety among clients, reinforcing the perception that the space is safe from certain racialized *elementos suspeitos* and upholding the impression of the mall as a luxury space that is associated with whiteness and affluence. But the strategy for securitization is also revealing of just how close criminal networks (and questionably legal law enforcement) are to this process. Security is also created by activating these networks to protect elite property and to build a consensus around what is acceptable crime and where such crimes can occur. As I have shown, utilizing different networks, building appropriate human and other infrastructure, all work to cultivate feelings of well-being in a setting such as City Mall.

Branded Stadiums and Securing Elite Leisure

Just as mall shopping security procedures intersect with issues around the potential buying power of consumers, security strategies for prominent sporting venues in Rio, which were largely in flux during the time of my fieldwork, drew on similar tactics that linked security work to the cultivation of desired clientele and the exclusion of those from the so-called popular classes. While the security managers that I interviewed did not always frame it so explicitly (though some did), there was an implicit subtext that operational risks were lower when dealing with an elite population, a framing which drew on long-standing discourses that equate low class with criminality. Enclaving, or restricting access in order to ensure a more "manageable" sector of the population, was seen as a positive and attractive strategy for managing risk and creating the valuable sensation of security.

Ricardo, an operations manager at a global security firm, explained the connection between economics, access, and security to me in this way. "Let's talk about what Maracanã (Rio's iconic soccer stadium) used to be like. You probably went there when it was like this, right? Flamengo x Vasco on a Sunday afternoon. The stadium is full of people from communities (favelas). Drinking beer all day." I nod, remembering going to these games with friends from the Rocinha and drinking beer all day myself. "Who did the security back then?" He continues. "The police. These people (favela residents) hate the police. So, then all the sudden someone is throwing bottles or cups full of piss at the police and then the police are going to come at them hard. And it is all going to be on live TV. This is terrible for the image of a sporting industry which is there to generate capital. Because make no mistake that is exactly what is going on in these stadiums. It's a billion-dollar industry. Something had to be done. People started to be afraid to go to stadiums. They didn't feel like stadiums were safe places." I remember this too, as my "Brazilian parents," the older couple who lived next door to me in the community during my first long stint of PhD fieldwork and who watched out for me, were horrified at the idea of me going to matches that they considered to be majorly dangerous.

With the arrival of the World Cup in 2014, there was a radical shift in both the population of fans and in the security regime. When Maracanã (and indeed all Cup stadiums) was upgraded in order to serve as the focal point for the World Cup, the infrastructural upgrade to the stadium came with a concerted and centralized effort to change the audience that could attend games. Security efforts became more preemptive. Ticket price—much like the 10,000-dollar handbag or the 900-dollar Speedo at the City Mall—worked as a form of access control, sending a clear message about who was a welcome guest and who was not. As Christopher Gaffney noted at the time: "Ticket prices for Brazilian football matches have increased 300 percent in ten years and are the most expensive in the world relative to minimum wage. The people's game has been taken from them" (Gaffney 2014, n.p.). A higher priced ticket worked as an exclusionary device, which in turn allowed for the rebranding of stadiums and successful recruitment of higher-income patrons.[7] As the security company managers consistently said, the more exclusive the ticket, the easier the public is to manage. Such a mindset relies on an assumed connection between poverty and the inability to control, a belief commonly held among mid-level security personnel who routinely told me that the poor don't respond to hospitality models but only to brute force. Such sentiment was also reflected in discourses around the mall that claimed that visible, spectacular, and more overtly violent forms of security were needed to control more lower-class establishments. Many company owners and managers identified such an application of violence as outside the purview of private security and did not want to risk their whole enterprise by placing their guards in challenging circumstances and set them up for the ever-possible overreaction.

One security firm owner, whose firm worked sporting events insisted the cost of any event ticket price was the single most important factor in shaping the operational plan. "It's not just *futebol*. It's the same thing with big shows, like Rock in Rio. We consider bidding for the contracts of those only because of the public they will draw. It's a public that we think we can offer a reasonable service to. Would I agree to have my company do the security for a free *baile funk* on the beach? No way. I would have to be *um louco*. But these other publics, I know I can provide a good service without risking the reputation of my company. So, it's a good job, an attractive contract." As this owner attests, from a security standpoint, raising ticket prices for entrance into these spaces neutralizes certain security concerns.

Carmen Rial adds additional nuance, arguing for an understanding of stadium security which relies on "hard" measures, such as blacklisting unruly fans, but also increasingly on "soft" measures, which she explains worked to change the habitus of stadiums. Upgrading interiors by restricting seating rules to limit flow and movement, imposing new forms of bodily control on fans, including enforcing staying seated during matches, prohibiting smoking and alcohol, and prohibiting excessive profanity, all "contributed to sense that workers were out of place in spaces designed with other class *tastes*" (2019, 106).

The economics of access control and subtler changes in crowd management were therefore part of a series of larger infrastructural changes that transformed popular venues into elite enclaves. Once the population inside the stadium had shifted, a new security figure was introduced: the steward, the sporting parallel of the hospitality-oriented guard used in shopping malls. According to the owner of a private security company who initially provided stewards to Maracanã, the steward model, where private security actors maintain law and order inside stadiums, had been successfully used in previous World Cups, and was the preference of FIFA organizers. When I asked him about the qualities required of the steward, he says that they are "polite, professional, and good at offering directions to the bathroom," both in Portuguese and in English. Indeed, when I completed the steward training course myself, I found that a great portion of the training was focused on imparting precisely these qualities to spectators through racialized performances of professionalism identical to those discussed in hospitality training settings that I talked about in the previous chapters. In classes on becoming a steward, training focused on grooming, being friendly, and defusing situations so as not to cause issues (see chapter 2).

When I conducted interviews with private security company owners in Rio after the Cup, nearly every company told me a story about how it was they who had invented and implemented the steward concept. The shift to the stewards was only possible, everyone agreed, because the economics of access to the stadiums had changed as well. Another manager, Carlos, who worked for a multinational

FIGURE 18. Steward watching the press corps. January 2021. Photo: Guito Moreto.

company, explained: "We were the first private security force to take over security from the military police. The tension was high and they laughed at us saying that our unarmed guards (stewards) were going to get beaten up. But I am not stupid. I don't accept missions that I can't complete. What the police didn't realize was that we didn't need them anymore because the public had changed." One owner, an active-duty police officer who also owned a private security company, said that he was initially laughed out of meetings because he had designed the reflective vest that made up the steward uniform, because it looked too much like the vests worn by Rio's garbage workers. "You are replacing the military police with janitors," he was told derisively by his colleagues from both the private security sector and from the military police they were replacing. But what was really happening was that the stadium was being remade as a hospitality space.

"The steward is a more sympathetic character," explained Ricardo, referencing the way in which a steward is viewed as a citizen rather than a political authority per se so there's more sense of the steward as "one of us" doing his job, not on a power trip, and so on. "The population doesn't have the kind of *ódio* and *desconforto* that it has with the police. And even if they did, you have changed the public to one that is more rule abiding and less confrontational. And so the steward just has to maintain the space, as it says in the law, '*seguro, harmônico, e confortável.*'"

The rise of the steward as an appropriate security presence for elite space—be it in the mall or in the stadium—indicates just how bifurcated the policing of

FIGURE 19. Steward directing flow of foot traffic. December 2020. Photo: Guito Moreto.

different spaces has become in Rio. As with trends in the development of urban spaces and infrastructure more broadly, policing is being gentrified. Those in wealthy enclaves, including the global megaevent going public, can afford to purchase hospitality-oriented private security and not have to interface with the rougher and less polished military police. Genteel spaces and their occupants demand gentrified police.

Not All Security Feelings Are the Same

If the work of security is to manage feelings on limited resources, the fraught nature of this charge was especially apparent in moments when people's perceptions about what security "felt like" differed. While private security owners and managers eventually embraced the steward model, it was initially not well received, in my opinion, because Brazil has always favored a more ostentatious and spectacular approach to policing (Robb Larkins 2015). At both the World Cup and the Olympics, local Brazilian security norms were in direct conflict with the ideas brought by global security personnel, who often had very different sets of expectations around the minimum conditions necessary to impart "security feelings" to their constituents. This, importantly, reminds us that security is part of a culturally specific model of policing and rooted in particular histories and perceptions.

For example, Tom, the inhouse security manager of a North American global firm, elaborated on his and his clients' perspective on the steward model and on full-blown tensions between Brazilian event organizers and his own clients. "For my clients, security is a guy in a polo shirt not a guy with a machine gun. No one wants to come to a world-sporting event with an armed escort."[8] Getting Brazilians on board with this proposed model of understated security, however, was far from easy for Tom and his team. In fact, it was a frequent and near-daily topic of discussion at morning meetings. He further explained: "Look, their models are different. It's all about guns ablazing [sic!]. It is about BOPE (elite squad) training with the Israelis to become an antiterror squad. They like to show they have the toys, the hardware to make that convincing. Even if they really have no clue what they are doing." For foreigners accustomed to the kind of "invisible" or "hospitality" model described and promoted by Tom, Brazilian security was experienced as exotic ostentation.

Being skilled at security Tom says, "is about being an organized administrator. It is planning." For the global consultants I interviewed, Brazil's lack of planning was flagged as concerning. It did not convey the sensation of security. In their eyes, meticulous, advance preparation was a necessary element in winning global organizers', sponsors', and spectators' confidence and conveying positive security feelings. "Why can't the Brazilians get on board with this?" I heard over and over. Tom's model of efficiency and foresight engages with stereotypes of Brazilians as "always late" or "always doing everything at the last minute," as another global consultant once complained. This then had direct consequences for the provision of security. "Because they can't plan, they have no choice but to use a heavily armed presence," grumbles Tom.

While there is little doubt that increased planning might have helped with operationalizing security, I question whether or not this was an ignorant failure on the part of Brazilian security personnel, or, at least partially, a choice to do things according to local customs in such a way that reflected Brazilian cultural norms around the sensation of security. After spending several months observing Brazilian agents (public and private) prepare for the Olympics, I noted how important it was to local organizers to maintain the local way of doing things and to keep global influences in check. It was a matter of resistance, pride, and nationalism. After all, these were Brazilian Olympics, not foreign ones.[9]

At a 2016 press conference, where military officials and security personnel from the local organizing committee for the Games announced the completion of the tactical plans for the Olympic installations, the top official presenting the plans declared to thunderous applause, that he was especially "proud of the fact that the security effort had been a 100 percent native one." As one security leader told me after the event, "Security is the only part of organizing for the Games that doesn't come with an instruction booklet from the IOC. Why? Because it's the only part of organizing that must be evaluated and designed locally, in accordance with local realities." The *sensação de segurança*, it seemed, was to be crafted according to Rio-based understandings of what that meant.

The importance of localized knowledge extended even to the city level. People from outside of Rio "don't understand how the Rio criminal thinks," said one Brazilian private security provider. So the role of "expert" is closed off even to Brazilians from other states whose officials simply could not comprehend Rio's craziness. I think about Tom's frustration with Brazil's "failures" to establish global planning models and wonder whether it was not willful ignorance at all but rather a desire for recognition that there is a Brazilian way of doing things, a resistance to a North-to-South model of knowledge transfer (cf. Amar 2013; Graham 2011). In this way, the megaevents were about creating a *Brazilian* security structure and imparting feelings of security in Brazilian fashion, instead of complying with the imposition of foreign expectations.

In June 2019, I watched a robbery take place in the upscale Rio de Janeiro neighborhood of Leblon. It was a Saturday. The sidewalks were filled with people on their way to the beach to catch the first warm rays of summer. I sat in an outdoor café while multigenerational families ate a late breakfast at the tables around me. The hum of conversation and the sound of silverware against plates was interrupted by a scream, as a young man reached over the decorative hedge of the patio (infrastructure intended to protect the café from the street) and grabbed an iPhone from the table next to me. He sprinted down the crowded street, parting the crowd like a wave for the first half block. Then cries of *"pega ladrão"* (get the thief) erupted. One of the bank's armed private and uniformed security guards came out to watch but didn't leave his post or join in the chase as a group of men who had been drinking breakfast beer at the corner *boteco* pursued the thief. They were followed, more slowly, by a heavyset man with *barriga de chope*, who I had often seen sitting on a chair outside one of the stores, watching the block. One of the beer drinkers tackled the thief, and Barriga began to punch and kick him while onlookers enthusiastically cheered him on. When blood started pooling on the sidewalk, he stepped back. The thief remained quiet, motionless. By then the military police that were stationed on the beach corner had sauntered to the scene. Barriga retreated to the café, admirers in tow. Serenaded by thundering applause from the patrons, he ceremoniously returned the phone to its owner. Someone brought him a cold bottle of water and a towel which he used to swipe at the wetness on his thick neck. I asked the server who he was. She shrugged. Police? I asked. Maybe, she replied. But he doesn't wear a uniform, I said. She shrugged again. He went back to his stool, watching the block.

In this specific case, we see insecurity and security as intertwined with other forms of economic and social inequality; who can have an iPhone, who can have leisure on a Saturday afternoon, and who can employ an informal and shady lookout to resolve any threats to right those experiences. Security is a commodity connected to the flow of other commodities. Barriga isn't employed simply to protect cell phones; his performance demonstrates that he is also working the affective realm, reassuring consumers, passing the *sensação de segurança*, providing the comfort required for consumption in the stores he guards, or creating the possibility for a leisurely stroll on an upscale city block.

This episode illustrates the incredible and omnipresent plurality of security actors stationed on a single block of elite space on a sunny Saturday afternoon in one of Brazil's most exclusive neighborhoods. These actors are organized according to jurisdiction and job function, in alignment with the kind of space they are charged with securing. Formal private guards work inside their designated space of the bank or within the confines of a specific store that they are charged with protecting; informal *vigilantes*, fed up with crime give chase, leaving the dirty work to the "maybe police" like Barriga, working as a "maybe private security guard," while the formal police do the clean-up.

When I told Gomes about this episode, he nodded his head. "This is why I always say, besides the closed condominium, where risk can be nearly totally contained, Leblon is the safest neighborhood in Rio." Why exactly, I asked? "Because it is where all the famous and powerful, not to mention rich, people live. They can demand better policing. They can afford everything. Better cameras, gated entrances, and lots and lots of off-duty police." Taken together, these forms of security work to produce a kind of securitized bubble, which is in turn connected to other securitized bubbles of urban life and leisure, such as the fortified office building, the condominium, the shopping, the stadium. What we see here is how the same dynamics that are ever present in the stadiums and shopping malls, dynamics of manning checkpoints and controlling access, of performing security, migrate into entire elite neighborhoods, migrating from private to public spaces.

A few months later, I visited Gomes on the train station and we sat in the station McDonalds to talk away from the noise of the arrivals terminal. I told him about the *sensação de segurança* that he had talked about and how I was using it as a frame for this chapter. "*Olha*," he said, "I can give you another example." He told me that his boss had recently made him fire a guard who was overweight because he didn't look like he could run very fast. Gomes explained to me that this was ridiculous. Not only was it Christmas and he was angry that he had to dismiss the man at the holiday season but the logic behind firing him was bogus. "The whole point here is that this guy was fired not because of his operational inability. The guys' job is not to run after anyone—that would be the police's job, or public security job, right? But this guy's job is to make the public feel a *sensação de segurança*. And since he was heavy, people wouldn't *feel* like he could run after anyone. So he gets fired. See, illusions and feelings! That's what makes security!"

FIGURE 20. Road monitored twenty-four hours a day. January 2021. Photo: Guito Moreto.

FIGURE 21. Ubiquitous sign posted on condominium wall announces, "You are being filmed." Copacabana, Rio de Janeiro. January 2021. Photo: Guito Moreto.

FIGURE 22. Low-tech barbed wire against the perfect summer sky. Tijuca, Rio de Janeiro. January 2021. Photo: Guito Moreto.

ROUTINE SUFFERING

This one time there was an attempted assault. An attempted armed robbery. I worked in a big company, one of the biggest security companies in the city. The company had more than 13,000 employees. They had contracts all over the state. And I worked with them for ten years. Ten years of service. One day, I was working in a school in the metro area, outside the city proper. I was napping, watching television. When all the sudden, I hear a voice ordering me to get up. "*Levanta!*" "*Levanta!*" And I thought, huh? Who is calling me? Get up, get up? And so, I stood up and looked around the perimeter. I saw a *cidadão* (citizen) with a knife. He had just scaled the fence and was coming in through the perimeter where I was sitting. We had a chair there where we would sit and watch television but there weren't any cameras, you know. So, I stood there. There was like a standoff, me and him. Then he turned around and fled.

—Romario, thirty-seven years old. Twelve years in the security field.

This didn't happen to me, but it happened to one of my *colegas no serviço* (work colleagues). At the time, I was a *vigilante de ronda*, patrolling around this really large condominium, contracted by this company. I won't say the name so as not to complicate matters. But the condominium was in the *zona oeste* (the city's west zone). What happened had to do with one of the *porteiros* that worked the afternoon shift. A kite fell onto our side of the condominium gate. And he didn't give the kite back to the *molecada* (group of kids) that came looking for it. He got all *machão*—tough guy—because Brazil has a lot of *machão*. So, what did he do? Not only did he not return the kite to the kids, but instead he broke it in half in front of them, all confrontational and stuff. What happened? Well, a week later. Maybe a little more than a week later, because it's always a little while later that the shit goes down. The *porteiro* was found in the morning. He was inside the security *guarita*. *Morto*. Dead. He took three bullets to the chest. The condominium complex was really large and of course no one saw anything. But afterward, through the *boca pequena* (lit. little mouth, the grapevine) we found out that one of the kids involved in the kite incident was the son of the manager of the *boca de fumo* (drug selling point) in the community adjacent to the complex. And so this drug dealer ordered our colleague's death.

The media didn't pay much attention. This was probably because the guy was just a simple *porteiro*, a simple security guard, but maybe also because our company was one of the big ones, the powerful ones and things about them just didn't get published in the newspaper.

—Richard, fifty years old. A lifetime in the security field.

Once, I had this situation in the condominium that I worked at. Here is what happened. A resident of one of the apartments told us that we should start working armed. The manager didn't allow this but this one resident, he really wanted it. And he had a gun. I don't know if it was his dad's or what. I just know that because he liked us a lot, he let us use the gun. It was me and one other friend. He only left the gun with the two of us, never with the third guard, just us. He liked us.

So, one day, I was sitting in the guard house, working, and the *porteiro* (doorman) asked me to watch his post so that he could go to the bathroom. No, wait, it was to make a coffee actually. He went to the kitchen to make a coffee. It was like one or two in the morning. Right after he left, this guy started messing around right outside the perimeter. He started banging on the metal fence out front, maybe like he was trying to get my attention or distract me from my post. But I couldn't tell exactly because my view was partially blocked by some trees. Without knowing exactly what was going on, I could tell the guy was up to something and so I put my hand on the gun and I stood up. As he approached and got closer to the *portão* (gate), I realized he was drunk. He was climbing up on the fence and then falling off again because he was so drunk. So, I put the gun back inside the drawer of the *guarita* (guardhouse). But pooooofffff! The gun went off. It went off inside the drawer. I sat my butt back down in the chair. I swear I thought I had shot myself in the leg. I swear that I even felt the heat and this burning sensation.

But when I looked, I saw that the bullet had lodged itself not in my leg but in the *livro de atas* (the legal statute book that is standard to keep on-site; like the Bible in the hotel nightstand). And then, well, the sound of the gunshot created a *bafafá*, a huge fuss. Residents woke up. I told everyone that it was a motorcycle that had gone by shooting and so on. And then next day the *sindicato* (manager of the condo, like the head of the building co-op) called me for a talk and even the *porteiro* that asked me to sit in his place backed me up but it all kind of hung over me. Two weeks later I was fired.

—Cesar, forty years old. Eighteen years in the security field.

I was just finishing up my shift in the evening when it happened. The day had been *esquisito*. I had spent the whole day guarding this place in the woods. *No meio da mata*. It wasn't even a house or an office yet. It was just a construction site. I spent the whole day there. In the middle of the woods. Alone. Just me and God. There was no electricity. Actually, there was just one lightbulb, so I guess there was light. I sat there alone. In the middle of this concrete foundation. There were a few shipping containers full of tools and materials. A lot of rolls of cable.

At some point, I got up to stretch and drink some water. I was supposed to walk around and patrol the site. Over near the area where the construction workers took their breaks, there was a drinking fountain. There was no one there but me. I went inside to the place where the drinking fountain was and to my surprise, the drinking fountain was turned on and running. But there was no one there in that area but me. There was another guard that worked with us on the site and he was working alone like me in another area really, really far away. So of course, I called him and said "Oi, Fulano, did you come over here and turn on the water, turn on the drinking fountain?" And he said "No, no it wasn't me. I didn't leave my post all day. And I went off duty around 3:00 a.m. anyway. It wasn't me." When he said that, I felt cold, a cold creeping sensation. Was there someone else there with me? I turned off the water.

I went outside and I did another round of patrolling. I thought to myself, it's not possible that there is anyone else out here with me. But I was scared and so I yelled in very loud voice: "If there is someone here . . . If there is someone here, well *amigão*, you better come out?" I said stuff like: "There is a bunch of us, and we are all armed. You better come out." I said this just to see what happened. But no one came out. Eventually, I came back around, back to the same spot that I had started the *ronda*. The water was turned on again! *Novamente*. I didn't see anyone. This gave me the worst feeling. Like ice. You know sometimes we hear these stories. People say things like about *assombração*, ghosts, spirits. I swear to God that there was no one else on-site. But the water that I had just turned off was on again! I started looking around outside the building. It was a rainy day and muddy, but I could see only my footprints.

—Paulo, forty-five years old. Thirty years in the security field.

It happened when I was working at the condominium. There had been some problems with the community next door and so our *chefe* told us that we needed to do more frequent patrols. One day, we got an anonymous tip that someone was selling drugs right outside the entrance. We located the suspect and when he saw us, he took off. As it happened, there was a train line, train tracks, that ran right next to the location. The *menino* was so concentrated on running from us that he didn't seem to see the train coming. He was running but he kept looking back to see if we were getting close to catching up with him. He misjudged the distance. He collided with the train. He fell. And the train wheels passed right over his legs. The scene was (voice catches), *bastante, uh bastante triste*. This was someone's life. He wasn't older than sixteen. After it happened, all these people started running out from the community. People that knew him. Holding his hand. Others were lamenting that he had chosen that life. That they had always told him to *largar aquela vida*, give up that life. *Mas não tem jeito*. In the life of crime, it's either jail or death. About half an hour later, he died. I have to confess that the image, in my mind the picture of this scene is imprinted in me. It doesn't ever leave my head.

—Sebastião, twenty-eight years old. Six years in the security field.

I am ex-militar of the Forças, from the Marines. I have technical training in the field, I am a good security worker, but this doesn't mean that stuff still doesn't come up. When I started my very first security job in the 1990s, my work post was in an office, but it was under construction. So basically, we were guarding a construction site. One day, one of the other guards on the site turned up dead.

He was killed by *bandidos*. He had been out drinking and there was a fight. Then he came to work the nightshift and they came to kill him. This happened at midnight. Things were really tense. Really tense. The guy was always really disrespectful of all of us other guards. During the day, he would walk around brandishing his gun in an ostentatious manner. Sometimes on the weekends, he would bring his guitar and play instead of working. Other times, he would sleep half the day away while on the job. He would go lie down in the *guarita* and just sleep.

One night, after he had had this fight, you know, three *bandidos* came after him on the job site. They scaled the walls, high walls, mind you, with two revolvers and a shotgun and started to shoot. And they killed the guy. Afterward, we were all called in to answer to the building manager, to talk about what had happened. And after the manager had asked all his questions then we were asked more by the bosses of the company we worked for. As I went to leave, they stopped me and said, "Wait, we just have two more questions about your dead *parceiro*." I had been working that day and so they just asked me whether I saw anyone or anything suspicious during the day shift and I said no. And the other *pergunta*, I asked? The boss laughed and asked, "Was that guy an idiot or what?"

—Reginaldo, fifty years old. Thirty years in the security field.

So, the episode happened in a calm, super tranquil place. (A gated housing complex). We never thought that anything sinister would ever go down there. But it happened, *né*? It was the shift change. We did the change, I passed responsibility over to my colleague. A few hours later, four or five hours later they called me, saying that some heavily armed guys broke in to the *posto* and held the guards hostage, including Francisco, Chico. He worked there in the road, he was what we called a *guarda de rua* (*vigia*) just watching houses of the *bacana* (lit., cool but meaning wealthy) people. He resisted the guys. I guess they were ordering him into the *guarita* and told him to lie on the floor. He tried to run but they got him. And my God, they started to beat him. The beat him so bad that when I got to work the next day, there was blood all over the walls. He barely survived. He barely lived.

And to top it all off, three months later, the same guys came back. This time during the day. The first time, it was at night but the second time, in broad daylight. Plain day! First thing in the morning in fact. *Bem cedinho*. They held up us four guards in the *guarita*. Took us hostage. Tied us to the chairs. Bound our arms and legs with duct tape. They had stolen a company car, from Vivo (the phone company). The kind of car they send for repairs, you know, and set it up so that it made things look less suspicious. They took the service ladder from the car and set it up in front of one of the houses next door, up to the window, the house of this Japanese guy, so that it would look like it was legit you know. And then they climbed over and opened the gate, letting in two or three or four guys. *Caras todas armadas*. Everyone totally armed. Two of them just holding us hostage. They took our phones. Pulled the SIM cards out, pulled the batteries out. Saying that they didn't want to hurt us, they just wanted to rob the house next to us. The Polícia Civil came later to do the investigation and they said the guys stole a lot of cash, $250,000 in total that the guy had in the house.

—JP, thirty-eight years old. Twelve years in the security field.

With me, well, it happened only once, an *assalto*. I was working for a building company, on a construction site. Well, rather, I was working for a security company that was contracted by the building company. The construction site was a complex of towers, six towers. Each was two stories. And the *vigilância*, the monitoring, well there were a lot of access points where someone could enter the construction site. What happened? Six guys came in. They grabbed me out of the *guarita*. *Me espancaram*. They hit me. They beat me. They took the other two guards who were with me, but they didn't hit them. Only me. They said they were going to kill me. They made me kneel. Said again they were going to kill me. While doing this, they kept calling me by the wrong name. They were calling me by the name of another guy! Another guy who worked in security. They were told to kill this guy and, in their confusion, they were going to kill me instead, thinking I was him. Mistaken identity.

Moral of the story. I was able to reverse the situation. I could prove that I was not the guy. They got my *carteira de identidade* out of my wallet to verify. They apologized. They said they were sorry for the whole confusion. Thank God, right? Because I had two guns to my head as I kneeled there, and I was bleeding. In addition to this, they had kicked me in the ribs and in the kidneys. But in the end, they believed me. They believed that I was not the guy. But then they went in and well, they robbed the whole construction site. The copper pipes, the wiring, everything.

This all happened very fast. They had been staking out the site for more than a week, preparing. Just waiting for the chance to kill the guy and steal from the site. And so, what happened afterward, *professora*, well, security is a very thankless job. I got no psychological support for what happened. I didn't even get a day off. The very next day after I was beaten and threatened, my employers put me right back in the exact same post where it happened. Understand? The owner of the company I worked for was military police. Two military police actually, partners. I learned that in this area, in the security world, we are just a number. The traumas that stay with us, the pain that stays with us . . . No support from the company at all for this. Not a single acknowledgment of what had happened to me. I didn't have any help. I had to figure it all out myself. I sought assistance in the SUS (the public health system) to help me recover from the trauma. (Sighs deeply). This is what happened.

—Clovis, fifty-two years old. Twelve years in the security field.

4
EMOTIONAL LABOR IN THE SECURITY COMMAND CENTER

"Begin every communication with the words 'simulation, simulation.' This will help others to discern that the incident you speak of is not real. Next, identify yourself by name, function, and complete location," instructs the commander, standing in front of our assembled group. On the command center's wall, behind my head, are two clocks. One clock, a normal clock, shows the big hand inching closer to the start of the simulation. The other is like a doomsday clock, red numbers in digital descent toward what we called "Games Time," the opening of the XXXI (31st) Olympiad, hosted for the very first time by a South American nation, in the city of Rio de Janeiro.

On the first day of the games-wide simulation, the little hand hits the 12 sharp and, because we operate with military precision here, the phone rings, marking the start to the simulation. The voice on the other end says: "Simulation, simulation." Gripping my pen tightly, I listen, nervous and overwhelmed. I scribble, scratch at my notebook. I can't write fast enough to make the notes in any one language so I mix English acronyms with Portuguese verbs, a choice I will woefully regret when I look at these same notes later trying to make sense of them for the daily reports.

I stand to address the assembled security personnel, all twenty-five of them. I know it's twenty-five because as a no-rank woman, I had placed a pen and paper next to each phone. I was typically asked to do this kind of work. Assistant-level. Secretarial. *Trabalho doméstico*. Domestic work. Woman's work.

I repeat the details of the incident exactly as I heard them: "Simulation, simulation. Erika Larkins, Security Analyst, Main Operation Command, Olympic Park,

Barra de Tijuca, Rio de Janeiro, Brazil. Opening incident reported by Venue Security Manager (VSM) Moises, Maracanã Stadium. 01:00 hours. The west ramp of the stadium has been taken over by Indigenous peoples, or as they called them 'Indians,' protesting the demolition of the Museum of the Indian which made room for the parking lot adjacent to the stadium. Apparently, they are practically naked, have spears, are holding approximately four Games personnel hostage. Venue Security Manager requests notification of police liaison in Center for Integrated Command and Control. Incident has potential to impact the field of play."

As the description of the incident leaves my mouth, I fear that I heard the message wrong because this seems ridiculous but, then again, I once read that George W. Bush blamed 9/11 on the "failure of the imagination" of the security personnel. Since no one teeters toward laughter, I conclude that this scenario must be somehow probable for people whose racist conceptions of Indians clearly included savagery and archaic weapons.[1]

I sit. I key the incident into the reporting system, try to classify it within the confines of the prepopulated drop-down menus. There is no entry for "povos indígenas" or even "índios." Seeing me struggle, the analyst next to me suggests "terrorists," but I am not about to accept that that's what they are so I leave it blank. In the white box that asks for a written summary of the incident, I spell lots of things wrong, activating the red squiggly underline of the spell-check. Before I can fix the absent accents and misplaced vowels, the phone rings again, as it will now ring in five-minute intervals for the next twelve hours as part of the rules of the simulation. My spelling errors become part of history, archived forever, but for now another minor humiliation pinned up on the monitors at the front of the command center for scrutiny in a room full of "real" security analysts.

The room discusses the situation at hand. Since it is only the opening lobby, they settle on a reasonable solution: isolate the perimeter and notify the *Fundação Nacional do Índio* (FUNAI), the Indian Protection Agency. After I key this in, we receive a second call from the VSM that informs us that the imaginary Indians don't speak Portuguese. Can I request a translator to negotiate? And a hostage team since they are using some of the food and beverage staff as human shields. As the day goes on, one of the senior analysts will jokingly suggest nuking them. Someone else will propose shooting everyone, even the hostages. "*Mata logo*," another guy says laughingly, turning the common expression, "get it done" into a double entendre with its literal meaning, "kill soon" hanging in the air. This solution is bandied about but gets dismissed due to the presence of international media crews congregating outside the stadium. The Indian incident blinks as a red "unresolved" on the central screen.

Meanwhile the phone trills again and again, relentless, as the simulated crises spread across the entire Olympic City like a wet oil spill. The anarchist protest group the Black Blocs shuts down the highway so that the athletes' buses can't pass. Anarchists let poisonous snakes loose on the tennis courts. A bomb threat is made to the marina. A truck filled with hazardous, airborne material topples over in front of the Park. A small plane crashes onto the beach adjacent to the volleyball venue. A duffle bag filled with explosives is tossed onto the marathon route. Scalpers hawk tickets everywhere. Petty thieves rob everyone everywhere. A foreign delegation tries to cover its cheating by stealing a van carrying dirty doping samples to the lab. *Os índios* continue with their protest.

At some point in the day, a freezer full of Kibon ice cream bars is delivered to the break room adjacent to the command center. "Do you think all of this could actually happen?" I ask the commander while we eat popsicles, our mouths stained purple with grape. "That is not the point," he counters, taking on the slightly superior pedagogical tone he used when pointing out to me what he considered to be obvious. "It's not the small details of the scenario that matter, it's the opportunity to test, to rehearse, to get prepared."[2]

Drawing on nine months of fieldwork with high-level security forces, this chapter examines the logic of "security preparedness" as I observed and experienced it and shows how preparedness worked to foster the creation of the sensation of security for megaevent fans, television audiences, employees from other areas beyond security, corporate sponsors, and other members of the "Olympic family," as it was called.[3] "The rationality of preparedness," according to the anthropologist Limor Samimian-Darash, "addresses a seemingly inevitable future disaster that can only be managed once it happens. Intervention is aimed at reducing the resulting damage rather than preventing particular threats" (Samimian-Darash 2016, 362). Similarly, as noted by Andrew Lakoff in regard to domestic security personnel in the United States, preparedness "provides security experts with a way of grasping uncertain future events and bringing them into a space of present intervention" (2007, 247). As I understood it from my interlocutors, preparedness was about mitigating catastrophe by expecting and accepting the worst and training on basics like the chain of command or communication instead of directing energy toward preventing threats. Beyond engaging with a well-established and widespread modality for training and readying teams for high-risk events, preparedness was at the heart of the production of the sensation of security. Indeed, the capabilities of the local organizing team and the Brazilian government and its security forces were created, articulated, and performed through this notion, which signaled foresight, contingency plans, and clear organizational chains of command. Together, these all worked as evidence to support an image of Brazil and its security forces, be they public or private, as capable of ensuring that the Games went off without major incident. The provision of the sensation of security was aimed at a diverse group of people, with competing interests and different cultural expectations around what good security looked like, including ticket-holding fans attending events, upper-level employees working in other parts of the planning and executing apparatus, corporate sponsors and their security teams, foreign delegations and their security teams, government officials, and so forth.

In what follows, I track the elaboration of preparedness, as a way of performing the sensation of security, through exploration of two overlapping realms. One, which I have just described, focused on simulations, practice sessions where the team could rehearse responses to potential security incidents while also performing the capability necessary to build feelings of confidence for observers.[4] The other involved an incident-reporting system that I call CrimeBase.[5] Both of these arenas conditioned us to classify and codify issues according to the norms of the institutional context in which they were working. Preparedness, therefore, accomplished two central feats. It trained, directed, and conditioned emotional responses and taught employees to perform in ways which would (hopefully) shape the emotional responses of others. Put differently, if preparedness was an inner exercise of disciplining feelings and reactions, it was also a performative modality necessary to convey professional competence and the marketability of the security apparatus to outside observers, contributing to the presence of the sensation of security. To be prepared, we tamed our own emotions and then performed for other parts of the event's organizing body, for security industry leaders, for global contractors, and for corporate sponsors.

Setting the Scene

The security operations were located on the eighth floor of a tall, mirrored building that towered above the Olympic Park. With still-fresh paint on the walls, so fresh that its smell lingered on our uniforms, in our hair, and on our skin; the smell even permeated our homes at night. Fixtures had not been closed and ceiling panels displayed wires. The incompleteness of the building, which made it feel like an unfinished shell, did not evoke the sensation of security. Rather, it revealed the fact that everything had come together to look barely presentable at exactly the last minute, and suggested a lack of preparation. Luckily, outer spaces were more carefully curated. Though the command center floors were under construction, on the ground level, which we shared with the international media, there was a row of newly installed ATM machines from Bradesco, the official sponsor bank. A brand-new souvenir store relentlessly peddled merchandise.

Visible through the window were shelves of stuffed Tom and Vinicius toys, the Rio2016 mascots designed to represent a combination of all Brazilian plants and animals. Tom and Vinicius also graced key chains and appeared on overpriced T-shirts.

The security command center was at the back corner of the west end of the floor, past the situation rooms and the director's private and never-used office. The plans called for a password-protected, bulletproof security door to gatekeep this wing but it was never installed. The other wing of our floor was never finished at all, just taped off with plastic to keep the plaster from making a mess and to dispel any hazardous material. The door to the security command eventually got a fingerprint scan pad, intended to recognize our registered biometric information, but there were so many problems programming it that we eventually just propped the door a few inches open instead. The room was freezing from the constant blow of the air conditioning, a form of climate control typical of secured spaces, a sensorial element of the sensation of security, which communicates modernity and civilization in the context of the tropical climate and its associations (Frazier 2019).

At some point, someone tacked two flags up over the room's only windows, the ones that looked down at Vila Autódromo, the adjacent favela that successfully resisted removal, a small part of which was still standing right outside the entrance. My colleagues regularly looked out at it with scorn and suspicion, imagining the community as a potential locus of protest and saying things like how it was full of "sports-hating communists." I think it was partly in an attempt not to see it that someone hung the flags. One, the Brazilian flag. The other, representing Rio's notoriously murderous elite special forces from which a number of the more important members of the security team originated, displayed a skull with a knife through it. The flags effectively blocked most of the natural light out of the room, leaving it lit primarily by screens.

Security cameras reporting from different sectors of the park were on three of the monitors in front of the room, gesturing toward the presence of an advanced surveillance system, but a closer look would reveal the grainy flickering quality of the feed, too macro to yield much information. Live coverage of key competitions graced another screen. Yet a third screen displayed the running list of open security incidents, not just from the main park but from all parks, competition venues, and transportation routes, color-coded according to level of severity. These were our outstanding incidents, our problems to be solved. All energy was to be directed toward closing them out.

On a typical day, when I came in to my early morning shift, I would switch the login information on the computer with the overnight analyst and he would verbally brief me on the open incidents in CrimeBase,[6] the system that we used to record all *ocorrências* (lit. occurrences) as we called them, that affected the competition.[7] CrimeBase *ocorrências* ranged from internal security issues in venues—like suspicious packages or ticket scalping to external issues like gunfire in nearby favelas or the shenanigans of US swimmer Ryan Lochte. A digital clock on the corner of each incident window counted how many hours had passed without resolution of the *ocorrência*.

The incidents were usually resolved in a decentralized manner—our structure awarded considerable autonomy to field managers where *ocorrências* were actually happening. The job of the analysts in the command center was, as we were told in one training with counterterrorism experts, to see the big picture—beyond the limited vision of the operatives in the venues, which were like fragmented islands. We had to discern if patterns of *ocorrências* were related. Such a discourse was far grander than what we actually did. The narrative of there being a central monitoring center keeping an eye on the big picture was a useful part of the performance of security.

Ocorrências entered the system in several different ways. There were always external reporting lines, since our phone number was listed as the contact point for all security incidents for the public. But for our internal security team, the initial idea was that an app, also developed by the same company that had designed CrimeBase, would be used by all the area managers on the ground who would input incident information, which would then emerge on the screens of analysts like me, accompanied by a gentle and unobtrusive chime alert.[8]

However, the app—itself a performative device intended to communicate the modernity and efficiency of our team—was far less effective than the narrative suggested. Days after rolling it out, people began to complain that it sucked all the battery life out of their phones in a matter of minutes and refused to use it. Members of the security team then resorted to calling the command center to verbally log the incident which we then keyed into the system. Alternately, they posted incidents in a group WhatsApp thread from which we had to extract them. In other cases, people from other sectors like transportation, having realized that the incident reporting system that they were using didn't speak to our system due to a different glitch altogether and suddenly realizing that the technology was a mirage, came in the propped-open door of the command center, usually wringing their hands or reporting in frustrated tones that there was yet another theft, or yet another scalper, yet another problem. The useless nature of the app and its associated reporting platform thus reiterates its performative function and attests to the way in which security-related technology was largely a performative tool intended to cultivate the *sensação de segurança*.

Professionalism as Archive

My participant observation during this time of my fieldwork revolved centrally around being an interface with CrimeBase. I was instructed by my superiors to do two things. First, I needed to meticulously register every action related to (almost) all *ocorrências* into CrimeBase, thus creating an archive that could be presented as evidence of transparency and efficiency. Second, if anyone from other areas of the organizing committee asked for an update on an *ocorrência*, I was to respond that we were working on resolving it. "Resolving it" didn't mean that the problem would go away. It meant that we were trying to close it out of our system, demonstrating that we took appropriate steps to deal with the matter.

CrimeBase wasn't the only program that was beta tested during the event. Mind bogglingly, everything was being simultaneously logged on a parallel system, "OcorrênciaOne," developed by another police *coronel* for a security company he owned. OcorrênciaOne was not integrated with CrimeBase. In addition to the two *ocorrência* systems, operational personnel also had to submit what were called "daily run sheets," summary forms of all reported incidents, which answered the same questions as the other systems in yet another form. These sat in a central email account and were not opened. These competing systems undermined the sensation of security for anyone up close to the event, as the unnecessary duplication of tracking suggested parallel agendas at play.

The seasoned security workers who had to engage with all of these parallel systems totally understood what was going on—that they are being asked to perform triple the amount of work for the future financial or career benefit of higher-ups. It was initially a source of frustration. I remember one venue manager in particular whose diatribe included calling out the record keeping systems as *para inglês ver*, a colloquial expression that means "for the English to see," and signifies the performance for outsiders.[9] While this was annoying and the source of a fair amount of grumbling and overtime, when I called (at the commander's behest, something which I never failed to mention!) to remind the field managers to fill out report x or file form y, I heard a weary resignation that signaled they also understood their work as reinforcing their ties to those higher-ups in ways which were deemed potentially useful. In short, the duplication of labor, of work, of performance was understood as a strategic element for winning security "markets," meeting their demands and requirements through performance. Security actors at all levels used the systems to perform competence and professionalism for the outside. All of us were co-opted in the performance.

If CrimeBase was an ineffective program that only served the performance of security, its success as such depended on the cooperation of those who interfaced with it. We, me and analysts like me, were trained to perform by a CrimeBase representative, a petite woman in high heels with Pat Benatar style 1980s jet black hair, that I later found out was one of the commanders' girlfriend. Her bird-like features matched a sharp, shrill disposition and a laser-like focus on making CrimeBase seem like a viable program so that it stood a chance of securing future contracts.[10] Unfortunately for those of us who had to try to demonstrate its worth, CrimeBase was buggy and molasses-slow. It was originally designed for police operations, a fact which was evident, as it included buttons to dispatch a patrol car or call a judge, actions that had little relevance for our work. Ironically, like so much of the preparedness world, the system itself was aspirational, since it was still deemed so ineffective that no police force would buy it. But that did not mean we would not be required to try to perform its competence. The whole idea was that the Olympics would generate important PR for CrimeBase, and its executives could advertise that Rio 2016 was an official client on their promotional materials, thus raising the company's international profile because it was unthinkable that such an important global brand with considerable resources would use and depend on a system that was so clunky.[11]

In addition to being a way to perform professionalism and to create future economic opportunities for security entrepreneurs, incident reporting systems like CrimeBase justified our existence as a security unit. In this way, the burden of preparedness was that of documentation, of archive. The constant registration of minute time-consuming steps was necessary to demonstrate, and thereby legitimize, the work we carried out. And the ability to generate reports—and informative analytics, so we could see from where most of the *ocorrências* were coming or what type they were—were part and parcel of the performance of modernity that underpinned the entire Rio Olympics. The fact that we never actually generated reports like these, let alone talked about them or analyzed them, was beside the point. The mere *potential* to generate data if needed was sufficient to lend itself to the *sensação de segurança*.

Performing Preparedness for Others

Conveying a sensation of security to others through the use of monitoring systems was just one part of the performance of preparedness. With frequency, actual performances were required, and the command center was a frequent destination for foreign delegation security personnel and International Olympic Committee personnel. The ritual for these visits was as follows. The commander would usually gesture for me to come and translate for him as he proudly interpreted the summary data for CrimeBase that was scrolling on the big screen. He would typically ask me to give visitors an example of how the system worked, using a sample incident. Because I lived in constant fear of having my security clearance revoked for being too honest, I played the part and always opted for benign or incomplete examples that highlighted success, not abject failure.

For example, in one demonstration for two observers from Tokyo, the city slated to host the 2020 Games, I pulled up a case of a hole in the perimeter fence that was logged in overnight. "It works like this," I said, explaining the system in the hypothetical so as to avoid all-out lying. The person in charge of this sector of the Park would have logged the incident through his cell phone. With an app on each field manager's phone, it would allow them to seamlessly input data in real time. Once registered, a push notification would come through on the security command center screens. We would then look up the location on the Park camera, see if there was anything of interest there to complement the case, and then route it to maintenance for resolution. Someone—probably the field manager in that particular sector—would have moved a private security guard on-site while that happened. The guard would form a physical barrier to the movement of any goods or people until the requisite repairs could be made. My Japanese audience nodded encouragingly as if to say, this all seems so reasonable and efficient. I exchanged niceties with the visitors about my Portuguese and the day's competitions. The commander smiles and pats me on the back: "Aren't we lucky to have Erika here?" he says with a smile, igniting a by then familiar sense of discomfort that I was colluding with the enemy.[12]

The performance of professional competence and the deception that it sometimes entailed was not undertaken out of malfeasance; there were simply no resources to finance increases in security. The sensation of security would have to do. For example, I remember a particular incident at the Marina da Glória, where a very persistent British representative from the Olympic nomad team, a team that traveled from Olympics to Olympics, called every single day for a week straight to report that employees were feeling unsafe walking from the venue to the metro stop due to an increase of in-park muggings at knife point. While at first, I was just instructed to tell her that we were looking into it and that we were checking the cameras in the region, after four or five complaints, I was told to tell her that we were stationing a patrol car along the walking route. After passing on this message, I asked the shift manager if I should then call our police liaison to request the car. "Of course not," he said to me, with an expression that conveyed his annoyance and low opinion of me. "Do you see any extra money around here for increasing security? If I had the budget, *claro*, I would send the car. But I have no budget." "Well, why did I tell her that then?" I asked. "*Querida*," he said diminishingly, "You told her that to make her feel better. If we can't give her the actual car, at least we can give her the feeling that we are going to send the car. Now go and close out the incident in the system." Through this sort of preparedness work, security workers are taught that the security problem is not the actual problem to be solved. We were creating the *sensação de segurança*. When seen through this prism, it didn't matter if we actually solved the problem but only that we gave the impression that we had solved it. The *ocorrências* became manageable, or even controllable, because the metric for judgment was the efficacy of our impression management skills not the actual resolution of the security issue at play.

Furthermore, a very much intended side effect of this mode of thinking, or disillusionment if you will, is that it functioned to downplay the human costs of a security incident, reducing it to something not to be felt but to be managed. Our work entailed choreographing our performances, not engaging with the suffering or losses outside the command center. This suggests the other element that I argue to be key to preparedness thinking as I experienced it: simulations and systems emotionally and cognitively condition workers to think about *ocorrências* in ways which favor detachment and which place brand security on par with human lives. If the idea behind the sensation of security is to make guests and clients feel safe enough to consume—not to actually be safe—the whole enterprise becomes one which values and strives for the conditions for consumption rather than human well-being.

Classifying the World, Favoring the Brand

Inputting *ocorrências* meant transforming messy, complex worlds according to overly simplistic taxonomies. In my command center research, I openly struggled to learn this skill, often wanting to write large blocks of notes describing the incident, a tendency which I eventually realized ran counter to the entire goal. I was consistently begging the Pat Benatar look-alike manager to add more categories in the incident drop down menus so that I could be more specific. With time, I began to realize that I was to use the system as it was intended to be used, not to try to improve it. I was supposed to keep quiet and master its limited semantics, a semantics which mirrored the organization's vocabulary, and perhaps more important, its priorities. All the terms in the system were prepopulated and fed into the system by Benatar. The big bosses were the ones that helped to determine the words but after the initial input, those of us who worked with the system were to play with it during the simulations, noting any missing terms which would then be considered for inclusion. We would jot these down on a communal notepad kept in the middle of the table for Benatar's consideration. While she did not welcome conversation with me about her rejection of terms that I suggested, *assalto* (assault) or *sangue* (blood), she did accept *manifestação* (protest). The terms themselves indicate the parameters of corporate concern. Bodily harm or injury wasn't the problem, the problem was if it stopped the competition. The details of what stopped it didn't so much matter. However, political protest could be included directly because it was damaging to the brand reputation.

Another particular incident serves to illustrate the way in which security is aimed at protecting the viability of the event and the Olympic brand. The Venue Security Manager of the road race (bicycle) called to say that there was a report of gunfire in a favela near the course route. The competition was scheduled to begin in one hour. "Is there police action in the favela?" he wanted to know. How would I have entered this event into the system? I started with "gunfire" but there was no pull-down menu item on the incident tab for gunfire, despite its routine daily occurrence all over Rio. I debated using the "other" tab and typing in gunfire. But I got reprimanded if I did this too often since it wasn't good for aggregate data. Additionally, I was told that I was thinking about it all wrong.

I called the commander over to ask how to classify it. "Think about it from our perspective," he said to me, the "our" accompanied by a sweep of the hand which embraced both the room of security personnel and asked me to imagine myself as part of a vast Olympic family. "I see," I said. The Olympics doesn't care about gunfire in and of itself, it doesn't care about dead bodies, or weeping mothers, it cares about the threat these things pose to the field of play. Aha! It's not the incident itself per se but its possible ramifications to the event. "Disruption to field of play?" I asked cautiously. "There you go, *querida*," he said with a nod.[13]

I find this category as an entry on the dropdown menu. I entered it and clicked the radio button which was supposed to notify our representative in the city-wide police command and control center downtown. That button never worked, though, so I consulted the kinship chart and called Carlos. "Hi," I said. "It's the Gringa," as he called me. "Hi, Gringa." I could hear him smiling. "The VSM said there is gunfire in Cidade de Deus, is that you guys?" "Hold on," he replied. A few minutes later he returned. "Yes, that's us. What time does the race start? Thirty minutes from now? Okay, yay, I will tell them to hurry up in there and be out of the way in time."

This kind of incident illustrates the overbearing concern with one kind of disturbance, toward which all our preparedness was to be directed: mitigating interruptions to the field of play.[14] Interruptions would signal to all that things were decidedly *not* in control, undermining the delicately established *sensação de segurança*. Furthermore, interruptions to competitions meant disrupted television broadcast; interrupted television meant revenue loss. The security world we created was one that was oriented toward the brand's profitability and the preeminence of markets. If the system revealed priorities, it did so through semantics.

The emphasis on the "field of play" signaled the preeminence of corporate profit, while other terms were more about corporate image protection. This is best illustrated by the shifting terminology we were instructed to use to address potential bombs or explosive devices, or as we initially were implored to call them "suspicious packages." During simulations, the term "suspicious packages" appeared as a drop-down menu selection and it was one we used frequently, as backpacks, plastic bags, suitcases, duffle bags, and food carts were abandoned constantly, testing our ability to treat each and every one as an instrument that could reduce a stadium to dust.

However, as Games time approached, this terminology was replaced, by the higher-ups that liaised with the international security agents, by a new one: suspicious item. *Item suspeito*. Just before the opening ceremonies, we saw a further sanitation. Potential bombs became simply *itens de interesse*, items of interest. The language here mirrored what I personally experienced as a shifting reaction to the possibility of real bombs. I found the simulations concerning, and dealing with them, namely, calling for the bomb dogs and disabling robots, made me very anxious. However, by the time that I was required to *call* potential explosives mere "items of interest" during the actual event, I found myself only mildly annoyed with them, even the ones that had appeared real with fake liquids and wires and which had been intentionally planted by Olympic foes to scare us. This attitude was evidenced on the team by the frequent use of the adjective *chato*, or annoying, to describe the incidents that we had to deal with or to disparage the civilians from other divisions who were characterized as *cheia de frescura* (fresh) for asking us to look into incidents that they, with their untrained vision, saw as security risks.[15] All of this, I argue, is revealing of the emotional registers through which preparedness develops.

Thus, while it is a critical part of test-driving plans, security preparedness is also about redefining what, precisely, constitutes a security problem. Crisis is not limited to the kinds of conventional carnage that people might associate with laymen's notions of the term security but extends to any occurrence that disrupts markets and the flow of people and capital needed to maintain and secure them. To return to the simulation from the opening of the chapter, the problem of the Indians wasn't so much a question of the potential for violence as it was about the interruption of the event itself. Through simulations, I learned that disruption of the field of play and risks to the integrity of the brand were the incidents with the highest risk classifications. They were deemed both dangerous and far more likely to happen because they included supply chain logistics, infrastructure, and crowd control. For security personnel, a breakdown in any of these (and other) areas was treated as a security incident; the hierarchy of threat bowed to the market. By this rationale, a strike in the employee cafeteria or a long line at the soccer stadium concession stand became as critical to prepare for as faulty metal detectors. The examination of preparedness, therefore, allows us a window into understanding the processes by which myriad things come to be securitized, a way to understand how a "securitize everything" logic is operationalized and enables us to observe how the sensation of security is cultivated in these settings.

The Emotional Labor of Preparedness

Simulations test communication protocols, but they also prepare security personnel for the emotional work and toll of crisis. As Lakoff notes, simulations work "to generate an affect of urgency among officials in the absence of the event itself (and) to generate knowledge about vulnerabilities in response to capability that could then guide anticipatory intervention" (2008, 401). Here, I spectacularly failed; I might have been an effective field worker but I was a novice security operator. I initially found the simulations to be agonizing. My experience stood in stark contrast to that of the seasoned professionals, for whom the simulations seemed to be mildly interesting from an operational standpoint at first, but which by day two, had been largely abandoned in order to complete the real work of dealing with incomplete fences and broken surveillance cameras. I think that my experience, as it initially diverged from theirs, but eventually came to better reflect their stance, is illustrative of the ways that security workers are conditioned to adapt to a constant state of emergency that defines the emotional labor of preparedness. If a detached and even-keeled stance is necessary to impart the sensation of security to nonsecurity personnel, corporate sponsors, television audiences, and fans, it took time to learn.

The worst part of the simulation was not the problems being presented for resolution, it was the relentless pace at which disaster unfolded, flooding the office with the sound of nonstop, ringing phones. The second worst part was the harried, barking voices reporting the problems when I picked up the line; riddled by anxiety, it was nearly impossible for me to understand the jumble of security-related vocabulary and names of streets and intersections, which I knew quite well, but that poured out before the phone slammed down.[16] For me, the stress of the simulation was exacerbated by the social pressure of having to stand up and address large groups of security professionals as (almost) the only woman, the only person without a security background, the only non-Brazilian, and the only nonnative speaker of Portuguese on the team.[17] To allow the team to see cracks in my façade, however, would have revealed me as an unreliable colleague and one who could potentially damage the delicate sensation of security under construction.

Managing emotions was not only related to withstanding the constant barrage of imagined disasters cooked up by simulation authors. Once the event began, we also struggled to remain positive and motivated. In the command center, our morale, like our location, was precarious since we were removed from the competition, whereas other security personnel were energized by their proximity to the action. We knew they were catching glimpses of famous athletes and hearing the applause, an applause that they could interpret as validation that their efforts had helped to produce a successful event. It was only doom and gloom in the command center. After a few weeks, the higher-ups began to realize the psychological toll on the team. Suddenly, we received gifts of free food, drinks, and unlimited Ben and Jerry's ice cream bars. We were also offered free tickets to less popular events (shot put; table tennis) to use on our days off, a strategy which had the dual purpose of appeasing us and filling seats for better television optics.

Ironically, the detachment from the competition that was identified in this case to be a point of potential demoralization, was the same emotional distance on which our work depended. Simulation had already trained and rewarded us in detachment. We were not supposed to bridge the cognitive distance between incidents and bodies and pain. The point of our isolation was to experience the incidents on the screen not through the kinds of things that make disaster real or potential disaster real—no flesh, no gore, no tears. Yet this detachment had another, albeit unexpected, consequence.

Inhabiting a preparedness space was also about the feelings of impatience or even disillusionment that came from having practiced for futures that never materialized. Our jobs depended on the possibility of threat. If there wasn't a real possibility that something was going to go wrong, our skills were no longer marketable. We were just used, in service to a false sensation of security rather than to actual safety. Slow days, when few incidents came into the system, left everyone listless, bored, and grumpy. And while clearly, I could know on a deep level how wrong it was to want bad, violent things to happen and none of us really wanted people to be hurt of course, we did want problems to resolve. Thus, preparedness mentalities also created a contradictory desire for something to actually go wrong. We began to long for the chance to practice all the procedures and protocols rehearsed on real incidents.

In this chapter, I have described how the preparedness mentality was operationalized in the space of the command center. Starting with simulations, analysts like myself were instructed in the rules of the game—how to think about, how to document, how to report security incidents. We were also taught to see what constituted an incident through the particular lens of the Olympics, a unique organization with its own brand-sensitive priorities. All of this involved interfacing with software systems which shaped our ability to archive events.

Security work, in this context, was also emotional work, where preparedness meant the emotional stability and the sanitization of danger. The one kind of emotional involvement that was encouraged, however, prioritized loyalty and fealty. Simulations and pregames prep often functioned to create security team solidarity and allegiance to the local organizing committee. Interestingly, loyalty among security personnel was not so much loyalty to the larger Olympics but specifically to these Olympics, the Rio ones. Security work was cast as essential to cultivate a positive national image for the global audience, a sentiment that resonated with the breed of intense nationalism already present among the men.

Even if they frequently criticized the government and felt that Brazil was going in the wrong direction under the leadership of the progressive Partido dos Trabalhadores or PT, the world was watching and they did not want to risk Brazil's (and their own) tenuous entrance on the global stage with an Olympic-size security disaster. Furthermore, personal ineptitude would jeopardize the professional standing of the entire team, principally that of leadership. On this point, strong feelings of fealty to those above oneself in the hierarchical structure were abundant, particularly because so many of the members of the security team had leveraged their positions through preexisting networks of professional kinship. I even found myself affected by such a climate of fealty, as I engaged in emotional caretaking for the higher-ups by covering for them while they slept at their desks after pulling all-nighters, for example.

On the last day of the simulation, the "Indian incident" was still pending. It just wouldn't go away. The director, half exasperated at what I think he saw as an unlikely scenario and a potential waste of his time, jokingly announced to the room that he had thought of a solution to the Indian problem. "We will just send Erika. She's an anthropologist! She can round them up and bring them to her house. Problem solved. Those human rights people will be happy!" I could be their tool for performing cultural sensitivity.

FIGURE 23. View from the guardhouse. January 2021. Photo: Guito Moreto.

FIGURE 24. 24-hour cameras and alarm grace the wall of a high-end apartment. January 2021. Photo: Guito Moreto.

FIGURE 25. Resident, Visitor, Pedestrian. Everyone in their lane. January 2021. Photo: Guito Moreto.

SECURING LIFE

I remember an incident which really marked me. It really affected me. I was working on the train, just doing a regular patrol between the cars as it traveled. As I entered one of the cars, I encountered a *menina*, an adolescent. She was seventeen years old, I would find out later. She had just attempted suicide after her boyfriend had raped her. She had taken a whole box of pills.

I was alone with her in that train car.

I sat with her until we arrived at the next station. I called for help. Once my security colleagues arrived, we called for the *bombeiros*. And did all of the first aid things that we had been taught and what they told us to do on the phone while we waited for the paramedics to arrive.

Thanks be to God, the girl came out of the whole situation alive. And the family was so grateful to me. I had been the first person to find her. I had been the first responder. I was so grateful and relieved that I had been able to help keep her alive. I think it's really interesting, you know, to think about this. Because it shows you that we don't work just in the area of security. It is proof that we aren't just there to do security. We are usually the front line of contact with passengers, with the public, with clients, with people.

And we are there, you know, making a difference all the time. Even in situations when it's not really a typical security job. We are there to give all the necessary help to who needs it. I guess you could say that we protect life.

—Jonathan, twenty-five years old. Three years in the security field.

It happened way back at the beginning, just when I started out working as security. In fact, it was my first job. My first company. Thirteen years ago now. Wow, I guess I have been in this field for thirteen years. *Patrimônio, escolta armada*, I have done it all. So, it was funny because I was just walking around with my daughter yesterday and I went by the place where this happened. It was a bank. I was working at the Banco do Brasil. It was a Saturday. I had just arrived at work and I heard a gunshot and took cover, thinking immediately that there was going to be something going on in the bank. It was the twelfth of October.

After the gunshot, it got so quiet. Like total silence. So, I went outside to see what the situation was. A little ways down the street, there was movement, a certain *correira*. I am also a paramedic, I did a first responder class. And so I partly went out to see if I could help with something. I walked a little way down, what did I see? There was a child on the ground, people gathered all around, a woman wailing and supporting herself with a hand on the church fence, Nossa Senhora da Lapa. I broke into a run. The child had just been shot. The mother and child, it seemed, had just left the bank and had been assaulted in the street. The mother was hysterical. I said to her, "We are going to stop this bleeding and save your son." There were no cars passing in the road since it was a Saturday and the area was less *movimentado* than normal, so I ran to a nearby taxi stand and begged them to help us. We put the child in the car and began to drive to the hospital. I made a tourniquet and tried to stop the bleeding while we drove. When we got to the hospital, the hospital workers moved him to the gurney, and I told them what happened. What I remember the most is that the child looked at me, and said "*Tio*, don't let me die." "No," I said, "You are going to live, little dude. It's going to be okay."

But what I didn't know then is that the dad had been with them too. I was so focused on the child and getting him to the hospital that I didn't realize that the father also had been shot. He was a ways up the road, so I didn't see him. I could have saved them both. But I didn't even know he was there in the confusion, so I concentrated on saving the child. I remember it all so clearly because the child was the same age as my son.

The next week, my boss told me that I was going to receive a phone call at work. And to my great joy, it was the kid. The kid that I saved was alive. I am so proud of this.

—Francislei, thirty-eight years old. Thirteen years in the security field.

We had an occurrence at work, just today actually. A seventy-eight-year-old woman had a stroke in the shopping. She fell to the ground. We were able to be with her until the paramedics came. I do not know if she lived.

—Cristiano, twenty-eight years old. Two years in the security field.

We had this incident a few weeks ago. At the Deodoro station. A fifteen-year-old kid was getting off the train. I noticed immediately that something seemed wrong with him, like something was going on with his body. He didn't seem right. He was moving weird. So, I went over and asked him if he was feeling okay, and just then he fell over! Onto the train tracks! He started convulsing. I immediately radioed my superiors letting them know. Because the next train was going to arrive and we had to stop it, to divert it. We were able to get him out of there and secure his safety without any further harm. We called his mom, who came to pick him up. I guess he hadn't taken his medication, a medication he needed to prevent seizures. But we were able to protect him and help him return home.

—Anderson, thirty years old. Seven years in the security field.

Something that happened to me. At the time, I was doing some jobs for the CCR (consortium that manages toll roads). My patrol was a forty-kilometer area. I was coming back to the base when I encountered an accident in the middle of the road. It was 7:00 p.m. and I was on my motorcycle. Patrolling the highway on the *moto*. And there was a major collision. A car smashed into the guardrail. A head-on collision. The car had flipped over. Wheels to the sky. So, of course I pulled over. I was in my uniform. I can picture the scene. I went over to the car. Three people in the car were already dead. There was a young child who had been thrown from the car. He was nine meters away from the car. Splayed on the road, calling out to me, asking for help. Arms broken. I went over and, simply, I tried to calm him. I put him in my arms, gently, and I said, I am calling an ambulance. It's already on its way. Then I heard his mother, crying from inside the car. She was alive. She was upside down, suspended upside down, held prisoner by the seatbelt. I ran and cut the seatbelt away from her. The other people, like I said, the two in the back seat and the driver were already dead. Only the mother and the small child were alive. Besides the bodies, which were prisoners inside the car, it was as if the whole car had been shaken out on the highway. I went around picking up papers. The family had been returning from grocery shopping in another city and so the food was all over the road. I picked it all up. There was even money blowing around. I gathered it all. I set it beside where the woman was, where she sat *completamente desesperada* (in complete despair). Her parents were the victims stuck in the back seat. I sat with her and the child waiting for the ambulance, which far away, some forty kilometers from the base. It was a really difficult scene. I think it's the most difficult thing I have ever seen in my work in security.

—Paulinho, fifty-two years old. Fifteen years in the security field.

Epilogue

SELLING THE SENSATION OF SECURITY

On November 19, 2020, João Alberto Silveira Freitas, a forty-year-old Black man, was beaten to death by white private security guards after an altercation inside a Carrefour grocery store in the southern city of Porto Alegre. Video footage shows that a misunderstanding with a cashier led to two of the store's private security guards escorting João Alberto to the exit. Right outside the establishment, the confrontation escalated, as guards delivered repeated blows to João Alberto's stomach and head, eventually wrestling him to the ground and kneeling on his back and neck while waiting for the police to come. During the several minutes he was restrained, gasping for air and calling for help, numerous bystanders, including a store manager, gathered around. On the cell phone videos they recorded, plaintive calls for mercy are audible. But the recordings also capture other passersby heaping insults on the pinned man, with some even adding their own kicks. Among those who witnessed the beating was João Alberto's wife, who was restrained by more guards, and whose desperate screams can be clearly heard. The incident, a macabre echo of the death of George Floyd in the United States, ignited similar outrage on Brazil's streets and on social media. The beating took place just one day before Brazil's Black Consciousness Day.

The Carrefour case, as it came to be called, was a clear manifestation of the spectacular violence of antiblackness at work in contemporary Brazilian cities. Despite its shocking brutality, the incident was not especially exceptional but reflected the routine terror experienced by Brazil's Black population and the tacit societal acceptance of that terror (Alves 2014; 2018). Yet the incident and its aftermath also brought to light issues that are especially revealing to the understanding of private security.

While extreme violence toward Brazil's Black population has long been understood as the purview of police, the Carrefour case put *private* security into the spotlight in a new way. As I discussed in chapter 1, the industry prides itself on being distanced from such displays of overt police violence, which are often framed as "unprofessional." João Alberto's death underscored private security's complicity in larger patterns of violence and led to calls for further regulation and (ironically) additional police oversight of private forces. What the incident laid bare, however, was the way that all security actors operate out of a similar ethos, independent of whether they are employed by the state or by a private corporation.[1] Public police and the private industry enjoy a symbiotic and enmeshed relationship and both reflect and reproduce a racist and classist social order.

While João Alberto's murder reflected long-standing norms of antiblackness, it also represented a sort of rupture, a break with implicit agreements about violence and its enactment. The spectacular violence that is typically confined to favelas or peripheries—the "socially accepted" places for the enactment of racialized terror—erupted into an "unacceptable" hospitality context. As expressed by observers, it was not just that João Alberto was so savagely beaten, it was that it happened while he was doing something as quotidian as shopping for groceries in a place as safe and neutral as a chain grocery store. Aside from the obvious grief and outrage that the beating generated for Black Brazilians, and the negative effect it had on any fragile sensation of security that they experience in the antiblack lethal democracy, the Carrefour case and its aftermath must also be understood for how it produced an unsettling and undesirable crack in the *sensação de segurança* for non-Black Brazilians. The sensation of security is built on the idea that white society does not have to confront or be exposed to the horrific violence that upholds racial privilege. In this fashion, the fact of João Alberto's highly mediated murder produced a fissure in the unspoken racial contract, which relies on denying the presence of systemic racialized violence in order to uphold white supremacy.

When I asked security laborers I knew about the Carrefour case, many referenced the kinds of discourses about security work that I have explored throughout this book. Mauro, for example, told me with obvious disdain that the guards responsible had failed by "allowing their emotions to take over." They had not acted as professionals. Others talked about the incident in language that sought to distance their own good work and professionalism from the murderous guards that killed João Alberto, referring to the perpetrators as the "supposed guards" or "those they are calling *vigilantes*." The bad apple narrative, which many readers will recognize as a standard trope used to dismiss systemic police brutality, quickly formed around the two guards in question, eliding discussions about how their actions reflected larger values in Brazil and making it much more challenging to center discussions of institutional racism in the security industry. Alternate narratives about the victim as somehow deserving of this rough treatment—it was quicky revealed that he had a criminal record and was known to the workers of the store for causing problems—also contributed to the advancement of a set of "explanations" for his murder, which attempted to explain it away and reinstate and rebuild the sensation of security.

If security work is work that upholds the unequal status quo, widespread protests in the wake of João Alberto's death threatened to break open the hypocrisy of the racial contract and were cast as illegitimate sources of terror by those seeking to uphold it. As the case drew more global attention to Brazil's deadly racist security forces, President Jair Bolsonaro came out in support of security personnel and in support of the racial contract, vehemently denying that the incident was related to racism, and framing the antiracist work of social movements and those who took to the streets in protest as the *real* danger to national unity. Such a denial of ongoing systemic and structural racial inequality was, of course, irreconcilable with the empirical reality of violence toward Black Brazilians. But it was also paradigmatic of ongoing resistance to engaging with the white supremacist underpinnings of security labor and illustrative of the kind of discursive support that Bolsonaro has offered to security actors throughout his career. With his praise, he renewed his promise to advocate for a vision of the social order which protected the rights of security personnel to administer violence as they saw fit, without oversight or repercussion. In making these comments, he also constituted security workers as an imagined group, defined by a strong sense of righteousness and morality, in opposition to those taking to the streets in protest and calling for oversight, accountability, and justice.

Along with discourses that circulate in the industry around race, modernity, technology, and masculinity, which I have discussed in previous chapters, I would like, by way of closing, to consider an additional factor, an additional affective register at play, one that shapes the desires of security personnel to enter the profession and to do their work and which is well demonstrated by the aftermath of the Carrefour case. For security workers, feelings of loyalty, fealty, and belonging, are the backbone of *their own* sensation of security. Being part of the "security family" means activating an imagined network of influential colleagues, united by professional calling and a shared sense of moral righteousness. Thus, while much of this book has explored how private security workers across the hierarchy cultivate the sensation of security through resonant performances, we must also consider how the security sector offers its workers a chance to experience this desirable sensation.

EPILOGUE

The Security Family

Bespectacled in wire-rimmed glasses, Formiga was an unimposing, dark-haired man, the child of Portuguese immigrants. In his free time, he read books about wine, fancying himself as a recreational sommelier. The regional manager for one of southern Brazil's largest private security companies, he cultivated and supervised its most valued local contracts. Inviting me to his company's headquarters, he dispatched a bodyguard doubling as a driver to fetch me at the airport, who accompanied me to the company's main hub, a towering, mirrored glass building nestled among the city's nondescript bursts of endless skyscrapers. The series of sleek, Brutalist fountains out front, combined with the posh lobby, made it feel as if I were on holiday, checking into a hotel rather than getting a tour of a private security company.

Formiga, teeth bared and smiling with pleasure, greeted me at the elevators. We exchanged customary kisses, his heavily cologned *beijos* landing a little too close to my mouth. Remembering my purpose, I successfully resisted the urge to wipe them off with the back of my hand. We exited on the top floor into a room full of cubicles. En route to his corner office, he introduced me to the young women on his secretarial team. In front of his office door waited his personal assistant, Flor. It was the Monday after Semana Santa (Holy Week), and everyone had been away from the office enjoying the last gasp of summer. "Get out here and let me look at those new tits!" Formiga called out to Flor as he approached, a devilish grin spreading across his face. Flor, herself smiling from ear to ear, threw her shoulders back, presenting the telltale conical perfection of implants. "Do you like them?" she asked. Formiga leaned in for a closer look. Then calling to the other managers, "Hey, Zé Carlos, Lucas, did you see? Flor's tits look *ma-ra-vi-lho-sa*," the word drawn out for emphasis. He let out a low whistle. As Flor preened for her adoring audience, butterflies fluttered in my stomach, on cue with a terror that I myself might be the next object of intense male scrutiny. Putting his arm around her, and affectionately calling her *filha*, or daughter, Formiga said kindly, "You look great, dear."

Finished, Formiga extended his hand to me and I followed him into his glass office, which glowed blue from the slight tint of the light-filled windows. Adding to the corporate fishbowl effect, I could see those in the next office building moving like ants. "See," said Formiga, gesturing back at the appreciative murmur of people assembled around Flor's desk, "We are a family here. We support one another."

A few hours later, I heard the reference to family once again. After a posh business lunch in which he rapidly detailed the history of the company while I tried to take notes in between bites of salad and two bottles of Beaujolais, Formiga spent the better part of an hour going through his phone like a Rolodex, picking out dozens of phone numbers of movers and shakers in the industry, calling them and introducing me as "part of the company family" by virtue of his relationship with me, and then handing me the phone so that I could present myself and my research project with promises to follow up. As he went, he gave me a shorthand running narration of the cast of characters. "Oh *fulano* (so and so), he invented private prisons in Brazil, he'd be great to talk to. Really nice guy. Plays a mean game of beach racquetball." Or *fulano*, military guy, he helped to write the legislation for *Portaria 3.233*. *Fulano*, ex-PM, does the security for Cargill. "You should really talk to the guys that do the multinationals. They have interesting stuff to say," he added, reminding me just how vast and varied the family was.

As he escorted me back to the elevator at the end of the day, Formiga lingered again at Flor's desk. "Put a blazer on or something so I don't have to tell my wife I spent the whole work day staring at your boobs," he told her laughingly. I thanked him for his hospitality. He brushed it off, reminding me to make sure to follow up with the kingpins he had introduced me to. "We are a family, all of us in the sector. We go back to the *infância* (childhood) of private security. These guys are real professionals. They can help you, *filha*," he concludes, assigning me the same gendered kinship term as Flor. *Filha*, now tangled with both patriarchy and paternalism.

As the above scenes illustrate, powerful private security actors like Formiga drew on and emphasized the metaphors of family in order to describe the companies they managed as well as the larger security industry, evoking the promise of kinship for newbies like me, seeking access to a web of connections and resources. Yet as the above episode also suggests, this family is hardly a functional or equitable one, being instead built on and reinforced by hierarchy, patriarchy, and power. The security family, as an idea not as empirical reality, is used to cultivate a *sensação de segurança* for security laborers themselves.

For security workers, to be part of an imagined family, as Formiga describes it, is to *belong* in this highly masculine and authoritarian kinship group. Guards are no longer mere individuals but part of a larger professional web. Crucially, the security family also offered a community and a professional identity precisely at a historical juncture where emerging far right wing and conservative religious discourses were building radical narratives around the idea of disorder, chaos and change in the racial and gender hierarchy. The security family—a traditional family based on the bonds of men, and where belonging was determined by being an upstanding moral professional on the side of the law—was extremely appealing.

As I observed it, a great part of the appeal of the security family was the idea that it was composed of members with shared ideological beliefs, a vision of how the world should be, hard, honest workers, and around an imagined set of conditions that would give security laborers themselves the greatest sensation of security. Often, this entailed a desire for a return to an idealized, "traditional" past—a more natural state of security embodied by authoritarian rule. This was often, but not exclusively, represented by Brazil's military dictatorship. Nostalgic longings here also came as calls for clarity in a world which guards characterized as increasingly unstable and complex. As Guilherme, the security manager at a chain of malls where I conducted fieldwork, explained to me, there was an ease to being able to tell who the good guys are and who the bad guys are. But now, he complained, "You can't tell who anyone is! The only thing to do is to suspect everyone! It is exhausting." The nefarious and shifting nature of organized crime, he further clarified, had destabilized things, as had social mobility for the lower classes under the many decades of leftist government rule. As traditionally excluded demographics entered the space of the shopping mall as potential consumers for the first time, it made it harder for guards to know who was a suspect and who was an honest client; it was harder to know how to treat people without making a mistake. The social order was in flux.

In addition to a sense of security built on an idealized order, where people could be easily categorized as rightful guests or obvious undesirables, the sensation of security was constructed in contrast to its imagined opposite—the things that would create a state of *in*security. This opposite often entailed an imagined reality of urban chaos, which relied on the criminalization of poverty and located the source of alleged disorder with the low-income, nonwhite dwellers in favelas or urban peripheries. It was the imagined territory of *vagabundos*, a multivalent term which was used to defame and insult the political left as suspicious and presumably dishonest subjects, and which served as the foil against which righteous security family members were cast.[2]

This paradigm—of militarized moral righteousness set against an imagined enemy—will be familiar to anyone who has followed recent Brazilian politics. For many of those I accompanied for this book, Bolsonaro's election as head of state perfectly befitted his role as the *pater famílias* of police, military, and military personnel. Security workers' proximity to him also brought a renewed sense of security. During the whole election cycle, the same group WhatsApp that I used to extract *ocurrências* from in order to enter them into CrimeBase looked like a different kind of archive—one attesting to Bolsonaro's role and centrality to the security family while showing how potentially empowered certain members of this group would be if he won the election. The thread regularly featured pictures of all the major players in the family with Bolsonaro himself. Some were of the professional variety, depicting men in their police or military uniforms, gathered around Bolsonaro with smiles wide enough to suggest a pride in togetherness.

Other photos were also of the personal variety, as one or two members of the team appeared alongside him in swimming trunks, securing beer koozies at what appeared to be poolside Sunday afternoon family barbeques. These images, which performed professional deference to the patriarch, also underscored the power of the upper echelons of the security hierarchy. They suggested the personal connections, safety, and privilege of those who already enjoyed such a familial intimacy with the soon-to-be president.

Indeed, the security family, like any other family, had clear hierarchies. Owners and managers usually fit one of two profiles. Either they migrated to private security from other areas of the *carreira das armas*—for example, from the police. In this case, their claims to authority as top dogs stemmed from their own personal reputations as violent actors—which they often sought to bring with them into the private realm—think about the skull and dagger BOPE flag in the command center for example. This was a sensation of security which emanated from their relationship to the state and their recognition (and impunity) as legitimate violence workers that came as a result. In contrast, the other possible leadership model, represented by men like Formiga, was linked to corporate connections, global business acumen, and education level—symbolized by drinking first-growth French wine. Here, the sensation of security was built on (the impunity) of class status and international networks. It bears noting that neither of these types of managerial aspirations and success are available to low-level guards, who generally are not able to achieve the level of education necessary to enter the police forces nor possess the skills, connections, or whiteness to follow in Formiga's footsteps.

Thus, family organization had already privileged (relatively speaking) men at the top, whose livelihood was built on the backs of those less fortunate, less educated, and largely darker-skinned masses of guards who protected cargo, stadiums, or shopping malls. Racialized dimensions of the masculine hierarchy were reflected, for example, by the term *guardinha*, from the word *guarda*, or guard, marked by the use of the diminutive *-inha*, little guard. Through the widespread use of this term, which was used to feminize them and their work, guards were demasculinized and placed on par with women. The low-level labor of private security was thereby rendered largely invisible work, women's work, even if the sum total of this work was what pays for the Brutalist fountains and wine tours. White men elevated themselves above Black men by exploiting their labor and feminizing them through derogatory nicknames which painted their work as equivalent to the unseen work of women.

Security as a learned behavior is cultivated in training facilities, on the job, and in the family. As I have demonstrated, in all the security spaces studied, ideas circulate about success through hard work, self-improvement, and individual responsibility, not on demands for corporate accountability or structural change—those would be viewed as leftist values. If private security is about the commodification of the right to feel safe in one's city—the ability to enjoy the sensation of security—individual workers in the industry are also indoctrinated to feel as if they are the authors of their own destiny, displaying a different side of neoliberal ideology that continues to prominently shape security personnel thinking. Guards are encouraged to bootstrap, *not* take on the systemic issues that lead to their death, injury, or ongoing poverty. It is with the individual guard that the responsibility for cultivating the sensation of security ultimately lies.

Webs of Patronage

The private security hierarchy, like clientelist governments everywhere, relies on the establishment of systems of patronage, where more powerful company owners and managers command powerful networks of allies, enjoying their own sensation of security surrounded by loyalists. Leaders of both the "former police chief turned private security owner" type and the "global businessman" type of patriarch deployed these kinds of governing family relationships. In the case of military or police leadership, company owners tapped into their vast extant networks of armed actors, bound to them by rank and a deference to hierarchy. Regardless of their crossover into the sphere of private enterprise, they carried these networks with them and were able to marshal them in the service of their companies. For actors like Formiga, the realm of mobilization was the corporate world, multinationals, global contractors, global suppliers, and policy wonks in Brasilia.

As corporate leaders that run their companies through the utilization of a career's worth of connections, they also modeled a form of governance built on patronage and favor-granting that would trickle down to the lowest levels of the family, as guards themselves sought to forge the kinds of connections that would get them hired in an industry which relied on knowing someone or having an "in," to be hired. Such was the case with the team of men in the security command center, many of whom came from the very same graduating class of military police and who had forged careers in connection to and in tandem with one another. The team relied on a breed of nepotism based on fealty and trust, qualities that the family cultivates at all levels.

An ex-cop, Lucia, famed for her beauty in her youth who had once served as a police public relations officer, and who worked with me at the Olympics well illustrated the importance of connections and loyalty to Rio's private security enterprise. As two of the only women in the office, we sometimes ate lunch together, or rode the metro home to the South Zone. I don't know if Lucia sought me out because it was lonely to be in a sea of men (though she was probably used to it) or because the love of her life had been a LAPD officer who was killed in the line of duty at the height of their relationship, and she wanted me to tell her more about life in California as a way to remember him. Regardless, it was clear that even though she was ostensibly part of the team and a longtime member of the security family by virtue of her role as the lipsticked mouthpiece for the corps, she did not feel part of things, as evidenced by a lot of "them" or "those guys'" language.

After one particularly fraught day on the job, with stressful visits from the International Olympic Committee looking over everyone's shoulder, Lucia complained to me about what she conceived of as the poor organization of the security plans. I asked her about the root cause of this and she said that it was because the whole show was led by security professionals who ascended to their role by virtue of their reputation of having successfully worked on other events or in other warzones, such as the UN mission to Haiti, or the pacification of favelas. But it is not really about qualifications, she mused. "The only reason this shit holds together at all is because it is run by men with deep ties to one another. They serve those bonds." I found this statement to be especially revealing because it shows how, in the construction of the team itself, nepotism was intentionally cultivated to serve the security endeavor in a useful way. Success in the security family meant showing deference to the power structure. Loyalty keeps the patriarchs in power but also functions to hold together what is perhaps a shaky security apparatus, since it is built so heavily on the idea of shared aims, on personal connections, on being a name in Formiga's Rolodex, and not on actual skills or education. The sensation of security is an illusion, an ethereal performance, which privileges capital and protects the racialized status quo, for security workers and for those they guard.

As I have argued in this book, security laborers perform the quotidian work of cultivating the sensation of security necessary to promote the consumptive habits, leisure, and pleasure of their compatriots. Even with the widespread growth of and demand for private security in Brazil, outsourcing and other structural failures have further impoverished security workers, making their work more precarious. These conditions are part of a racist system that is built to maintain low-wage and disposable labor while promising guards social mobility and respect as dignified security entrepreneurs and servants of the social order.

FIGURE 26. Residential enclosure names often reference ionic North American places. January 2021. Photo: Guito Moreto.

FIGURE 27. Cameras outside a closed condominium in Barra de Tijuca, Rio de Janeiro. Sign reads: For your safety, this area is being filmed. January 2021. Photo: Guito Moreto.

FIGURE 28. Condominium monitoring sign reminds passersby that camera figures are shared with the local police battalion. January 2021. Photo: Guito Moreto.

THE POST OF THE FUTURE

Why is the company executive more respected than the company janitor, even if the janitor is a king in his field? Society rewards the executive for his education and admires him for the complexity of his job. People don't think the janitor can do the same kind of work. And that is why, nowadays, even though it has become more common, people are amazed to hear about a security guard who is attending college or who has a degree.

The best job is one in which you are respected for your professional behavior and *não pelo número de "canudos" que você tenha*, not for the number of diplomas you have.

A good job has decent working conditions. As in, the location and equipment are in line with the needs of the post. The workers are people who respect their own role as the maintainers of the order and security of the place.

I know I am responding for the majority when I say decent working conditions include a *clean* guardhouse (*guarita*) with a bathroom, equipment that actually works. Equipment that helps you to do your job. Equipment say, like, a radio, or a telephone, or closed-circuit television, a desk, a computer. Basic tools. A clean place to eat your lunch.

Something else. A good job means being respected as relevant. Today, we are seen as outcasts. Like a pariah that since they had no other options, could only become a security guard, where they are always hated. Yes, hated and judged because our job requires us to regulate and guide even those who have more important jobs in society than us. They hate having to obey "*the guardinha*" (little guard, in feminine so demasculinized). This term is disliked by all of us, by all security professionals. It implies that we are inferior.

—Reginaldo, fifty years old. Thirty years in the security field.

Listen, we just want to work, receive our agreed upon salary, be known and acknowledged for the work we do. My job as a driver, my post is the car. The patrol car. In the traffic. In the rain. We just do our jobs, you know? Just obey, just be obedient.

Not complain. You are paid to not complain.

—Andre, thirty-five years old. Ten years in the security field.

The ideal post for me, and I have worked in various, is the one that has good interpersonal dynamics. The relationships between employee and employer are *essencial*.

Get it? This is the ideal post for me. Because if I am hired to perform X security service, I am a professional and I am going to do professional work. And so maybe the bosses will observe me, analyze me and like the quality of my service. Maybe they keep me on.

They trust me in my ability as a security guard. *Beleza*. Or maybe they don't like my work. They let me go and find themselves another person that pleases them. So what we really want, what makes the work *agradável*, pleasant, is good, respectful relationships. The necessary respect between men.

Respect! It's just respect, man. Because the first impression that people have of us is that they don't like us. This is because the Brazilian, well, he is not accustomed to respecting. He isn't used to having a good, respectful relationship with others. He doesn't naturally respect his neighbor. The Brazilian, the first thing he thinks when he comes up to the guardhouse is "the security guard is *chato*, annoying." He has already decided not to like us.

The best post is that which has all that I need to work well: a chair, an umbrella if I have to sit in the sun. A gate that opens, that works. Water fountain, bathroom, microwave.

A post where you arrive and are *acolhido pelo posto*. The post holds you, cares for you so that you can do your best work. Its like this: how can you ask people to do their best work when you don't do your best work for them? How can you not give a *rapaz* a chair to sit in and think that he will do his best work for you?

—Romario, thirty-seven years old. Twelve years in the security field.

Achieving dignity in this line of work, work where we are *tão esquecida*, so forgotten, is basically impossible. Even our labor unions are poorly organized and bad intentioned.

Our employers don't care about us, their miserable employees.

What would it mean to live with dignity? To do our work with dignity? It would mean being respected for the uniform, respected for the way in which we give our energy and even our whole body to protect the company's assets. We would have clean water to drink, maybe even warm coffee to make the night go by easier.

It would be a job where the supervisor isn't playing favorites protecting Guard A or B over others and where he doesn't lift even his little finger to help the professional who works twelve hours on his feet, with only twenty or thirty minutes to choke down his food. It would be a post where we were not treated like numbers. Where it was clean. Where we have honest colleagues and partners. Where we are not called *guardinhas*.

I have worked so many posts in over twenty years in this field and even the basic dignity hides from us. To work with respect that would be enough. To work without humiliation would be enough.

—Marcos Antônio, forty-six years old. Twenty-three years in the security field.

If this were dignified work, we would be given benefits like health insurance for ourselves and our children. Lately, we have learned that health is, *de fato*, the most important thing in this life. Without our health, we cannot work.

My dream post, where there are basic clean conditions and where the other guards can also help to keep the worksite well organized and *cheiroso* (fragrant, nice smelling). Afterall, no one should have to leave home to spend twelve hours in pigsty.

My dream post where we are respected by the client, where *all* of us in this profession are respected. We are so *jogada as traças* (thrown to the moths), so abandoned. I want to work in a place that is properly monitored, managed, and where the *ocorrências* are well documented and dealt with correctly.

My dream post? Work conditions are, in fact, the hardest part to change. Perhaps because the *vigilante* is treated as a thing, as any old thing. We have to comply with the rules governing the application of force in all the places where we perform our service. But what is missing in the majority of our working environments is a healthy respect for *nossa farda*, for our uniform.

We haven't been able to properly look after ourselves for a long time.

—Richard, fifty-two years old. A lifetime in the security field.

The best working condition would be to have a contract where the client has no ulterior motives. Where they just expect the best from the professional and just give the professional the opportunity to get involved in important decisions.

The details of the post don't matter. What I want is to have the tools to do my work, to do a good job. To have a good team. To have good leaders. Listen, I like to have excitement on the job. I want things to happen. I have a lot of energy. I feel the most adverse conditions are what make the most prepared professional. We don't just automatically get respect. Respect must be earned by performing excellent service.

One of the problems that happens a lot ... Well, I guess I would say that something that I have experienced is that with outsourcing, it is routine and normal for there to be some kind of bribe going on. This happens especially with public contracts. In the end of the day, it is us, at the ground level, that always end up paying the bill.

—Roberto, thirty-five years old. Five years in the security field.

Dignified work for me is leaving my house at the right time, clocking in for my shift at the right time, working my twelve hours, taking my one hour of lunch. Dignified work is having harmony in the workplace. People treating you well. With all that you need to be well. A kitchen, a bathroom. And an umbrella to sit under if you have to work outside. It's just to have your own small corner. A place where you are respected and where you can respect others.

—Herbert, forty-six years old. Twenty years in the security field.

Dignity, *cara*, is health insurance. I am a father, the head of my family. Dignity, *cara*, is a *cesta básica* (month food staples) or at least a warm meal on the job, a real dignified meal. Because to buy one near the places we work *é tudo caro*, man, all expensive shit around us.

Everything is so hard. No help. We are in the middle of this pandemic. There is a crisis all around us. We are barely making it. 104 degrees Fahrenheit in the sun. No sunscreen and that stuff is expensive. Repellant for mosquitos too.

We have to work in suit and tie in this kind of heat. No one deserves that kind of condition. I wish they would have more compassion. An ideal post, *nunca vai ser*. It will never be. We have to work in a team. Teams are the hardest thing on earth. Someone is always unhappy. Someone is always making trouble.

You'd need people actually helping each other. People would have to actually be on time. No post can be unattended so we depend on the other person to show up to arrive before we can leave for our homes. After twelve hours, you are impatient, you can't get home soon enough. When no one comes to replace you, you miss the bus. Sometimes the only time you can go to the store is when you are not working, and with the pandemic everything closes earlier. If my colleague is even a little late...

I can't buy bread in the bakery for my children.

—Douglass, thirty-two years old. Six years in the security field.

In all places, all places, all places, if you are a *segurança*, guard, *guardinha*, *vigilante*, if you don't have a title but you are watching and guarding something, you will never, never, never be worth something for the company.

A guy jumps over the fence and he steals three cameras and a bunch of copper wire and the guard doesn't see. This happens, you know. Your cameras weren't working, your alarm wasn't working. The company will come looking for you, cracking heads. You aren't worth anything. You didn't see anything? What, did you sleep on the job? You are fired.

When the security guard saves the day, when he stops the theft, no one comes to say "You did good work," or "You are a good person." Or "You pay attention." Or "My guards are good." "My guards are sharp." "My guards paid attention." Oh, *não*. None of this is said. Everything, everything, everything, be it in a shopping or a condominium, falls on the shoulders of the guards. All of it. Here, the only question they ask is why did the security guard not notice? Why didn't the security guard say something? Why didn't he sound the alarm? Why wasn't he patrolling? Sometimes, yes. I do wonder why we do this. A guy told me once: time is the irreversible currency of life. You are selling your time. You don't get it back.

—Cesar, forty years old. Eighteen years in the security field.

Notes

INTRODUCTION

1. Because of potential confusion with the English term "vigilante," which carries a different connotation, I maintain the term *vigilante* in italics throughout this text. In addition, to avoid potential confusion for English speaking readers, I have opted to use the translation, "guard," as much as possible.

2. Private security work is very poorly paid work. The 2022 union-negotiated contract for guards working full-time in the state of Rio de Janeiro is R$1662.20 per month, which is slightly above the minimum wage and equals approximately US$325.00.

3. Hard security in this context is intended to refer to armed work in settings conventionally associated with security work, such as guarding banks, guarding valuable cargo, guarding an airport or something that is considered to be a military target. Beyond the private sector, hard security involves ostensive policing and the policing of favelas through military-style operations. Soft security refers to unarmed or lightly armed work in locations that are not so associated with threats, such as shopping malls, schools, country clubs, condominium access control. As I will show throughout this text, soft security settings require subtler and less ostensive techniques and may use collaboration and dialogue to resolve conflicts.

4. While in this particular moment, Mauro browbeat the guards with the stark reality of profit-driven enterprise and the lack of care for laborers, at other moments, he gave guards encouragement and gestured toward ways for them to find meaning, for example through discourses of personal responsibility including caring for imaginary mothers like Mauro's. As I will explore throughout the chapters, this sort of ambivalence was widely expressed by guards. The declaration that security is about money and the encouragement for guards to find moral superiority in their work are often in tension with one another.

5. Tessa Diphoorn, writing in the context of South African private security, describes a similar dynamic, noting how private protection became a highly desirable "club good" (2016a; Diphoorn and Kyed 2016).

6. https://www.gov.br/pf/pt-br/assuntos/seguranca-privada/legislacao-normas-e-orientacoes/portarias/portaria-3233-2012-2.pdf/view.

7. As Jaffe and Diphoorn note in their analysis of the postcolonial roots of private security in Jamaica, several important parallels with the slave-holding past bear mentioning: the racialized antagonism between lighter-skinned and more affluent company owners and managers and the masses of guards, and the dominance of "old boys" networks of nepotism and paternalism (2019). These dynamics are also clearly present in the context of Brazil.

8. Work in these two fields is not mutually exclusive. Some people working in the formal part of the sector also work in unregulated settings on their days off, a practice that is referred to as *bico* and is also common among low-ranking police officers.

9. Although, as I will demonstrate in this text, mobility is more a promise than a reality. Like political subjects in other contexts, private security workers experience what Lauren Berlant has described as "cruel optimism" or the ways in which "people have remained attached to unachievable fantasies of the good life—with its promises of upward mobility, job security, political and social equality, and durable intimacy—despite evidence that

liberal-capitalist societies can no longer be counted on to provide opportunities for individuals to make their lives 'add up to something'" (2011, n.p.).

10. This discourse resonates with what Jaffe and Diphoorn note in the analogous case of private security in Jamaica, as one of the side effects of outsourcing: "a neoliberal mode of labour control that works through self-disciplining and the responsibilization of workers for their own conditions" (2019, 922.) In addition, the emphasis on personal responsibility and effort as the path to class mobility is prevalent far beyond the security world and is common to narratives on the relationship between meritocracy and hard work in the context of Brazil's "new middle class." See Klein, Mitchell, and Junge, 2018.

11. As Denise Ferreira da Silva puts it, "Raciality almost immediately justifies the state's decision to kill certain persons.... 'Such killings do not unleash an ethical crisis because these persons' bodies and the territories they inhabit always-already signify violence'" (quoted in Alves 2018, 8). See also Christen Smith (2016) on necropolitics and the Brazilian state.

12. They are also likely to suffer other deadly side effects of systemic racism, the effects of the "afterlife of slavery": "skewed life chances, limited access to health and education, premature death, incarceration, and impoverishment" (Hartman 1997, 6).

13. Thus it reflects the larger dynamics of racial capitalism. As Bledsoe and Wright say of the United States and Brazil, "Capitalism is actually *dependent* on anti-Blackness to realize itself" (2019, 11).

14. The nine-minute figure is based on 2018 numbers, as reported by the Instituto de Segurança Publica (http://www.ispdados.rj.gov.br/).

15. In this way, private security work also reflects what Rebecca Bartel, writing about Colombian financial and debt markets, calls "necrofinance," or the process by which fiscal value is elevated above human life (2021). She explains: "Necrofinance arises out of late capitalist economic structures that generate systemic socio-economic precarity to the point of generating violence in order to generate profit" (2021, n.p.).

16. Ruth Wilson Gilmore eloquently describes racial capitalism in this way: "Capitalism requires inequality and racism enshrines it" (2020, n.p.).

17. Patricia Pinho's analysis of whiteness in Brazil is useful for understanding what performing whiteness means in this context. She writes that "behavioral whitening" is related to distancing from Afro-Brazilian and Indigenous cultural practices and emulating white society's habits related to health, hygiene, and education. However, as she notes, "if education and health were tools that allowed for one's internal whitening, they were not capable of erasing the blackness from the surface of the body" (2009, 43). It is this tension that defines the work of guards in hospitality settings.

18. To return again to Sharpe's concept of the wake, she writes, "Living in the wake means living in and with terror in that much of what passes for public discourses *about* terror we, Black people, become the *carriers* of terror, terror's embodiment, and not the primary objects of terror's multiple enactments" (2016, 15).

19. Blackness and whiteness in Brazil are not only about skin color but also index other embodied behaviors, postures, and ways of speaking (Roth Gordon 2017).

20. As Tomas Salem and I note in our exploration of gendered hierarchies of police work, security actors generally elevate violent forms of policing above softer forms of conflict resolution and tend to use feminizing metaphors to debase work they do not perceive as inherently masculine (2021).

21. Throughout the book, I use the term "we" when writing about times that I was engaged as an ethnographic participant in a group activity. My usage is intended as a narrative device that helps readers to envision the context under description and should not be taken to signal a kind of belonging or unity. I explore this dynamic more later in the introduction when I talk about methodology and research access.

22. Here, Samimian-Darash and Stalcup note that for Deleuze and Guattari assemblages are "complex structures of elements that communicate not hierarchically or through linear connections, but rather as a rhizome (in contrast to trees)" (2017, 80). Deleuze and Guattari identify two different kinds of communications, that of the tree structure and the rhizome. "While the logic of the tree, like the state, is that of a central power from which twigs branch out, the rhizome grows as a multiplicity, not subject to a single center. The emphasis, for Deleuze and Guattari, is on the connections between the infinite number of roots, and the fact that the rhizome form is in perpetual motion, and, therefore not given in advance; the units composing a rhizome are themselves changing" (Samimian-Darash and Stalcup 2017, 80).

23. The multiscalar approach to the study of security assemblages has also been explored by Abrahamsen and Williams, who call for attention to the possibility of breaking with conventionally stacked levels of scalar analysis—local, national, global—to consider how "different elements within the same assemblage can inhabit either the local or the global or both simultaneously. The local, in other words, is multi-scalar and need not run through the national to function at the global level" (2017, 15). See also Glück and Low (2017) for another discussion of the spatial and scalar dynamics of security.

24. For example, a private security company owner who also happens to be military police might use his police role when he needs to transport a weapon from one post to another, rather than filing for the permit he needs if he is acting as a private company owner. Unsurprisingly, rank-and-file private security guards, who have less ability to do this, are consistently at the bottom of the security hierarchy due to their extant position in wider class and racial hierarchies. For an excellent overview of the sociological and criminological literature on the relationship between public and private policing, see Diphoorn 2016a.

25. During this period, I often navigated between the humble and the elite security worlds in a single day, rising in the dawn-dark to commute to the training centers, which were located in high-crime parts of Rio's *zona norte*, close to where the majority of the guards-in-training lived. After lunch, I would trek back across the city on the decrepit trains, where I would often run into guards with whom I had trained at one of the schools and who were now employed to guard the trains, to the immaculate offices of the organizing committee. It must be acknowledged here that the ability to traverse these worlds in this way was part of my privilege as a researcher and that I was able to negotiate access to both of these worlds due to my own particular gender, class, and racial identity.

26. Here, I was inspired by Derek Pardue's assertion "that certain arguments require multi-modal material and a thoughtful mixture or juxtaposition of language and the sensorial" (2019, n.p.).

27. In order to maintain the anonymity of research participants, *none* of the images included in the book are taken at security schools or with guards with whom I did fieldwork. The reader should understand these pictures as generally representative of the places, people, and environments under study.

1. THE *CARREIRA DAS ARMAS*

1. The time period of significant growth in cargo theft (2013–2017) coincides with one of the sustained time periods of my fieldwork. While cargo theft has declined some in the interim, along with a general decrease in crime nationally since 2019, it remains prevalent. Experts attribute the decrease in incidences to better monitoring technology and to a specific police policy which made cargo theft as high priority as violent crime. Despite a dip in cases, experts note that as of 2021 thefts are again on

the rise, up 7 percent from last year. See https://estradao.estadao.com.br/caminhoes/sao-paulo-e-rio-de-janeiro-concentram-80-dos-roubos-de-carga-no-pais/.

2. While favelas controlled by drug traffickers have traditionally had managers that oversee drug distribution, e.g., the manager of the white (cocaine) and the manager of the green (marijuana), many now have a manager of cargo, who works directly to provision weapons for heists and redistribute stolen cargo after theft.

3. The cargo industry—and the security companies that are contracted by the industry—is fundamentally unconcerned with securing territory or even the lives of its employees. Their focus and principal priority is to open a safe passage for capital to move to market; guards are solely tools for the creation of this safe passage. Therefore, at the same time that guards are to a certain extent integrated into the city through the performance of relatively stable, formalized work, inclusion occurs in highly asymmetrical fashion; the terms of inclusion demand the potential sacrifice of parts of their bodies (on the job injury) or their lives (death during confrontation).

4. In this chapter, I draw on material collected from three different introductory escolta classes (each lasting three weeks for seven hours a day) that I attended, along with two "recycling classes," where guards that are already in the workforce are required to complete continuing education to renew their licensure. In addition, I draw from fifteen interviews with escolta guards and interviews with three escolta instructors.

5. Hazard pay is defined as extra compensation that comes from performing hazardous work, including that which produces physical or psychological distress. In addition to escolta, other forms of hazardous work in Brazil include labor involving exposure to chemicals or medical waste. While there are no statistics on the racial identification of those working in private security, when I posed questions on the racial demographics of guards to company owners, instructors, managers, and classmates, everyone conceded that the majority of guards are Black. However, in keeping with the Brazilian conventions of not talking about race, most appeared uncomfortable with the question and made subsequent reference to class or schooling or place of residence as an explanatory factor as a way to sidestep the implications of racism, saying things like, "This is a profession that requires little schooling and the group that has the least schooling has the darkest skin," or "Most people who work in the sector live in favelas, where many Black people live." See Roth Gordon (2017) on cordial racism and the correlational discourses between race, class, and education.

6. The multivalent term *bandido* translates literally as "bandit," and denotes a criminal in the general sense and was often employed to refer to drug traffickers. The term *marginal* was also used frequently by my research subjects. Translated literally as "marginal," it can be used to refer to someone who behaves in legally questionable fashion and to a person viewed as morally compromised and unethical. In addition, the marginal also has connotations that are related to the person's standing within larger society and can be evoked to refer to someone who has little social worth or who doesn't count as a full citizen (Perlman 1976). To do war against *marginalidade* is also to claim status for oneself as a nonmarginal.

7. According to the guidelines established in the 2012 legislation, for the entire training course, guards are permitted thirty-three .380 bullets and eighteen .12 gauge bullets.

8. In order to save money, private security companies and the clients that contract them, often skirt the legally required team of four guards—where one drives, one sits in the passenger seat, and two ride in back—opting instead for a pared down team of two. Since the driver has to watch the road, this really only leaves one person to monitor threats.

9. The certification to work as an escolta guard is combined with another armed variety of work, the *transporte de valores*, done in the armored car, which is predominately used to transport cash. I do not address armored car work in as much detail in this book because few of the guards that I encountered or trained with in courses were employed in this part of the sector.

10. With few notable exceptions, such as Souza Cruz, the cigarette company, and Correiros, the mail service, escolta work is outsourced labor. The client is a large corporation. They contract the private security work to be performed by a firm. The firm provides the guards.

11. According to Lei N. 7.102 (20 de junho 1983) and Portaria no. 3.233 2012-DG/DPF (10 de dezembro 2012), *vigilantes* working in escolta are limited to a single long barrel weapon, a .12-gauge shotgun. The rationale for this has to do with the very minimal amount of weapons training that is provided by schools. The schools in turn say that their job is only to train guards on the weapons they can legally carry.

12. I base this on anecdotal data drawn from professionals in the field. Official statistics are very hard to locate since the data is held by private companies who have a stake in not publicizing the failures of their guards.

13. Pay scale by year available here: http://sindvig.org.br/tabela-de-salarios/.

14. As I also noticed in my research on drug traffickers that within their communities, death was discussed as almost an expected outcome of this career path.

2. HOSPITALITY SECURITY

1. Vivian and her husband, a powerful police officer, perfectly embodied the balance between hard and soft security that is paradigmatic of success in today's industry. She was responsible for the front of the house and the hospitality-oriented work but was simultaneously backed by someone with the connections to police and more hard-line interventions. The setup mirrors the way in which hospitality security relies on violent policing even as it seeks to distance itself from the dirty work of harder forms of security.

2. Following Nielsen, Sumich, and Bertelsen, I consider enclaving to be more than a "physical manifestation of dominance and privilege" (2020, 1). Rather, it functions as an "aesthetics of imagination," a conduit for "new urban imaginaries based on the idea of the materially segregated spatial unit" (2020, 4). Security, as noted by Caldeira (2002) in her seminal work on São Paulo, is part of this imagination. Furthermore, the proliferation of these spaces in the period under study must also be understood in relation to the general economic and social changes of the period and analyzed in the context of the overall reduction of inequality characteristic of the progressive governments of the Worker's Party (2003–2016). During this time period, Brazil saw the growth of a new lower middle class, known as "Classe C." Because emerging middle-class status was so linked to emulating the status markers of the more traditional middle and upper classes, including the gated lifestyles and presence of security as a consumer good and class marker, private guards were in further demand by a new group of consumers (da Silva and and Robb Larkins 2019). At the same time, as this new middle class—which was less white and not as highly educated as the traditional elite—sought access to status-laden consumer goods and experiences like international travel that had long been the purview of the upper classes, it created a backlash that both had long-term political ramifications and also grew the market for private security.

3. I follow Jen Roth Gordon (2017) in using phenotypical descriptions to communicate information about race to readers. Roth Gordon—like Fry 1996; Sansone 2003; Owensby 2005; and Burdick 1998—argues for a situational understanding of race that depends not only on skin color but also on contextual factors like language, class status, and behavior. In this particular case, phenotypical information along with their profession as guards offers clues about how to locate individuals in social and racial hierarchies. Furthermore, geographic place of residence sends signals about class and racial hierarchies in Brazil. See Vargas 2004 on the link between blackness and favelas; and McCallum 2005 on how racialization is connected to social practice, which is in turn connected to place and city geography.

4. It is important to state at the outset that this methodology is complicated by the fact that my own experiences of the labor of private security work are very different from those of the people I was studying due to my own identity as a middle-class, white woman. This difference, combined with the fact that security was not my profession, both facilitated and inhibited research access, and needs to be accounted for when trying to interpret what my own experiences as a participant-observer reveal about private security workers' understandings regarding the training of their own bodies. Nonetheless, even as a woman who didn't belong in the overall climate of what Paul Higate calls the "fratriarchy" of the security industry (2012a), embodied participation in private security worlds allowed me to understand aspects of the training experience beyond just asking about the body.

5. On the connection between race, cleanliness, and hygiene in the North American context, see Zimring 2017. On race, class, and smell in the United States see Hsu 2020 and Denyer Willis (2018) for the Rio suburbs.

6. See Ramos and Musumeci 2005 on clothing and criminality in Rio.

7. Part of my fieldwork involved following one of the private security guard unions as representatives evaluated Olympic sites for compliance with labor laws. Union representatives were concerned with ensuring the safety of their guards. They checked the availability of shade for guards to avoid strong tropical rays, whether or not there was clean water available or a chair to sit in to rest weary legs. They also asked about the location of bathrooms and whether or not employers were providing areas for breaks and lunch. The absences of these things not only violated workers' rights but also undermined guards' efforts at body management. When they did observe violations, union leaders described them as a "lack of respect for the category," the category meaning the profession itself. Guards could not effectively manage their bodies nor could they command respect in these subpar conditions.

8. No one arrived at the school with their shirts on, but changed upon arrival, precisely to avoid these kinds of confrontations. In other cases, however, there seemed to be a peaceful coexistence between organized crime and private security. One of the schools even had a functioning *boca de fumo*, or drug-selling point, located at the end of the block it was located on. Everyone just ignored each other.

9. While guards were concerned with managing the polyvocal qualities of their bodies, I was engaged in a different, yet parallel management of my own body in the research setting. As a white foreigner, my body represented affluence and mobility. Going to higher crime parts of the city meant that I had to work to downplay as many signs of affluence as possible; to counter the "natural" interpretations of my white body. This was necessary so that I did not present myself as a good target for assault on the train or bus and because I knew that it would be harder to establish rapport if I appeared elitist. In order to combat that, I removed designer labels. I wore plain jeans and tops that I purchased at an open-air market in the favela. Lower-class Brazilian fashion features tighter and more revealing clothing than I was used to. When trying to dress more like those at the school and "class" my own body to make it more appropriate to the setting, I often inadvertently gendered myself more strongly. Although to do otherwise would have actually marked me as more strongly foreign and less knowledgeable of Brazilian norms, I also felt uncomfortable in my own skin.

10. In another class, Eduardo set up an elaborate scenario involving a bar fight caused by one patron acting inappropriately to another patron's girlfriend. Again, as the only body that was a good fit for this role, I was to play the victim. The guard assigned to acting in a lewd manner was visibly embarrassed when he had to heckle me. For the sake of training purposes, he had to embody the vulgar category he was performing against in the hospitality model. Afterward he apologized profusely, reminding me that he would never act that way in real life. He wanted to make sure I understand that he was not the

negative stereotype he had performed in the simulation. Nonetheless, he wouldn't look at me for the rest of class.

11. There was one topic that was, for me, surprising in how little attention it received: how to profile a potential assailant; to find signs on other bodies that would suggest danger. We simply didn't spend any time on identifying suspects. One possibility for the omission was that it was understood that they all knew what criminals looked like, as if all *marginais* were easily knowable.

3. SECURING AFFECTIVE LANDSCAPES OF LEISURE AND CONSUMPTION

1. While more attention has been devoted to the elite enclave, Dinzey-Flores argues for a perspective that includes forms of punitive enclaving as well. In her work, *Locked in, Locked Out: Gated Communities in a Puerto Rican City*, she shows how while fences and gates might work as technologies of protection in the case of wealthy areas, in housing projects they are used as mechanisms of surveillance, monitoring, and enclosure (2013, 53–72).

2. Rather than focus purely on these urban enclaves as forms of social exclusion and segregation, or as Davis even characterized them as a form of "class warfare" (1992, 228), as they have so often been cast by observers, it is important, as Nielsen, Sumich, and Bertelsen note, to examine their utopian nature as well. That is, they imagine a certain future; a utopia of "things in their place" (2020, 7).

3. It also bears noting that less affluent neighborhoods often mimic the spatial security dynamics of closed condominiums. Contrasting the different technologies present in Rio and São Paulo's security scene, Rial and Grossi write, "We have on the one hand sophisticated state-of-the-art computerized equipment and on the other artifacts used with cruel intent, such as glass shards embedded on wall tops; iron fences topped with spearheads or spikes that are capable of terminally perforating or impaling a human body; plain barbed-wire fences; electric fences electrocuting the invader; or fences constructed from razor-sharp wire (sold in packages of twelve to sixty metres)" (2002, 113). Cruder and less expensive technologies are commonplace in low-income areas.

4. Guilherme was especially eager to talk with me about his work because he viewed me as a way to achieve some measure of validation from his two adult children, both of whom were ashamed of their father and his former and current line of employment, even though his work was supporting them financially while they attended the universities he described as having converted them to leftist beliefs (commies, he joked in English). They objected to his role in what they perceived as oppressive structures of governance. The fact that a university professor like me was interested in Guilherme's work and had positioned him as an expert holder of useful knowledge gave him a counterargument for their dismissal and criticism. My research project became a routine topic of interest at the family's Sunday lunches.

5. What he describes here is a fantastic example of crime-deterring design and the way in which security intersects with architecture and shapes built spaces. See Coaffee (2009); Coaffee, O'Hare, and Hawkesworth (2009); and Boddy (2008).

6. He went on to describe another way that networks were cultivated in order to secure the shopping. "Listen, in shoppings that are close to poor areas—take Shopping North, surrounded on all sides by favelas—we work really hard in the marketing. We create and promote propaganda around the image of the mall as theirs. We say it's their space, their home. Nobody robs their own house, right?"

7. In the case of the World Cup and the Olympics, "accreditation" was required of staff and many ticketholders. As Vida Bajc notes, accreditation is a surveillance procedure. "To be 'accredited' means to be subjected to precise identification and clear classification

into categories of privilege. These correspond to segmentation of the enclosure into sub-areas that are themselves stratified on the basis of privilege of access. The various codes and designations on the cards are pictural abstractions of how this procedure of hierarchy of classification of participants works" (2016, 21).

8. Here, Tom reflected a dominant attitude which I heard from non-Brazilian security personnel working with sponsors, in which part of their job was negotiating local security manifestations with regard to "the degree of security presence that corporate sponsors were willing to stomach" (Bennett and Haggerty 2011, 5).

9. In many of our group social events, nationalism or a sense of pride in the "Brazilian Olympics," was foregrounded in the discourse. Such a framing reflected an understanding of the implications of successful events on a geopolitical scale (Boyle and Haggerty 2009)

4. EMOTIONAL LABOR IN THE SECURITY COMMAND CENTER

1. Later, I realized that this simulation was inspired by a protest at the 2014 World Cup which produced a recognizable and famous photograph of a Native man in traditional dress, aiming his bow and arrow at suited security guards.

2. This sentiment is also reflected in what Samimian-Darash was told by informants in her own fieldwork at Israeli emergency preparedness exercises. Scenarios were "serious and reasonable," "not a worst case but plausible and serious." Simulation was "not prophecy, it's a decision, and we need to be ready for it" (2016, 359).

3. It is important to underscore that the subjects of this chapter are at the top echelons of the security structure and are involved in the strategic planning exercises that are then operationalized on the ground by the less powerful security actors, security personnel who have been the focal point in previous chapters.

4. Observers, in this context, include other members of the Olympic team from other areas outside of security, foreign delegations, the press, etc.

5. This is a pseudonym intended to mask the identity of the system.

6. The occurrence database was, like everything else in the preparedness world, an acronym. Sometimes I heard whole sentences of acronyms strung together like a code that it took me considerable effort to decode. I frequently felt that I was learning a new language—made worse by the fact that sometimes the acronym was in English but pronounced in Portuguese. For example, "Field of Play" or FOP was pronounced "foppy." I recall one early meeting where I sat through the entire thing without deducing what the term meant.

7. Other areas like food and beverage or transportation used different systems, none of which were integrated with the security software we were using. We had another security officer who sat in the main Games command with representatives from each area and who inputted things into their system as needed.

8. Even in the case of extreme or more urgent incidents, the peaceful chime didn't change. It was just the auditory soundtrack for disaster as usual.

9. Such performances reflect what Carmen Rial describes as the "technological fetishism" of megaevent security, particularly in the soccer world (2019, 111).

10. This sort of effort is quite typical in the field. As Bennett and Haggerty note in their work on security and megaevents, "From security guards to fencing to high-tech sensors and monitoring devices, all these corporations see mega-events as an opportunity to secure lucrative contracts and to showcase their products for future events" (2012, 7).

11. The use of the system reflected the ambition of individual security entrepreneurs. Such an orientation toward a promising future was commonplace among Games security personnel who frequently characterized their participation as waged in the service of aspirations for postevent employment, particularly with multinational companies. As Vida

Bajc notes of Olympic and megaevent security more generally, "In recent years, we notice in the public sphere the appearance of security experts whose institutional knowledge of such original events seems to have become the measure of the past, the present and the future. These experts have positioned themselves in a privileged role of access to security-related information about past events, promoting the organizers to feel compelled to consult them in preparations for the next event" (Bacj 2016, 54).

12. But of course, the performed version is not what actually happened. In fact, the hole was discovered when R$50,000 worth of camera equipment was reportedly smuggled out through it.

13. Breach of perimeter or damage to property were some of the more popular ones in the drop-down menu, united in their reference to financial damage.

14. This illustrates just how powerful the Olympics was in its right to dictate security in the city at the time.

15. The one exception to my slightly annoyed state of mind was the time that I had to call the squad for an item that was left in a stairwell inside a stadium where my husband and children were watching a competition.

16. One of the very first calls involved an incident for which I flat-out did not understand a single critical detail. I could not decide whether or not to admit to this or just ignore the incident and hope no one noticed. I went for the latter and thankfully, it got buried under other problems to be resolved and no one reprimanded me. But this kind of imposter syndrome was not unique to me; all the lower-level people expressed it at some point. However, I might have been in the weirdest position among the analysts, when the higher-ups who authorized my research participation on the team decided that it made the most sense to invent a role for me so that I could better understand the security world.

17. The only non-far-right-winger.

EPILOGUE

1. The blurring of public and private was additionally underscored as additional details came to light. One of the guards responsible, twenty-four-year-old Giovane Gaspar da Silva, was actually himself a police officer who was working second shift as a guard on his day off in order to augment his low police salary. As mentioned in previous chapters, such work is quite common in the private security industry.

2. Such an image of social disorder, especially in the lead-up to the 2018 election, moved beyond the age-old tropes of urban criminality which have defined the political landscape, especially in cities like Rio and São Paulo. It incorporated a more explicitly gendered, moral discourse, locating the source of societal breakdown with people whose identities are constructed as an attack on "traditional family values": those in the LGBTQ+ community, women who aspire to careers and demand gender equality, anyone who evokes human rights, and so forth.

References

Abraham, Itty. 2009. "Segurança/Security in Brazil and the United States." In *Words in Motion*, edited by Carol Gluck and Anna Lowenhaupt Tsing, 21–39. Durham, NC: Duke University Press. https://doi.org/10.1215/9780822391104-003.

Abrahamsen, Rita, and Michael C. Williams. 2011. *Security beyond the State: Private Security in International Politics*. Cambridge: Cambridge University Press.

———. 2017. "Golden Assemblages: Security and Development in Tanzania's Gold Mines." In *Private Security in Africa: From the Global Assemblage to the Everyday*, edited by Paul Higate and Matas Utas, 15–31. London: Zed Books.

Adey, Peter. 2006. "If Mobility Is Everything Then It Is Nothing: Towards a Relational Politics of (Im)mobilities." *Mobilities* 1 (1): 75–94.

Adorno, Sérgio. 1993. "Criminalidade urbana violenta no Brasil: Um recorte temático." *Bib. Boletim Informativo e Bibliográfico de Ciências Sociais* 35: 3–24.

———. 1999. "Insegurança versus direitos humanos: Entre a lei e a ordem." *Tempo Social* 11 (2): 129–53.

Alves, Jaime Amparo. 2014. "From Necropolis to Blackpolis: Necropolitical Governance and Black Spatial Praxis in São Paulo, Brazil." *Antipode* 46 (2): 323–39. https://doi.org/10.1111/anti.12055.

———. 2014. "On Mules and Bodies: Black Captivities in the Brazilian Racial Democracy." *Critical Sociology* 42 (2): 229–48. https://doi.org/10.1177/0896920514536590.

———. 2016. "Blood in Reasoning: State Violence, Contested Territories and Black Criminal Agency in Urban Brazil." *Journal of Latin American Studies* 48 (1): 61–87. https://doi.org/10.1017/S0022216X15000838.

———. 2018. *The Anti-Black City: Police Terror and Black Urban Life in Brazil*. Minneapolis: University of Minnesota Press.

———. 2021. "F*ck the Police! Murderous Cops, the Myth of Police Fragility and the Case for an Insurgent Anthropology." FocaalBlog, April 27. https://www.focaalblog.com/2021/04/27/jaime-a-alves-fck-the-police-murderous-cops-the-myth-of-police-fragility-and-the-case-for-an-insurgent-anthropology/.

Alves, Jaime Amparo, and João Costa Vargas. 2015. "On Deaf Ears: Anti-Black Police Terror, Multiracial Protest and White Loyalty to the State." *Identities* 24 (3): 254–74. https://doi.org/10.1080/1070289x.2015.1111839.

Amar, Paul. 2013. *The Security Archipelago: Human-Security States, Sexuality Politics, and the End of Neoliberalism*. Durham, NC: Duke University Press.

Anderson, Ben. 2010. "Preemption, Precaution, Preparedness: Anticipatory Action and Future Geographies." *Progress in Human Geography* 34 (6): 777–98. https://doi.org/10.1177/0309132510362600.

Aquino, Jania, and Felipe Freitas. 2018. "Inserções etnográficas ao universo do crime: Algumas considerações sobre pesquisas realizadas no Brasil entre 2000 e 2017." *Revista Brasileira de Informação Bibliográfica em Ciências Sociais* 84 (October): 107–47. https://doi.org/10.17666/bib8404/2018.

Araújo, Angela Maria, and Maria Rosa Lombardi. 2013. "Trabalho informal, gênero e raça no Brasil do início do século XXI." *Cadernos de Pesquisa* 43 (149): 452–77. https://doi.org/10.1590/s0100-15742013000200005.

REFERENCES

Auyero, Javier. 2012. *Patients of the State: The Politics of Waiting in Argentina*. Durham, NC: Duke University Press.
Bajc, Vida, ed. 2016. *Surveilling and Securing the Olympics: From Tokyo 1964 to London 2012 and Beyond*. London: Palgrave Macmillan. https://doi.org/10.1057/9781137290694.
Bartel, Rebecca. 2021. *Card-Carrying Christians: Debt and the Making of Free Market Spirituality in Colombia*. Berkeley: University of California Press.
Bennett, Colin J., and Kevin Haggerty. 2011. *Security Games: Surveillance and Control at Mega-Events*. Oxfordshire: Routledge.
Berlant, Lauren Gail. 2011. *Cruel Optimism*. Durham, NC: Duke University Press.
Bledsoe, Adam, and Willie J. Wright. 2019. "The Anti-Blackness of Global Capital." *Environment and Planning D: Society and Space* 37 (1): 8–26. https://doi.org/10.1177/0263775818805102.
Boddy, Trevor. 2008. "Architecture Emblematic: Hardened Sites and Softened Symbols." In *Indefensible Space*, edited by Michael Sorkin, 277–304. Oxfordshire: Routledge.
Boyle, Philip. 2012. "Knowledge Networks: Mega-Events and Security Expertise." In *Security Games: Surveillance and Control at Mega-Events*, edited by Colin J. Bennett and Kevin Haggerty, 183–98. Oxfordshire: Routledge. https://www.routledge.com/Security-Games-Surveillance-and-Control-at-Mega-Events/Bennett-Haggerty/p/book/9780415619622.
Boyle, Philip, and Kevin D. Haggerty. 2009. "Spectacular Security: Mega-Events and the Security Complex." *International Political Sociology* 3 (3): 257–74. https://doi.org/10.1111/j.1749-5687.2009.00075.x.
Brum, Eliane. 2020. "Por que Bolsonaro tem problemas com furos." *El País*, March 11. https://brasil.elpais.com/opiniao/2020-03-11/por-que-bolsonaro-tem-problemas-com-furos.html?fbclid=IwAR3MVlg7CWakOXyLg_XHXuEVO30g9wTGrWM8CpfAVp_oiRqwoUVlyYuKP4s.
Burdick, John. 1998. *Blessed Anastacia: Women, Race, and Popular Christianity in Brazil*. New York: Routledge.
Button, Mark. 2007. *Security Officers and Policing: Powers, Culture and Control in the Governance of Private Space*. Oxfordshire: Routledge.
Caldeira, Teresa P. R. 2002. *City of Walls: Crime, Segregation, and Citizenship in São Paulo*. Berkeley: University of California Press.
———. 2013. "The Paradox of Police Violence in Democratic Brazil." In *Policing and Contemporary Governance*, edited by William Garriott, chapter 4. New York: Palgrave Macmillan.
Cano, Ignacio, and C. Ioot. 2008. "Segurança, tráfico e milícias no Rio de Janeiro." *Justiça Global*, August 26. Rio de Janeiro: Justiça Global and Fundação Heinrich Böll. http://www.global.org.br/blog/seguranca-trafico-e-milicias-no-rio-de-janeiro-2/.
Cardoso, Francilene. 2018. "Racismo e necropolítica: A lógica do genocídio de Negros e Negras no Brasil contemporâneo" (Racism and Necropolitics: The Logics of Black Genocide in Contemporary Brazil). *Revista de Políticas Públicas* 22: 949–68.
Carey, Grace A. 2019. "Anthropology's 'Repugnant Others.'" *American Ethnologist*, April 23. https://americanethnologist.org/features/reflections/anthropologys-repugnant-others#:~:text=For%20Harding%2C%20humanizing%20%E2%80%9Crepugnant%20others,necessary%20to%20do%20ethical%20anthropology.

Carranca, Adriana. 2018. "The Women-Led Opposition to Brazil's Far-Right Leader." *Atlantic*, November 2. https://www.theatlantic.com/international/archive/2018/11/brazil-women-bolsonaro-haddad-election/574792/.

Carvalho, Bruno, Mariana Cavalcanti, and Vyjayanthi Venuturupalli Rao. 2016. *Occupy All Streets: Olympic Urbanism and Contested Futures in Rio de Janeiro*. New York: Terreform.

Chakravartty, Paula, and Denise Ferreira da Silva. 2012. "Accumulation, Dispossession, and Debt: The Racial Logic of Global Capitalism—an Introduction." *American Quarterly* 64 (3): 361–85. https://doi.org/10.1353/aq.2012.0033.

Chisholm, Amanda, and Saskia Stachowitsch. 2016. "Everyday Matters in Global Private Security Supply Chains: A Feminist Global Political Economy Perspective on Gurkhas in Private Security." *Globalizations* 13 (6): 815–29. https://doi.org/10.1080/14747731.2016.1155796.

Coaffee, Jon. 2003. *Terrorism, Risk and the City: The Making of a Contemporary Urban Landscape*. London: Ashgate.

———. 2009. *Terrorism, Risk and the Global City: Towards Urban Resilience*. London: Ashgate.

Coaffee, Jon, Paul O'Hare, and Marian Hawkesworth. 2009. "The Visibility of (In)security: The Aesthetics of Planning Urban Defences against Terrorism." *Security Dialogue* 40 (4): 489–511.

Coaffee, Jon, and Peter Rogers. 2008. *Rebordering the City for New Security Challenges: From Counter-Terrorism to Community Resilience*. National Emergency Training Center.

Collier, Stephen J. 2008. "Enacting Catastrophe: Preparedness, Insurance, Budgetary Rationalization." *Economy and Society* 37 (2): 224–50. https://doi.org/10.1080/03085140801933280.

Collier, Stephen J., and Andrew Lakoff. 2008a. "Distributed Preparedness: The Spatial Logic of Domestic Security in the United States." *Environment and Planning D: Society and Space* 26 (1): 7–28. https://doi.org/10.1068/d446t.

Collier, Stephen J., and Andrew Lakoff. 2008b. "The Problem of Securing Health." In *Biosecurity Interventions: Global Health and Security in Question*, edited by Andrew Lakoff and Stephen J. Collier, 7–32. New York: Columbia University Press.

Costa, Arthur Trindade Maranhão. 2011. "Police Brutality in Brazil: Authoritarian Legacy or Institutional Weakness?" *Latin American Perspectives* 38 (5): 19–32. https://doi.org/10.1177/0094582X10391631.

———. 2021. "Bolsonaro e a lógica miliciana." *Piauí*, April 6. https://piaui.folha.uol.com.br/bolsonaro-e-logica-miliciana/.

Costa, Breno, Reinaldo Chaves, and Hyury Potter. 2018. "O lucrativo exército de segurança privada comandado por militares, milicianos e amigos de Eduardo Cunha no Rio." *The Intercept Brasil*. https://theintercept.com/2018/07/16/o-lucrativo-exercito-de-seguranca-privada-comandado-por-militares-milicianos-e-amigos-de-eduardo-cunha-no-rio/.

Cowan, Benjamin A. 2016. "Holy Ghosts of Brazil's Past." *NACLA Report on the Americas* 48 (4): 346–52. https://doi.org/10.1080/10714839.2016.1258277.

———. 2021. *Moral Majorities across the Americas: Brazil, the United States, and the Creation of the Religious Right*. Chapel Hill: University of North Carolina Press.

Cowen, Deborah. 2014. *The Deadly Life of Logistics: Mapping Violence in Global Trade*. Minneapolis: University of Minnesota Press.

Cubas, Viviane de Oliveira. 2002. "A expansão das empresas de segurança privada em São Paulo." PhD diss., University of São Paulo.

Cunha, José Marcos Pinto da. 2016. "Aglomerações urbanas e mobilidade populacional: O caso da Região Metropolitana de Campinas." *Revista Brasileira de Estudos de Populacao* 33 (1): 99–127. https://doi.org/10.20947/S0102-309820160006.

Damasceno, Caetana. 1998. "'Em casa de enforcado não se fala em corda': Notas sobre a construção social da 'boa aparência' no Brasil." In *Tirando a máscara: Ensaios sobre racismo no Brasil*, edited by Antonio Sergio Alfredo Guimares and Lynn Huntley, 165–69. Sao Paulo: Paz e Terra.

da Silva, Antonio José Bacelar, and Erika Robb Larkins. 2019. "The Bolsonaro Election, Antiblackness, and Changing Race Relations in Brazil." *Journal of Latin American and Caribbean Anthropology* 24 (4): 893–913.

da Silva, Luiz Antonio Machado. 2010. "'Violência urbana,' e segurança pública e favelas: O caso do Rio de Janeiro atual."*Caderno CRH* 23 (59): 283–300.

Dávila, Arlene. 2016. *El Mall: The Spatial and Class Politics of Shopping Malls in Latin America*. Berkeley: University of California Press.

Davis, Mike. 2006. *City of Quartz: Excavating the Future in Los Angeles*. New ed. London: Verso.

———. 2007. *Planet of Slums*. London: Verso.

Deleuze, Gilles, and Félix Guattari. 1987. *A Thousand Plateaus: Capitalism and Schizophrenia*. Translated and with a foreword by Brian Massumi. London: Continuum.

Denyer Willis, Graham. 2015. *The Killing Consensus: Police, Organized Crime, and the Regulation of Life and Death in Urban Brazil*. Oakland: University of California Press.

Denyer Willis, Laurie. 2018. "'It Smells Like a Thousand Angels Marching': The Salvific Sensorium in Rio de Janeiro's Western Subúrbios." *Cultural Anthropology* 33 (2): 324–48. https://doi.org/10.14506/ca33.2.10.

Dickins de Girón, Avery. 2011. "The Security Guard Industry in Guatemala." In *Securing the City*, edited by Kevin Lewis O'Neill and Kedron Thomas, 103–25. Durham, NC: Duke University Press. https://doi.org/10.1215/9780822393924-006.

Diniz, Debora, and Giselle Carino. 2019. "Política e misoginia: Por que é a hora de as mulheres levarem uma cadeira portátil à mesa." *El País*, January 31. https://brasil.elpais.com/brasil/2019/01/31/opinion/1548964060_458044.html.

Dinzey-Flores, Zaire Zenit. 2013. *Locked In, Locked Out: Gated Communities in a Puerto Rican City*. Philadelphia: University of Pennsylvania Press.

Diphoorn, Tessa G. 2015. "'It's All About the Body': The Bodily Capital of Armed Response Officers in South Africa." *Medical Anthropology: Cross Cultural Studies in Health and Illness* 34 (4): 336–52. https://doi.org/10.1080/01459740.2015.1027342.

———. 2016a. "Twilight Policing: Private Security Practices in South Africa." *British Journal of Criminology* 56 (2): 313–31. https://doi.org/10.1093/bjc/azv057.

———. 2016b. *Twilight Policing: Private Security and Violence in Urban South Africa*. Berkeley: University of California Press.

Diphoorn, Tessa G., and Erella Grassiani. 2016. "Securitizing Capital: A Processual-Relational Approach to Pluralized Security." *Theoretical Criminology* 20 (4): 430–45. https://doi.org/10.1177/1362480616659821.

———. 2019. *Security Blurs: The Politics of Plural Security Provision*. London: Routledge.

Diphoorn, Tessa G., and Helene M. Kyed. 2016. "Entanglements of Private Security and Community Policing in South Africa and Swaziland." *African Affairs* 115 (461): 710–32. https://doi.org/10.1093/afraf/adw028.

Duffield, Mark. 2011. "Environmental Terror: Uncertainty, Resilience and the Bunker." School of Sociology, Politics and International Studies, University of Bristol. Global Insecurities Centre. Working Paper no. 06-11.

Durão, Susana Soares Branco. 2008. *Patrulha e proximidade: Uma etnografia da polícia em Lisboa*. Lisboa: Almedina.

Durão, Susana, and Maria Claudia Coelho. 2020. "Do qeu fala quem fala sobre polícia no Brasil? Uma revisão da literatura." *Análise Social* 55 (234): 72–99. https://doi.org/10.31447/AS00032573.2020234.03.

Durão, Susana, and Márcio Darck. 2012. *Repositório da universidade de Lisboa: Polícia, segurança e ordem pública; Perspectivas portuguesas e brasileiras*. Lisbon: Imprensa de Ciências Sociais.

Durão, Susana, and Josué Correa Paes. 2021. *Caso Carrefour: Racismo e Segurança Privada*. 2nd ed. São Paulo: Editora Unipalmares.

Durão, Susana, Erika Robb Larkins, and Carolina Andrei Fischmann. 2021. "Securing the Mall: Daily Hospitality Security Practice in São Paulo." *Lua Nova* 114: 137–74. https://doi.org/10.1590/0102-137174/114.

Erie, Steven P. 1992. Review of *City of Quartz: Excavating the Future in Los Angeles*, by Mike Davis. *Political Science Quarterly* 107 (1): 177. https://doi.org/10.2307/2152158.

Fassin, Didier. 2017. *Writing the World of Policing: The Difference Ethnography Makes*. Chicago: University of Chicago Press.

Fassin, Didier, and Estelle d'Halluin. 2005. "The Truth from the Body: Medical Certificates as Ultimate Evidence for Asylum Seekers." *American Anthropologist* 107 (4): 597–608. https://doi.org/10.1525/aa.2005.107.4.597.

Fawaz, Mona, Mona Harb, and Ahmad Gharbieh. 2012. "Living Beirut's Security Zones: An Investigation of the Modalities and Practice of Urban Security." *City and Society* 24 (2): 173–95.

Feltran, Gabriel. 2020. *The Entangled City: Crime as Urban Fabric in São Paulo*. Manchester: Manchester University Press.

Frazier, Camille. 2019. "Urban Heat: Rising Temperatures as Critique in India's Air-Conditioned City." *City and Society* 31 (3): 441–61. https://doi.org/10.1111/ciso.12228.

French, Jan Hoffman. 2013. "Rethinking Police Violence in Brazil: Unmasking the Public Secret of Race." *Latin American Politics and Society* 55 (04): 161–81. https://doi.org/10.1111/j.1548-2456.2013.00212.x.

Fry, Peter. 1996. "O euue a Cinderela negra tem a dizer sobre a 'política racial' no Brasil." *Revista USP* 28: 1 22. http://doi.org/10.11606/issn.2316-9036.v0i28p122-135.

Gaffney, Christopher. 2010. "Mega-Events and Socio-Spatial Dynamics in Rio de Janeiro, 1919–2016." *Journal of Latin American Geography* 9 (1): 7– 29. http://doi.org/10.1353/lag.0.0068.

Gaffney, Christopher. 2014. "The Traumas and Dramas of Post-Cup, Pre-Olympic Brazil." *Roar*, August 25. https://roarmag.org/essays/brazil-world-cup-olympics/.

Garriott, William Campbell. 2011. *Policing Methamphetamine: Narcopolitics in Rural America*. New York: New York University Press.

Ghertner, D. Asher, Asher McFann, and Daniel Goldstein. 2020. *Futureproof: Security Aesthetics and the Management of Life*. Durham, NC: Duke University Press.

Gilmore, Ruth Wilson. 2020. *Geographies of Racial Capitalism with Ruth Wilson Gilmore*. https://www.youtube.com/watch?v=2CS627aKrJI.

Glück, Zoltán. 2017. "Security Urbanism and the Counterterror State in Kenya." *Anthropological Theory* 17 (3): 297–321. https://doi.org/10.1177/1463499617729295.

Glück, Zoltán, and Setha M. Low. 2017. "A Sociospatial Framework for the Anthropology of Security." *Anthropological Theory* 17 (3): 281–96. https://doi.org/10.1177/1463499617729229.

Goldstein, Donna. 2014. *Laughter Out of Place: Race, Class, Violence, and Sexuality in a Rio Shantytown*. Berkeley: University of California Press.

Graham, Stephen. 2011. *Cities under Siege: The New Military Urbanism*. London: Verso.

Grove, Kevin. 2012. "Preempting the Next Disaster: Catastrophe Insurance and the Financialization of Disaster Management." *Security Dialogue* 43 (2): 139–55. https://doi.org/10.1177/0967010612438434.

Guimarães, Antônio Sérgio A., and Lynn Huntley. 2000. *Tirando a máscara: Ensaios sobre o racismo no Brasil*. São Paulo: Paz e Terra.

Handelman, Kali, and Rebecca Bartel. 2021. "Credit Card Christianity, Debt, and Violence in Colombia." *Revealer*. https://therevealer.org/credit-card-christianity-debt-and-violence-in-colombia/.

Harding, Susan. 1991. "Representing Fundamentalism: The Problem of the Repugnant Cultural Other." *Social Research* 58 (2): 373–93.

Hartman, Saidiya. 1997. *Scenes of Subjection: Terror, Slavery, and Self-Making in Nineteenth-Century America*. Race and American Culture. New York: Oxford University Press.

Harvey, David. 2007. "Neoliberalism and the City." *Studies in Social Justice* 1 (1): 2–13.

———. 2008. "The Right to the City." *New Left Review*. https://newleftreview.org/issues/ii53/articles/david-harvey-the-right-to-the-city.

Higate, Paul. 2012a. "'Cowboys and Professionals': The Politics of Identity Work in the Private and Military Security Company." *Millennium: Journal of International Studies* 40 (2): 321–41. https://doi.org/10.1177/0305829811425752.

———. 2012b. "Drinking Vodka from the 'Butt-Crack': Men, Masculinities and Fratriarchy in the Private Militarized Security Company." *International Feminist Journal of Politics* 14 (4): 450–69. https://doi.org/10.1080/14616742.2012.726092.

———. 2012c. "The Private Militarized and Security Contractor as Geocorporeal Actor." *International Political Sociology* 6 (4): 355–72. http://doi.org/10.1111/ips.12004.

Higate, Paul, and Matas Utas. 2017. *Private Security in Africa: From the Global Assemblage to the Everyday*. London: Zed Books.

Hinton, Alexander Laban. 2002. *Annihilating Difference: The Anthropology of Genocide*. Berkeley: University of California Press.

Hinz, Kristina, and Juliana Vinuto. 2022. "Police Soldiers, Elite Squads, and Militia: Militarized Masculinities and Public Security Discourses in Rio de Janeiro (1995–2018)." *International Feminist Journal of Politics* 24 (1): 63–86. https://doi.org/10.1080/14616742.2021.2021099.

Hirata, Daniel. "The Government of Street Vending: Formalizations of Informality and Use of Force." Essay. In *Living (Il)Legalities in Brazil: Practices, Narratives and Institutions in a Country on the Edge*. London: Routledge, 2021.

Hobbs, Dick, Philip Hadfield, Stuart Lister, and Simon Winlow. 2002. "'Door Lore': The Art and Economics of Intimidation." *British Journal of Criminology* 42 (2): 352–70. https://doi.org/10.1093/bjc/42.2.352.

Huggins, Martha K. 2000. "Urban Violence and Police Privatization in Brazil: Blended Invisibility." *Social Justice* 27 (2): 113–34.

Hughes, Everett. 1958. *Men and Their Work*. London: Collier-Macmillan.

Hsu, Hsuan L. 2020. *The Smell of Risk: Environmental Disparities and Olfactory Aesthetics*. New York: New York University Press.

Instituto de Pesquisa Econômica Aplicada. 2020. *Atlas da violência 2020*. Ipea. https://www.ipea.gov.br/atlasviolencia/publicacoes.

Instituto de Pesquisa Econômica Aplicada. 2021. *Atlas da violência 2021*. Ipea. https://www.ipea.gov.br/atlasviolencia/publicacoes.

Jaffe, Rivke. 2019. "Speculative Policing." *Public Culture* 31 (3): 447–68. https://doi.org/10.1215/08992363-7532751.

———. 2020. "Security Aesthetics and Political Community Formation in Kingston, Jamaica." In *Futureproof: Security Aesthetics and the Management of Life*, edited by D. Asher Ghertner, Hudson McFann, and Daniel M. Goldstein, 134–55. Durham, NC: Duke University Press. https://doi.org/10.1215/9781478007517-006.

Jaffe, Rivke, and Tessa Diphoorn. 2019. "Old Boys and Badmen: Private Security in (Post)Colonial Jamaica." *Interventions* 21 (7): 909–27. https://doi.org/10.1080/1369801X.2019.1585906.

Jauregui, Beatrice. 2013a. "Beatings, Beacons, and Big Men: Police Disempowerment and Delegitimation in India." *Law and Social Inquiry* 38 (3): 643–69. https://doi.org/10.1111/lsi.12030.

———. 2013b. "Dirty Anthropology: Epistemologies of Violence and Ethical Entanglements in Police Ethnography." In *Policing and Contemporary Governance*, edited by William Garriott, 125–53. New York: Palgrave Macmillan. https://doi.org/10.1057/9781137309679_6.

Junge, Ben, Sean Mitchell, Alvaro Jarrín, and Lucia Cantero, eds. 2021. *Precarious Democracy: Ethnographies of Hope, Despair and Resistance in Brazil*. New Brunswick, NJ: Rutgers University Press.

Kant de Lima, Roberto, Michel Misse, and Ana Paula Mendes de Miranda. 2000. "Violência, criminalidade, segurança pública e justiça criminal no Brasil: Uma bibliografia." *BIB, Rio de Janeiro* 50 (2): 45–124.

Karpiak, Kevin G. 2010. "Of Heroes and Polemics: 'The Policeman' in Urban Ethnography." *PoLAR: Political and Legal Anthropology Review* 33: 7–31. https://doi.org/10.1111/j.1555-2934.2010.01063.x.

Karpiak, Kevin G., and William Garriott, eds. 2018. *The Anthropology of Police*. Abingdon: Routledge.

Kedron, Thomas, and Kevin Lewis O'Neill. 2011. *Securing the City: Neoliberalism, Space, and Insecurity in Postwar Guatemala*. Durham, NC: Duke University Press.

Klein, Charles, Sean Mitchell, and Benjamin Junge. 2018. "Naming Brazil's Previously Poor: 'New Middle Class' as an Economic, Political, and Experiential Category." *Economic Anthropology* 5 (1): 83–95.

Lakoff, Andrew. 2007. "Preparing for the Next Emergency." *Public Culture* 19 (2): 247–71. https://doi.org/10.1215/08992363-2006-035.

———. 2008. "The Generic Biothreat, or, How We Became Unprepared." *Cultural Anthropology* 23 (3): 399–423.

———. 2012. "The Risks of Preparedness: Mutant Bird Flu." *Public Culture* 24 (3): 457–64.

Lakoff, Andrew, and Stephen J. Collier. 2008. *Biosecurity Interventions: Global Health and Security in Question*. New York: Columbia University Press.

Lehman, Stan. 2018. "A Look at Offensive Comments by Brazil Candidate Bolsonaro." AP News, November 29. https://apnews.com/article/1f9b79df9b1d4f14aeb1694f0dc13276.

Linhares, Juliana. 2016. "Marcela Temer: Bela, recatada e 'do lar.'" *Veja*, April 18. https://veja.abril.com.br/brasil/marcela-temer-bela-recatada-e-do-lar/.

Loader, Ian, and Neil Walker. 2007. *Civilizing Security*. Cambridge: Cambridge University Press. https://doi.org/10.1017/CBO9780511611117.

Lopes, Cleber da Silva. 2013. "O setor de segurança privada da região metropolitana de São Paulo: Crescimento, dimensões." *Caderno CRH* 26 (69): 599–617.

———. 2014. "Assessing Private Security Accountability: A Study of Brazil." *Policing and Society* 25 (6): 641–62. https://doi.org/10.1080/10439463.2014.912649.

———. 2015a. "Como os paulistanos veem os setores de segurança pública e segurança privada." *Privado* 26: 207–31.

———. 2015b. "Segurança privada e direitos civis na cidade de São Paulo." *Sociedade e Estado* 30 (3): 651–71.

———. 2018. "Policing Labor: The Power of Private Security Guards to Search Workers in Brazil." *Crime, Law and Social Change* 70 (5): 583–602.

Low, Setha M. 2001. "The Edge and the Center: Gated Communities and the Discourse of Urban Fear." *American Anthropologist* 103 (1): 45–58. https://doi.org/10.1525/aa.2001.103.1.45.

———. 2013. "Securitization Strategies: Gated Communities and Market-Rate Co-Operatives in New York." In *Policing Cities: Urban Securitization and Regulation in a Twenty-First Century World*, edited by Randy K. Lippert and Kevin Walby, 222–30. London: Routledge.

———. 2017. *Spatializing Culture: The Ethnography of Space and Place*. New York: Routledge.

Low, Setha M., and Mark Maguire, eds. 2019. *Spaces of Security: Ethnographies of Securityscapes, Surveillance, and Control*. New York: New York University Press.

Maguire, Mark. 2014. "Counter-Terrorism in European Airports." In *The Anthropology of Security: Perspectives from the Frontline of Policing, Counter-Terrorism and Border Control*, edited by Mark Maguire, Catarina Frois, and Nils Zurawski, 118–31. London: Pluto Press.

Masco, Joseph. 2014. *The Theater of Operations: National Security Affect from the Cold War to the War on Terror*. Durham, NC: Duke University Press.

Mbembe, Achille. 2003. "Necropolitics." *Public Culture* 15 (1): 11–40. https://doi.org/10.1215/08992363-15-1-11.

McCallum, Cecilia. 2005. "Racialized Bodies, Naturalized Classes: Moving through the City of Salvador da Bahia." *American Ethnologist* 32 (1): 100–117. https://doi.org/10.1525/ae.2005.32.1.100.

McKenzie, Evan. 1994. *Privatopia: Homeowner Associations and the Rise of Residential Private Government*. New Haven: Yale University Press.

McKinson, Kimberley D. 2021. "Fortifying Home and Yard: Metal, Vegetation, and the Embodied Practice of Middle-Class In/Security in Jamaica." *Journal of Latin American and Caribbean Anthropology* 26 (2): 297–323. https://doi.org/10.1111/jlca.12528.

Melgaço, Lucas, and Nelson Arteaga Botello. 2015. "Introdução: A securização das cidades latino-americanas." *Urbe* 7 (2). https://doi.org/10.1590/2175-3369.007.002.IT01.

Mills, Charles W. 1999. *The Racial Contract*. Ithaca, NY: Cornell University Press.

———. 2001. "Black Trash." In *Faces of Environmental Racism: Confronting Issues of Global Justice*. 2nd ed., edited by Laura Westra and Bill E. Lawson, 73-91. Lanham, MD: Rowman and Littlefield.

Monaghan, Lee F. 2002. "Hard Men, Shop Boys and Others: Embodying Competence in a Masculinist Occupation." *Sociological Review* 50 (3): 334–55. https://doi.org/10.1111/1467-954X.00386.

Muniz, Jacqueline de Oliveira, and Eduardo Paes-Machado. 2010. "Polícia para quem precisa de polícia: Contribuições aos estudos sobre policiamento." *Caderno CRH* 23 (60): 437–47.

Musumeci, Leonarda. 1998. "Serviços privados de vigilância e guarda no Brasil: Um estudo a partir de informações da pnad–1985/95." http://repositorio.ipea.gov.br/bitstream/11058/2401/1/TD%200560.pdf.

Nascimento, Abdias do. 1989. *Brazil, Mixture or Massacre? Essays in the Genocide of a Black People*. Baltimore: Majority Press.

———. 2019. "The Myth of Racial Democracy." In *The Brazil Reader*, edited by James N. Green, Victoria Langland, and Lilia Moritz, 445–48. Durham, NC: Duke University Press. https://doi.org/10.1215/9780822371793-114.

Nielsen, Morten, Jason Sumich, and Bjørn Enge Bertelsen. 2021. "Enclaving: Spatial Detachment as an Aesthetics of Imagination in an Urban Sub-Saharan African Context." *Urban Studies*, June, 881-902. https://journals.sagepub.com/doi/pdf/10.1177/0042098020916095.

Nordstrom, Carolyn. 1995. *Fieldwork under Fire: Contemporary Studies of Violence and Culture*. Berkeley: University of California Press.

Oh, Sookhee. 2014. Review of *Locked In, Locked Out: Gated Communities in a Puerto Rican City*, by Zaire Zenit Dinzey-Flores. *American Journal of Sociology* 120 (1): 290–92. https://doi.org/10.1086/677245.

Oliveira, André de. 2016. "#AgoraNãoSãoElas? O ministério masculino de Michel Temer." *El País*, May 13. https://brasil.elpais.com/brasil/2016/05/12/politica/1463073214_630598.html.

O'Neil, Kevin Lewis, and Kedron Thomas. 2011. *Securing the City: Neoliberalism, Space, and Insecurity in Postwar Guatemala*. Durham, NC: Duke University Press.

Owensby, Brian. 2005. "Toward a History of Brazil's 'Cordial Racism': Race beyond Liberalism." *Comparative Studies in Society and History* 47 (2): 318–47. https://doi.org/10.1017/s0010417505000150.

Paes-Machado, Eduardo, and Ana Márcia Nascimento. 2014. "Conduzindo o perigo: Práticas e redes nodulares de governança da segurança entre taxistas." *Espacio Abierto* 23 (3): 403–33.

Paes-Machado, Eduardo, and Maria Angélica Riccio-Oliveira. 2009. "O jogo de esconde-esconde: Trabalho perigoso e ação social defensiva entre motoboys de Salvador." *Revista Brasileira de Ciências Sociais* 24 (70): 91–106.

Paes-Machado, Eduardo, and Silvia Viodres-Inoue. 2015. "O lado sombrio da estrada vitimização, gestão coercitiva e percepção de medo nos roubos a ônibus interurbanos." *Revista Brasileira de Ciências Sociais* 30 (89): 9–30.

Pardue, Derek. 2019. "Connotative Memories." *Writing with Light. Cultural Anthropology*, October 29. https://culanth.org/fieldsights/connotative-memories.

Penglase, Ben. 2014. *Living with Insecurity in a Brazilian Favela: Urban Violence and Daily Life*. New Brunswick, NJ: Rutgers University Press.

Perlman, Janice. 1976. *The Myth of Marginality: Urban Poverty and Politics in Rio de Janeiro*. Berkeley: University of California Press.

Perry, Keisha-Khan. 2013. *Black Women against the Land Grab: The Fight for Racial Justice in Brazil*. Minneapolis: University of Minnesota Press.

Pineau, Gaston. 2006. "As histórias de vida em formação: Gênese de uma corrente de pesquisa-ação-formação existencial." *Educação e Pesquisa* 32 (2). Faculdade de Educação da Universidade de São Paulo. https://doi.org/10.1590/s1517-97022006000200009.

Pinheiro-Machado, Rosana, and Lucia Mury Scalco. 2020. "From Hope to Hate: The Rise of Conservative Subjectivity in Brazil." *HAU: Journal of Ethnographic Theory* 10 (1): 21–31. https://doi.org/10.1086/708627.

Pinheiro-Machado, Rosana, and Lucia Mury Scalco. 2021. "Humanising Fascists? Nuance as an Anthropological Responsibility." *Social Anthropology* 29 (2): 329–36. https://doi.org/10.1111/1469-8676.13048.

Pinho, Patricia de Santana. 2009. "White but Not Quite: Tones and Overtones of Whiteness in Brazil." *Small Axe* 13 (2): 39–56.

———. 2015."The Dirty Body That Cleans: Representations of Domestic Workers in Brazilian Common Sense." *Meridians: Feminism, Race, Transnationalism* 13 (1): 103–28.

Quintella, José Pedro Guedes, and José Luis Felicio Carvalho. 2017. "Segurança pública, violência urbana e expansão do setor de segurança privada no município do Rio de Janeiro." *Revista Produção e Desenvolvimento* 3 (2): 1–20.

Rabinow, Paul. 1997. "Introduction: The History of Systems of Thought." In *Ethics: Subjectivity and Truth*, by Michel Foucault. New York: New Press.

Ramos, Silvia, and Leonarda Musumeci. 2005. "Elemento suspeito: Abordagem policial e discriminação na cidade do Rio de Janeiro." *Boletim Segurança e Cidadania*, no. 8.

Rial, Carmen. 2019. "From Panopticon to Panasonic." In *Spaces of Security: Ethnographies of Securityscapes, Surveillance, and Control*, edited by Setha M. Low and Mark Maguire, 99–121. New York: New York University Press.

Rial, Carmen, and Miriam Grossi. 2002. "Urban Fear in Brazil." In *Urban Ethnic Encounters: The Spatial Consequences*, edited by Aygen Erdentug and Freek Colombijn, 109–25. London: Routledge.

Ribeiro, Ludmila, and Roberto Correa. 2013. "Review Essay: Recent Books on Crime and Police in Brazil." *Police Practice and Research* 14 (4): 338–46.

Ribeiro, Ludmila, and Alexandre Diniz. 2020. "Pandemic and Public Safety in Brazil: How Bad Is Becoming Worse." Chatham House. https://americas.chathamhouse.org/article/pandemic-and-public-safety-in-brazil.

Rigakos, George S. 2002. *The New Parapolice: Risk Markets and Commodified Social Control*. Toronto: University of Toronto Press.

Robb Larkins, Erika. 2013. "Performances of Police Legitimacy in Rio's Hyper Favela." *Law and Social Inquiry* 38 (3): 553–75. https://doi.org/10.1111/lsi.12024.

———. 2015. *The Spectacular Favela: Violence in Modern Brazil*. Berkeley: University of California Press.

———. 2017. "Guarding the Body: Private Security Work in Rio de Janeiro." *Conflict and Society* 3 (1): 61–72.

———. 2018. "Police, Hospitality, and Mega-Event Security in Rio de Janeiro." In *The Anthropology of Police*, edited by William Garriott and Kevin Karpiak, 139–52. Abingdon: Routledge.

Robinson, Cedric. 2000. *Black Marxism: The Making of the Black Radical Tradition*. Chapel Hill: University of North Carolina Press.

Rodgers, Dennis. 2004. "'Disembedding' the City: Crime, Insecurity and Spatial Organization in Managua, Nicaragua." *Environment and Urbanization* 16 (2): 113–24. https://doi.org/10.1177/095624780401600202.

Roth Gordon, Jennifer. 2009. "The Language That Came Down the Hill: Slang, Crime, and Citizenship in Rio de Janeiro." *American Anthropologist* 111 (1): 57–68.

———. 2017. *Race and the Brazilian Body: Blackness, Whiteness, and Everyday Language in Rio de Janeiro*. Berkeley: University of California Press.
Salem, Tomas, and Erika Robb Larkins. 2021. "Violent Masculinities." *American Ethnologist* 48: 65–79. https://doi.org/10.1111/amet.13005.
Samimian-Darash, Limor. 2011. "Governing through Time: Preparing for Future Threats to Health and Security." *Sociology of Health and Illness* 33 (6): 930–45. https://doi.org/10.1111/j.1467-9566.2011.01340.x.
———. 2016. "Practicing Uncertainty: Scenario-Based Preparedness Exercises in Israel." *Cultural Anthropology* 31 (3): 359–86. https://doi.org/10.14506/ca31.3.06.
Samimian-Darash, Limor, and Meg Stalcup. 2017. "Anthropology of Security and Security in Anthropology: Cases of Counterterrorism in the United States." *Anthropological Theory* 17 (1): 60–87. https://doi.org/10.1177/1463499616678096.
Sansone, Livio. 2003. *Blackness without Ethnicity: Constructing Race in Brazil*. New York: Palgrave Macmillan.
Sassen, Saskia. 1991. *The Global City: New York, London, Tokyo*. Princeton: Princeton University Press.
———. 2015. "Who Owns Our Cities—and Why This Urban Takeover Should Concern Us All." *Guardian*, November 24. https://www.theguardian.com/cities/2015/nov/24/who-owns-our-cities-and-why-this-urban-takeover-should-concern-us-all.
Schwarcz, Lilia Moritz. 2019. *Sobre o autoritarismo brasileiro*. São Paulo: Companhia de Letras.
Serviço Público Federal MJ—Departamento de Polícia Federal. Portaria no. 3.233/2012-DG/DPF, de 10 de Dezembro de 2012.
Sharpe, Christina. 2016. *In the Wake: On Blackness and Being*. Durham, NC: Duke University Press.
Simone, AbdouMaliq. 2018. *Improvised Lives: Rhythms of Endurance in an Urban South*. London: Polity.
Sindicato da Empresas de Segurança Privada, Vigilancia Patrimonial, Sistemas de Segurança, Escolta, Segurança Pessoal e Cursos de Formação no Estado do Rio de Janeiro. Convenção Coletiva de Trabalho 2022/2023 (Report No. RJ000182/2022). http://sindesp-rj.com.br/.
Sluka, Jefferey A. 2010. *Death Squad: The Anthropology of State Terror*. Philadelphia: University of Pennsylvania Press.
Smith, Christen A. 2016. *Afro-Paradise: Blackness, Violence, and Performance in Brazil*. Urbana: University of Illinois Press.
Smith, Neil. 1982. "Gentrification and Uneven Development." *Economic Geography* 58 (2): 139–55. https://doi.org/10.2307/143793.
Soja, Edward W. 2000. *Postmetropolis: Critical Studies of Cities and Regions*. Oxford: Blackwell.
Sorkin, Michael, ed. 1992. *Variations on a Theme Park: The New American City and the End of Public Space*. New York: Hill and Want.
"Tabela salarial 2022." Sindicato dos Vigilantes. https://sindvig.org.br/confira-tabela-salarial-2022/.
Telles, Edward E. 2006. *Race in Another America: The Significance of Skin Color in Brazil*. Princeton: Princeton University Press.
Telles, Vera da Silva, and Daniel Veloso Hirata. 2007. "Cidade e práticas urbanas: Nas fronteiras incertas entre o ilegal, o informal e o ilícito." *Estudos Avançados* 21 (61): 173–91. https://doi.org/10.1590/s0103-40142007000300012.

Vargas, João H. Costa. 2004. "Hyperconsciousness of Race and Its Negation: The Dialectic of White Supremacy in Brazil." *Identities* 11 (4): 443–70. https://doi.org/10.1080/10702890490883803.

———. 2012. "Gendered Antiblackness and the Impossible Brazilian Project: Emerging Critical Black Brazilian Studies." *Cultural Dynamics* 24 (1): 3–11. https://doi.org/10.1177/0921374012452808.

———. 2013. "Taking Back the Land: Police Operations and Sport Megaevents in Rio de Janeiro." *Souls* 15 (4): 275–303. https://doi.org/10.1080/10999949.2013.884445.

Wacquant, Loïc J. D. 1995. "Pugs at Work: Bodily Capital and Bodily Labour among Professional Boxers." *Body and Society* 1 (1): 65–93. https://doi.org/10.1177/1357034x95001001005.

Whitehead, Neil L., ed. 2004. *Violence*. Santa Fe, NM: School for Advanced Research Press.

———. 2007. "Violence and the Cultural Order." *Daedalus* 136 (1): 40–50. http://www.jstor.org/stable/20028088.

Woronov, Terry. 2016. *Class Work: Vocational Schools and China's Urban Youth*. Redwood City, CA: Stanford University Press.

Zaluar, Alba. 1994. *Condomínio do diabo*. Rio de Janeiro: Editora Revan.

Zanetic, André. 2009. "Segurança privada: Características do setor e impacto sobre o policiamento." *Revista Brasileira de Segurança Pública* 3 (1): 135–50.

———. 2013. "Policiamento, segurança privada e uso da força: Conceito e características descritivas." *Dilemas-Revista de Estudos de Conflito e Controle Social* 6 (3): 411–33.

Zimring, Carl A. 2017. *Clean and White: A History of Environmental Racism in the United States*. New York: New York University Press.

Index

Page numbers in *italics* refer to figures.

Abrahamsen, Rita, 16, 163n23
access control, 88, 98–101, 105, 146, 167n7.
  See also gatekeeping
accreditation, 167n7
aesthetics, 3, 24, 72, 76, 165n2
affective logics, 3–4, 14, 87–105, 143
Alexandre (interlocutor), 57–59
Alves (interlocutor), 84
Alves, Jaime, 10
Anderson (interlocutor), 139
Andre (interlocutor), 156
antiblackness, 3, 10–12, 141–43. *See also* racial hierarchy
Antonio (interlocutor), 36–37, 39, 41, 45, 47
armed escort of cargo (*escolta armada*). *See* escolta guards
armored cars, 6, 18, 30, *37*, 45, 49–50, 59–60, 66, 164n9
assemblage: concept of, 15–16, 163n22; security assemblages, 15–16, 89, 91
authoritarianism, 17, 145–46

Bajc, Vida, 167n7, 168n11
bandidos, 30, 38, 43–44, 48, 51, 59, 114, 164n6
bank guards, 32–33
Barra de Tijuca (neighborhood), 94, 118, *152*
Barriga (interlocutor), 104
Bartel, Rebecca, 162n15
belonging, 22, 43, 70–71, 143, 145
Benatar (interlocutor), 124, 126
Bennett, Colin J., 168n10
Berlant, Lauren, 161n9
Bertelsen, Bjørn Enge, 165n2, 167n2
Black Consciousness Day, 141
Black low-income workers, 2–4; in hazardous occupations, 10–11, 164n5. *See also* racial capitalism
Bledsoe, Adam, 162n13
boa aparência (good appearance), 69, 76–77
bodily capital, 65–66, 70, 76
bodyguards, 14, 33–34, 70, 144
body management, 69–71, 76, 166n4, 166nn9–10
Bolsonaro, Jair, 10, 143, 146–47
boxing, 66, 68, 95, 97

brand protection, corporate, 9, 15, 89, 94, 126–29
Bruno (interlocutor), 29
Burdick, John, 165n3

Cabral, Sergio, 14
cafés, 103–5
Caldeira, Teresa P. R., 5, 90, 165n2
capital, flows of, 15, 89; cargo security, 36–37, 51–52, 164n3; Olympics and, 127–29, 149; private security companies and, 4–6, 161n4; protection of consumer goods from theft, 92–94, 103–5; shopping malls, 93. *See also* commodities; racial capitalism
cargo theft, 6, 11, 30, 36, 41–43, 163n1, 164n3. *See also* escolta guards
Carlos (interlocutor), 39–41, 43, 44, 51, 59–60, 83, 100–101, 127
Carrefour case, 141–43
carreira das armas (careers involving weapons), 38, 44–46, 50–51, 147. *See also* escolta guards
Carvalho, José Luis Felicio, 5
certification, 6–7, 164n9
Cesar (interlocutor), 112–13, 159
Charles (interlocutor), 84–85
Chisholm, Amanda, 65
city planning, 5; enclaving, 90 (*see also* enclaving); insecurity and, 91; megaevents and, 65; spatial exclusion and, 65, 77, 88–89, 95, 98
clandestine private security, 7
class hierarchy, 2–3, 9, 65; criminality and, 98; elite privilege and, 74–75; escolta guards and, 47–48; exclusion and, 88–90, 94–95, 99; gated communities and, 165n2; hygiene and, 69; markers of, 165n3; in private security, 147
cleaning services, 8, 12, 90
cleanliness, 2–3, 11, 47, 69–71, 155, 157
clientelist governments, 148
clothing, 70–71, 76
Clovis (interlocutor), 31–32, 115–16
Colombia, 91
commodification, 5, 15, 77, 148

183

INDEX

commodities, 2, 89–90, 104. *See also* capital, flows of
concert venues, 64
condominium guards, 32, *53–55*, 61, 105, 111–14, *151–53*. *See also* gated communities
construction sites, 84, 113–16
consumption: conditions for, 126; spaces of, 64, 87–105
contractors: global, 12, 13, 17, 120, 148; military, 65; third-party security, 8, 16, 19
corporate sponsorship of megaevents, 9, 119–21, 168n8(chap.3)
Correiros (mail service), 165n10
counterterrorism, 122
COVID-19 pandemic, 23, 158
credentialing processes, 88
crime: far-right approaches to, 17, 20–21; fear of, 2–5, 91. *See also* drug trafficking; organized crime
Cristiano (interlocutor), 138
"cruel optimism," 161n9

Dávila, Arlene, 91
Davis, Mike, 167n2
death and injury, risk of: drug trafficking and, 72, 114, 165n14; escolta guards and, 11, 30, 36–37, 43, 47–48, 52, 164n3; hospitality guards and, 112; normalization of Black death, 10–11. *See also* necropolitical logics
deescalation, 23, 74–75, 100
Deleuze, Gilles, 15, 163n22
Denyer Willis, Graham, 72
Dickins de Girón, Avery, 8
dignity, 68, 156–58
Dinzey-Flores, Zaire Zenit, 167n1
Diphoorn, Tessa, 16, 70, 161n5, 161n7, 162n10
"dirty work," 47, 64, 65, 104, 165n1
discrimination, 38, 48, 65
domestic workers, 65
Douglass (interlocutor), 158
drivers, 11, 14, 40–41, 61, 64, 70, 144, 156, 164n8
drug trafficking: attacks on off-duty security guards, 72; cargo theft and, 36; escolta guards' attitudes toward, 51–52; in favelas, 35, 72, 164n2; terminology, 164n6; violence and, 72, 114, 165n14
Duffield, Mark, 90
Durão, Susana, 9, 64, 73

Eduardo (interlocutor), 66–71, 73–76, 166n10
education, in private security. *See* security schools
education level, 2, 18, 38, 96, 147, 149, 155

elite spaces, 2–3, 11, 63; history of, 90–91; militarization and, 68; sensation of security and, 74, 87–88; whiteness and, 14–15, 65, 74–76. *See also* enclaving; gated communities; hospitality security; shopping malls
emotional labor, 4, 15, 74–75, 120; preparedness and, 126, 129–30
enclaving: as form of security, 90, 92, 98, 99, 165n2; punitive, 167n1; as utopian, 167n2
entrepreneurship, 9, 49–50, 124, 149, 168n11
escolta guards, 35–52; classes and training for, 35–37, 39–43, *40*, *45*, 48–52; images of, *40*, *42*; industry priorities, 164n3; legal regulations on armed cargo escort, 40–41, 164n8; militarized hypermasculinity, 38, 44–46, 48, 52, 64; moral righteousness and, 38, 50–52; mundane rituals of labor, 29–30; outsourcing and, 165n10; professionalism, 38, 43, 48–50, 52, 68; racialized and classed views about, 47–48; risk of injury and death, 11, 30, 36–37, 42, 43, 47–48, 52, 164n3; sensation of security and, 37–38, 43, 51–52; status of, 37–38, 44; subject formation, 37–52; transportation routes, 41; wages, 38, 47–48, 164n5. See also *carreira das armas* (careers involving weapons)
ethnographic research methodology, 17–21, 24, 74, 162n21, 164n4, 166n4, 166nn9–10
exclusion, 12; prices and, 88–90, 94–95, 99; spatial, 65, 77, 88–89, 95, 98

family, 32, 67–68, 169n2; "Olympic family," 119, 127; "security family," 68, 143–49
far-right politics, 17, 20–21, 145–46
Fassin, Didier, 19
favelas (urban peripheries), 2; blackness and, 165n3; cargo theft and, 40, 42; drug trafficking in, 35, 72, 164n2; hazardous work by residents of, 164n5; illegality and, 70; near Olympic Park, 121; petty crime and, 86; shopping malls near, 167n6; spectacular violence and, 20–21, 98, 127, 142; speech in, 73
Fawaz, Mona, 91
fealty, 131, 143, 148
Federal Police, 6
fences, 24, 88, 89, 111, 112, 125, 129, 159, 167n1; barbed wire, *81*, *109*, 167n3
Ferreira da Silva, Denise, 162n11
FIFA, 100. *See also* World Cup
fighting skills, 67–68, 72. *See also* martial arts/ MMA
first responders, 23
Fischmann, Carolina, 9, 73, 89
Floyd, George, 141

INDEX

formal sector, 5, 7, 38, 104, 161n8
Formiga (interlocutor), 144–45, 147–49
Francisco (interlocutor), 60–61
Francislei (interlocutor), 33–34, 137–38
Fry, Peter, 165n3

Gaffney, Christopher, 99
gardeners, 11, 64, 90
Gaspar da Silva, Giovane, 169n1
gated communities: class status and, 165n2; housing projects, 167n1; images of, 79–81; private security and, 5, 63, 88, 90, 115. *See also* condominium guards
gatekeeping, 74–75, 88, 94–95, 105. *See also* access control
gendered hierarchies, 3, 45–46, 68, 145, 147, 155–56, 162n20
gentrified spaces, 5, 11, 65, 102
Gharbieh, Ahmad, 91
Gilmore, Ruth Wilson, 162n16
global neoliberal capitalism, 5–6. *See also* neoliberal logics
global security market, 12–14, 17, 120, 148
Global South, urban spatial regimes, 90
Goldstein, Donna, 65
Gomes (interlocutor), 87–89, 105
grooming, 69–71, 100
Grossi, Miriam, 167n3
guards. *See* bodyguards; condominium guards; escolta guards; high-level security; hospitality security; low-level guards; mall security guards; middle managers
Guatemala, 8
Guattari, Félix, 15, 163n22
Guilherme (interlocutor), 92–94, 96, 97, 146, 167n4, 167n6

Haggerty, Kevin, 168n10
Harb, Mona, 91
Harding, Susan, 20
hard security settings, 4, 161n3, 165n1. *See also* escolta guards
hazardous occupations, 10–11
hazard pay, 38, 47–48, 164n5
health insurance, 157, 158
Henrique (interlocutor), 44, 46, 48–49, 51
Herbert (interlocutor), 158
Higate, Paul, 166n4
high-level security, 4, 117–31, 163n25; Brazilian politics and, 146–47; strategic planning, 168n3. *See also* megaevent security; Olympics security; World Cup
hospitality security, 63–77; body management, 69–71, 76; dangers of overperformance, 71–72; defined, 11; elite offenders and, 74–76; perimeters and, 88–89; posture of guards, 72–74, 76; professionalism, 68–69, 75; in shopping malls, 91; slaveholding history and, 64–65, 77; speech, 73; subject formation, 76; working conditions, 67, 71. *See also* elite spaces; low-level guards
hotels, 64, 83
hygiene, 69–71, 76

ideological beliefs, 17, 20–21, 145–46
inequality, 2–3, 104, 162n12
informal sector, 7–8, 38, 161n8
insecurity, sensation of, 2–4, 15, 68, 91, 104, 146
insurance, 6, 19, 41, 46, 157, 158
intelligence officers, 92
interludes (interlocutor narratives), 23–24, 29–34, 57–62, 83–86, 111–16, 137–39, 155–59
International Olympic Committee, 124–25. *See also* Olympics security
Ipanema (neighborhood), 83, 91
Israel, 13, 168n2

Jaffe, Rivke, 3, 161n7, 162n10
Jamaica, 3, 161n7, 162n10
João (interlocutor), 30–31
Jonathan (interlocutor), 137
Jorge (interlocutor), 32–33
JP (interlocutor), 115

kinship metaphors, 143–48
Kleber (interlocutor), 36, 37, 39–43, 45, 48–51

labor laws, 8, 166n7. *See also* Portaria 3.233
Lakoff, Andrew, 119, 129
law enforcement, 16. *See also* police
Leblon (neighborhood), 91, 103–5
leftist government, 146
leisure spaces, 64, 87–90, 98–105
licensing fees, 6
Lima (interlocutor), 61–62
Lochte, Ryan, 122
low-income communities, 3, 10; Black workers, 2–4, 10–11, 164n5; organized crime and, 36, 41. *See also* class hierarchy; favelas; poverty
low-level guards: conflicts with other men, 23, 57–62; embodied performances of, 4, 12; as first responders in medical emergencies, 137–39; hierarchies and, 147; images of work spaces, 27–29; mundane rituals of labor, 23, 29–34; professionalism and respect, 13, 155–58; protecting property from theft, 83–86, 159; reflections on ideal working conditions, 23, 155–59; residences of, 163n25; routine suffering and injuries, 111–16; side jobs, 23, 29, 31–32; training and

low-level guards (*continued*)
  certification, 6–7. *See also* escolta guards; hospitality security; mall security guards
loyalty, 59, 131, 143, 148–49
Lucas (interlocutor), 85, 144
Lucia (interlocutor), 148–49
Lula da Silva, Luiz Inácio, 17

maids, 11, 64, 90
maintenance workers, 31
mall security guards, 8, 30–31, 64, 73, 84–86, 91–98, 92. *See also* shopping malls
Maracanã stadium, 14, 98, 100, 118
Marcos (interlocutor), 36, 37, 39–41, 43–51
Marcos Antônio (interlocutor), 156–57
marginality, 51, 164n6
marginal/marginais, 38, 43, 48, 70, 71, 164n6, 167n11
Marina da Glória, 125
martial arts/MMA, 33, 68, 86, 95, 97
masculinity, 17, 38, 44–46, 48, 52, 64, 145–46
Mauro (interlocutor), 1–2, 4–7, 11, 13, 18, 142, 161n4
medical emergencies, 23, 137–39
megaevent security, 16–17; gentrified spaces and, 102; observers and, 73–74, 118; security preparedness and, 117–31; technology and, 120, 122–23, 168nn9–10. *See also* high-level security; Olympics security; World Cup
menial labor, 11
middle class, 162n10, 165n2. *See also* class hierarchy; elite spaces; gentrified spaces
middle managers, 4, 13–14, 87, 92, 144–45
military: former officers as security company owners, 7, 97, 148; insecurity and, 15, 68; Olympic security and, 103, 117; private security and, 16, 38–39, 44–47, 58, 63–64, 67–68, 72, 91, 114, 145–46, 161n3. *See also* escolta guards
military dictatorship, 5, 14, 92, 146
military police, 85, 97, 101–2, 104, 116, 148, 163n24
Mills, Charles, 3, 11
morale, 130–31
moral righteousness, 8, 12–13, 17, 143, 146, 161n4; escolta guards and, 38, 50–52
Moreto, Guito, 23–24, 25–27, 37, 39, 40, 42, 45, 53–55, 66, 79–81, 92, 101, 107–9, 133–35, 151–53
multinational companies, 19, 100–101, 145, 148, 168n11

Nabo (interlocutor), 83–84
nannies, 11, 64, 90
narcotraffic. *See* drug trafficking
Nascimento (interlocutor), 61–62

nationalism, 131, 168n9(chap.3)
necrofinance, 162n15
necropolitical logics: antiblackness and, 10–11; escolta guards and, 36–38, 44, 47. *See also* death and injury, risk of
neoliberal logics, 5–6, 8, 10, 21, 37, 49, 71, 148
nepotism, 148–49
networks of security actors, 96–98, 167n6
Nielsen, Morten, 165n2, 167n2
9/11 attacks, 118

Olympics security (2016, Rio de Janeiro), 7, 13–14; accreditation and, 167n7; brand protection and, 9, 126–29; Brazilian nationalism and, 131, 168n9(chap.3); command center, 19, 120–22, 130; corporate sponsorship, 120–21; emotional labor and, 126, 129–31; global security norms and, 102–3; hospitality security and, 64–65; incident-reporting systems, 120, 122–28, 130, 169n13; labor laws on guards' working conditions, 166n7; modernity and, 121–22, 124; "Olympic family," 119, 127; perimeter, 90, 125, 169n13; posture of guards, 76; preparedness, 19, 117–31; professionalism, 124–25, 131; research methodology, 19; simulation of incidents, 117–20, 126–31, 168n1; team solidarity and morale, 130–31; visiting security personnel, 124–26. *See also* International Olympic Committee
order, 2–4, 146, 169n2
"organic" employees, 8
organizational chains of command, 119
organized crime, 36, 41–42, 72, 97, 146, 166n8, 167n6. *See also* crime
outsourcing, 8, 149, 162n10, 165n10
Owensby, Brian, 165n3

paramedics, 137–38
Pardue, Derek, 163n26
Partido dos Trabalhadores (PT), 131
parties, 57–60
patriarchy, 22, 145, 147–49
patronage, 68, 148–49
Paulinho (interlocutor), 139
Paulo (interlocutor), 36, 95, 96–97, 113
Pedro (interlocutor), 85–86
perimeters, 88–90, 125, 169n13
personal responsibility, 10, 12–13, 21, 49, 71, 148, 161n4
petty crime, 23, 83–86
physical fitness, 33, 68–69, 97, 105
Pinheiro-Machado, Rosana, 21
Pinho, Patricia, 162n17
planning, 4, 14, 102–3. *See also* city planning; preparedness

"playboys," 74–75
police, 3; attitudes toward, 50–51, 98, 101–2; mall security guards and, 93–94; private security and, 6–7, 125, 142, 147, 169n1; reporting systems, 124; security companies and, 63; as symbolically "dirty," 47. *See also* military police
police violence, 10, 20–21, 46, 141–43
politics, 5, 14, 17, 20–21, 92, 146–47. *See also* Bolsonaro, Jair
Portaria 3.233 (legal satute, 2012), 6, 40, 145, 165n11
posture, 72–74, 76
poverty, 23, 99, 146, 148. *See also* low-income communities
preparedness, 4, 15, 19, 117–31, 168n2
prices, exclusionary, 88–90, 94–95, 99
private security: attitudes toward, 47–48, 50; Black men as disposable and interchangeable, 10–11, 36; development and expansion of, 5–6; ethnography of, 15–17; formal sector, 5, 7–8, 38, 104, 161n8; government regulation of, 6–7; hierarchies in, 147–49; honor, status, and respect, 13, 37–38, 44, 75, 149, 155–58; ideal working conditions, 155–56; informal sector, 7–8, 38, 161n8; quotidian aspects of, 23–24, 149 (*see also* interludes); race and, 2–3, 10–12; range of labor, 17–19, 163n25; standards of grooming, 12. *See also* bodyguards; condominium guards; contractors; escolta guards; high-level security; hospitality security; low-level guards; mall security guards; middle managers; outsourcing; sensation of security
private security companies, 7, 63–64, 66, 97, 148; profit-driven, 4–6, 161n4
professionalism, 1, 12–15; emotional detachment and, 15 (*see also* emotional labor); escolta guards, 38, 43, 48–50, 52, 68; gendered hierarchies and, 68; hospitality security guards and, 68–69, 75; low-level guards, 155–58; masculine and authoritarian kinship groups and, 17, 145–46; middle managers, 13–14; preparedness and, 120; racialized performances of, 100; respect and, 155–58; as symbolic capital, 48
profiling, 95–96, 167n11
psychological emergencies, 23

Quintella, José Pedro Guedes, 5

racial capitalism, 3, 11, 77, 162n13, 162n16. *See also* capital, flows of
racial contract, 3, 12, 142–43
racial democracy, 13

racial hierarchy, 2–3, 9, 12; colonial past and, 77; discourse on, 95–96; escolta guards and, 47–48; hygiene and, 69; phenotypical information and, 165n3; in security industry, 147; violence and, 46. *See also* antiblackness; white supremacy
racism, 96, 149, 164n5
Reginaldo (interlocutor), 29–30, 114, 155–56
respect, 75, 149, 155–58, 166n7
Rial, Carmen, 96, 99, 167n3, 168n9(chap.4)
Ricardo (interlocutor), 36, 98, 101
Richard (interlocutor), 111–12, 157
Rio de Janeiro: fear of crime in, 2–5, 91; private security in (*see* private security); racial and socioeconomic inequality, 2–3; state violence in, 3, 10 (*see also* police violence). *See also* city planning; private security
robberies. *See* cargo theft; theft
Roberto (interlocutor), 157–58
Rodrigo (interlocutor), 36
Rogerio (interlocutor), 86
Romario (interlocutor), 111, 156
Roth Gordon, Jen, 165n3
Rousseff, Dilma, 17

safety, 2–3. *See also* sensation of security
Salem, Tomas, 46, 162n20
Samimian-Darash, Limor, 15, 119, 163n22, 168n2
Sansone, Livio, 76, 165n3
São Paulo, Brazil, 5, 11, 36, 73, 90, 144, 165n2, 167n3, 169n2
scalar analysis, 163n23
Scalco, Lucia, 21
Sebastião (interlocutor), 113–14
securitized bubbles, 90, 105
security: public and private forms of, 16, 163n24, 169n1 (*see also* police; private security); as racialized "dirty work," 47, 64, 65, 104, 165n1; security logics, 20–21 (*see also* affective logics)
security assemblages, 15–16, 89, 91
"security family," 68, 143–49
security infrastructure, 23–24, 89, 92–96, 167n3; images of, 25–27, 37, 39, 40, 42, 45, 53–55, 66, 79–81, 80, 92, 101, 107–9, 133–35, 151–53. *See also* fences; surveillance cameras
security schools, 17–18; basic training, 66; bodily capital and, 65–66; combat classes, 68; escolta classes, 35–37, 39–43, 40, 45, 48–52; facilities, 39; hospitality security classes, 65–76, 67; images of, 163n27; megaevent courses, 66; moral discourses, 13 (*see also* moral righteousness); practical training exercises, 74–75; private security companies and, 66; professionalism, 9–10;

INDEX

security schools (*continued*)
  recycling (continuing education), 35–36, 39;
  registration forms, 66
self-respect, 75
sensation of security (*sensação de segurança*):
  antiblackness and, 3, 10–12, 141–43;
  Brazilian cultural norms, 102–3; concept
  of, 2–4; criminal gangs and, 72; deception
  and, 125–26; elite spaces and, 74, 87–88;
  embodied experiences of, 3–4; emotions and
  (*see* emotional labor); enclaving, 90, 92, 98,
  99, 165n2; escolta guards' performance of,
  37–38, 43, 51–52; hospitality security and,
  64, 66, 71, 73–77; infrastructure and, 92–93;
  minimum requirements for, 89; organized
  crime and, 97; as performance, 149;
  preparedness and, 119–20, 125–26; "security
  family" for workers, 143–48; in shopping
  malls, 91–94, 96–98; technology and, 122;
  uniforms and, 71
service industry, 2, 64, 90–91
Sharpe, Christina, 10, 162n18
shooting ranges, 44–46, 45
shoplifting, 73, 84–86
shopping malls: branded image of, 9, 94;
  capital flow, 93; commercial success of, 91;
  gatekeeping at, 94–95, 105; near favelas,
  167n6; security infrastructure, 92–96;
  surveillance cameras, 94. *See also* mall
  security guards
Silveira Freitas, João Alberto, 141–43
slaveholding history, 64–65, 77, 161n7, 162n12
social disorder, 169n2. *See also* order
social mobility, 7, 95, 146–49, 161n9, 162n10;
  patronage and, 68; "self-made" narratives,
  67–68
soft security settings, 4, 161n3, 165n1. *See also*
  hospitality security
South Africa, 16, 161n5
Souza Cruz (cigarette company), 165n10
space, public/private divisions, 5
spatial exclusion, 65, 77, 88–89, 95, 98
spectacular security: of escolta guards, 11–12,
  43; hospitality work and, 88, 91, 96, 99,
  142; megaevents and, 102; performances
  of whiteness, 14; violence of antiblackness,
  141–43
speech, 73, 100
sporting venues, 98–103. *See also* Olympics;
  stadium security teams; World Cup
Stachowitsch, Saskia, 65
stadium security teams, 9, 64, 98–103; arrests
  by, 73–74; steward model, *100–101*, 100–102.
  See also Olympics security; World Cup
Stalcup, Meg, 15, 163n22
stereotypes, 13, 75, 103, 167n10

stewards, *100–101*, 100–102
structural critiques, 12–13, 21
Sumich, Jason, 165n2, 167n2
surveillance cameras, 63, 89, 94, 121; images of,
  80, *107–8*, *134*, *152*
surveillance software, 95
suspects, identification of, 95–96, 167n11
systemic critiques, 21, 148, 162n12

theft, protection of consumer goods from,
  92–94, 103–5. *See also* cargo theft; petty
  crime
ticket prices, 99
Tom (interlocutor), 102–3, 168n8(chap.3)
toughness, 44–46
training, 1–2, 6–7, 17–18, 119. *See also*
  preparedness; security schools
train station guards, 67, 87, 89
transporte de valores, 164n9. *See also* armored
  cars
trauma, 23, 116
truck hijackings. *See* cargo theft

uniforms, 70–71, 166n8
unions, 32, 156, 166n7
United Kingdom, 13
United States, 13, 119
upper class. *See* class hierarchy; elite spaces;
  gentrified spaces
upward mobility. *See* social mobility
urban enclaves. *See* enclaving
urban spatial regimes, 90. *See also* city planning
urban violence, 5. *See also* crime; police
  violence

vigilante, use of term, 161n1
"*vigi-lícia*" (slang term), 46
Vila Autódromo (favela), 121
Vinicius (interlocutor), 36
violent situations: favelas and, 20–21, 98, 127,
  142; private security guards and, 22–23,
  43–48, 65, 68, 74, 111, 141–43; in Rio,
  5; at stadiums, 98–99, 128. *See also* drug
  trafficking; escolta guards; police violence
VIP bodies, security for, 15, 34
Vivian (interlocutor), 63–64, 66, 76, 165n1

Wacquant, Loïc, 65–66
wages, 31, 161n2; hazard pay, 38, 47–48,
  164n5
weapons: condition of, 49–50; training in use
  of, 39–41, 44–46, 165n11. *See also carreira
  das armas* (careers involving weapons)
well-being, 2–3, 64, 126
whiteness: "behavioral whitening," 162n17; elite
  spaces and, 14–15, 65, 74–75; performance

of, 12, 14, 76–77; research methodology and, 166n4, 166n9
white supremacy, 2–3, 22, 76, 142–43
Williams, Michael C., 16, 163n23
Worker's Party, 17, 165n2
World Cup (2014, Rio de Janeiro), 7, 13; accreditation and, 167n7; global security norms, 102–3; hospitality security and, 64–65; posture of guards, 76; protection of corporate brand, 9; protests and, 168n1; stadium infrastructure and, 98–99; steward model, 100
Wright, Willie J., 162n13

Zé Carlos (interlocutor), 57, 144

CPSIA information can be obtained
at www.ICGtesting.com
Printed in the USA
LVHW042329210423
744923LV00004B/382